Management Control of Multinational Enterprises in China

A Contracting and Management Accounting Perspective

NEALE G. O'CONNOR

The University of Hong Kong

Mc Graw Hill

Singapore • Boston • Burr Ridge, IL • Dubuque, IA • Madison, WI • New York
San Francisco • St. Louis • Bangkok • Bogotá • Caracas • Kuala Lumpur
Lisbon • London • Madrid • Mexico City • Milan • Montreal • New Delhi
Santiago • Seoul • Sydney • Taipei • Toronto

The McGraw·Hill Companies

Management Control of Multinational Enterprises in China
A Contracting and Management Accounting Perspective

McGraw Hill Education

2 3 4 5 6 7 8 9 10 SEP 09 08 07 06

When ordering this title, use ISBN 007-124738-6

Printed in Singapore

Brief Contents

Contents

Foreword

In a little over two decades, China has emerged as one of the world's dominant economies. It has developed an active capital market, and its domestic markets are increasingly being opened to competition. Barriers to entry by foreign investors and firms are steadily being dismantled, and foreign direct investments are pouring in at an ever-increasing rate. Together, these developments make it important that business managers, investors and students develop a better understanding of the nature and dynamics of the Chinese business environment.

This collection of text and cases goes a long way towards helping to develop such an understanding relating to the management of multinational enterprises in China. Its author is an active researcher and teacher in Hong Kong whose work on China is known worldwide. The materials cover a broad scope. Starting with a multinational enterprise's initial investment decision to enter China, the text and cases consider intricate transfer pricing strategies and issues, going all the way to the problems in liquidating a failed venture. In doing so, coverage is provided on areas that tend to be glossed over in both international business and management accounting textbooks to give a broad overview of areas where international management in China differs from practices in Western developed countries. Students of this book will also discover the complexity and some of the value conflicts in the China business context.

While no single book can impart all the knowledge and skills that one needs to be an effective international manager, what this collection does very well is to create an awareness and basic understanding of what is important to know. This awareness and understanding will be a firm foundation for acquiring further knowledge about business management issues in China.

Chee W. Chow, Ph.D.
Vern Odmark Professor of Accountancy
San Diego State University

Preface

My first aim in writing this book is to contribute to the multidisciplinary understanding of how multinational businesses operate through both the international business and accounting lenses. Generally, the issues of management accounting and control of multinational operations have been given a secondary role in most international business and accounting textbooks. For example, the control problems that are highlighted by agency theory and the complexity of international transfer pricing are glossed over in most international business texts, while the issues of global strategy, political risk and foreign market entry modes are glossed over in most international accounting textbooks. The aim here in filling the void is to frame and describe the complexity of such issues using an international business planning and management control framework.

The second contribution of this book is to add to our understanding of business in China. While there are a lot of books on China about the business experiences of individuals and companies, very few of these books provide a systematic understanding of the business issues from a theoretical standpoint. The aim of the 18 case studies in this book is to help the reader understand the challenges and difficulties of doing business in China within an international business planning and management control framework.

Target Audience

The target audience at the undergraduate level includes both final year business and accounting students. At the Masters level, students in all types of business programmes would benefit, especially if the programmes incorporate case studies in the teaching method. The emphasis of this book is on the China context in which international business and management accounting and control issues arise.

Outline

Management accounting serves to support management decisions through the provision of information. In the international business context, greater attention is given to the way in which management accounting information influences decisions due to the added complexity of the environment. For example, a domestic firm divides its structure and controls across functional and product lines, whereas the multinational enterprise has a further dimension to manage – the different geographical locations of its subsidiaries. The text chapters in this book take a theoretical approach to the issues that surround how international business is contracted for and controlled. The various theoretical frameworks are also used in the case studies of foreign-invested enterprises in China.

The book is divided into two parts. Part one deals with the planning and investment function of management, which, given a particular global strategy, involves the search for investment opportunities and the setting up of the appropriate external contracts to manage such arrangements. In this part, aspects of multinational enterprise strategy and the international environment are explained in terms of how such factors influence the type of external contracting. In the process, several mainstream theories – transactions costs, bargaining power and resource dependence theory – are used to explain the linkage. The aim is to help the reader to understand the basic determinants of contract choice in the international environment with particular reference to China.

Once the external contract is chosen, management requires information to monitor such contract, which comes from having planning and control mechanisms in place. The emphasis is on the nature of the information that is required to structure and monitor a contractual agreement, which varies according to the type of agreement. For example, the information that is required to monitor market-based contracts such as franchising or licensing agreements is generally explicit and set out in the contractual agreement, whereas the information that is required to monitor non-market-based contracts (e.g., wholly owned subsidiaries or joint ventures) is generally, in part, explicit (set out in the agreement) and in part implicit (part of a management control system).

Part two deals with the management control function of management, which involves the use of various control mechanisms to monitor two main types of non-market-based contracts: wholly owned subsidiaries and equity joint ventures. This part draws on frameworks from the management accounting and control literature to help explain the main influences on the choice and design of various management controls and transfer pricing policy.

In summary, the text highlights the range of contracting and control issues that often arise in managing a multinational enterprise (MNE), and the case studies provide a unique insight of these issues in the China context.

Structure of the Book

Part One: Planning and Investment Function of Management

Chapter 1 – The international business environment and information needs

Information is required to a) formulate global strategy, b) source international finance, and c) assess the risk and returns that are associated with each investment opportunity.

- Global environment
- Strategic motivation to go international
- Product/service nature

Chapter 2 – International expansion and external contracting

Information is required to structure and monitor contracts.

- Market exchange
- Franchising
- Licensing
- Joint venture
- Subsidiary

Part Two: Management Control Function of Management

Chapter 3 – Management control of wholly owned subsidiaries

Information is required to organise resources, and to monitor and evaluate the performance of the wholly owned subsidiary.

- Human resource selection
- Decision control
- Performance measurement
- Performance rewards

Chapter 4 – Management control of joint ventures

Information is required to organise resources, and to monitor and evaluate the performance of the joint venture.

- Partner contributions
- Joint venture agreement controls
- Joint venture management controls
- Joint venture performance

Chapter 5 – International transfer pricing
Information is required to set transfer prices within and between non-market-based contracts.

Regulatory environment	Competitive environment	Organisation efficiency

Pedagogy

Theoretical expectations model. The basic model used follows a four-step approach in the form of an independent/dependent variable framework with the external contracting or management control mechanisms as the dependent variable (see Figure 1). We discuss the steps in the context of head office and subsidiary management in a multinational enterprise.

Step 1. What is the strategic and operational decision-making role of management? The decision-making role of management is identified. The question is what specific decision does the contracting and management control mechanism system serve? For example, is the new contract for international expansion part of a global or a multidomestic strategy?

Step 2. Which contracting and management control mechanism (dependent variable) is likely to play a key role in facilitating the decision-making role of management? In this step we focus on the range of contracting and management control mechanisms that help to implement or monitor the strategic and operational decisions made by management. We need to keep in mind that one or many contracting and management control mechanisms may be useful in facilitating specific strategic and operational decisions. Which contracting or management control mechanisms are most relevant? These mechanisms are identified in the expectations model as dependent variables.

Step 3. Theory is used to provide structure to the factors and issues that are associated with the decision. Particular theories are chosen to match the context of the decision role or problem that is being investigated. We need to identify theories that can help us to understand the nature and extent of the information and/or incentive problem that may be associated with each decision. What is the rationale behind the behaviour of management? Knowing the basis on which various levels of management is expected to behave is important for selecting the best theory to use in guiding the expectations in the model. The theory or theories chosen generally

Figure 1 Theoretical Expectations Model

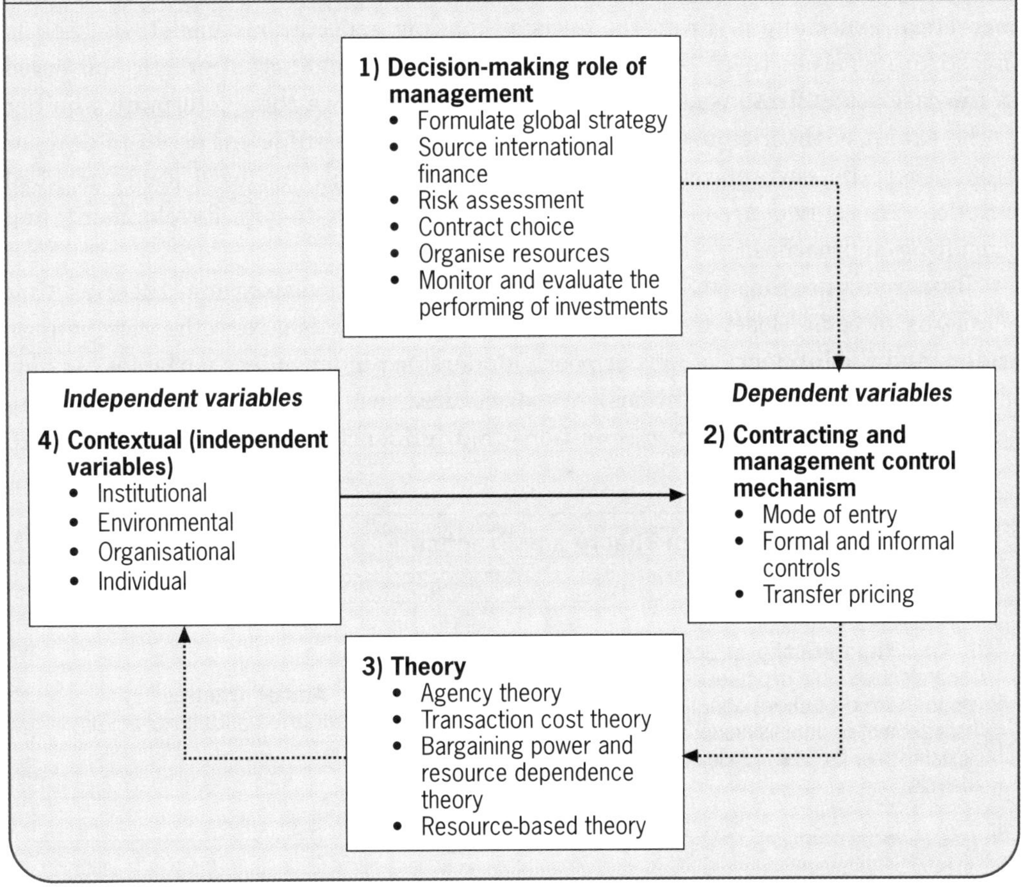

have specific assumptions about the purpose or role of management behaviour. This book takes a largely economic theoretical approach in that it assumes rational behaviour on the part of management, which has an interest in making decisions based on economic grounds.

Step 4. What contextual factors (independent variables) are likely to influence the use/non-use of the contracting or management control mechanism? The final step is using the theory to identify relevant independent variables that will help to formulate expectations about the ideal design (hypotheses) of the contracting or management control mechanism in facilitating particular decisions. We need to identify what (if any) independent variables exist to help us understand the extent to which particular contracting or management controls would be useful in facilitating decision making.

Case study approach. The cases that are presented in this book are designed around this framework of decision, contract and management control choice and theoretical expectations. From the decision-making expectations model, we seek to investigate whether there is a gap between the model and actual practice observed in the case study firm. Assuming that a gap does exist, we then determine whether a) the extent of theories used to develop expectations is sufficient or up to date, or b) whether the current practice that is represented in the case study is ideal practice. These two areas can also be referred to as theory development and consulting approaches.

Research into theory development focuses on discovering new theories that enable us to come closer to ideal practice or actual practice. New theories help us understand the influence of new or poorly understood independent variables. As new independent variables (conditions) are discovered, we are able to move closer to actual practice. The unobserved conditions that influence actual practice are hard to

Figure 2 The Gap between Theory and Practice

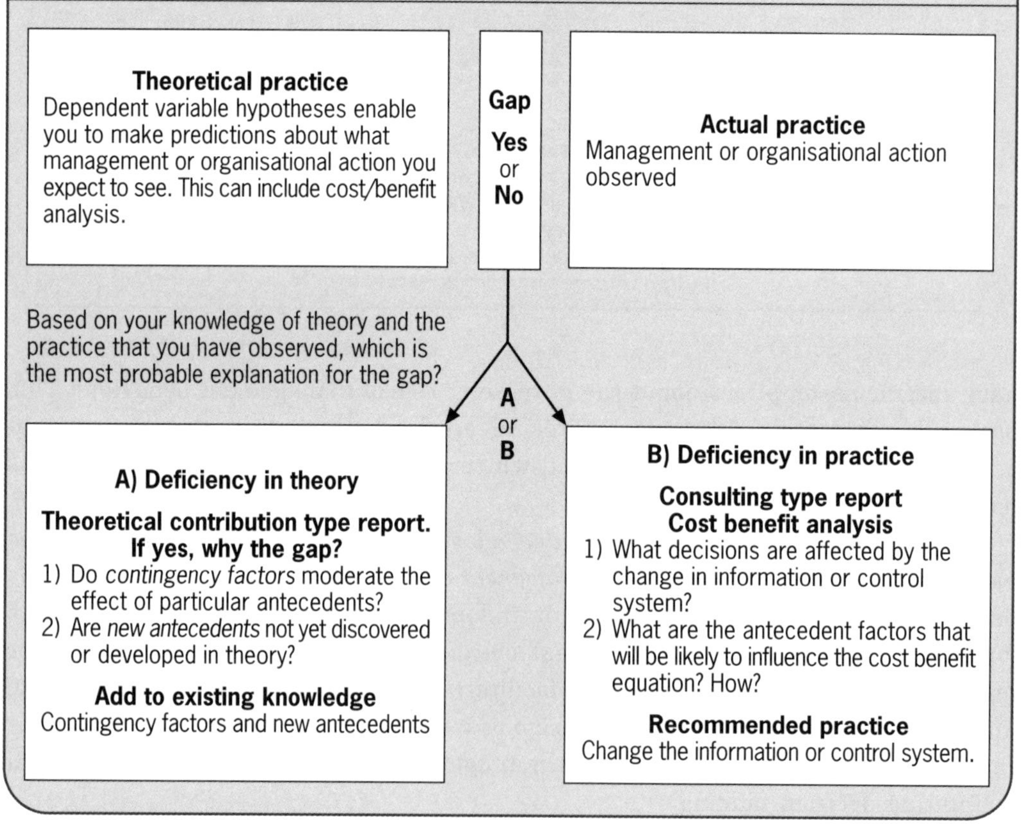

see, unless management is more sensitive and adequate information is available. To a certain extent, environmental uncertainties hinder management from taking further action to minimise the gap between theory and practice (see Figure 2). A lack of understanding of the theories also contributes to this uncertainty. In short, theory-directed research seeks to understand the new factors that are likely to influence the level of practice observed. The focus is on extending existing knowledge and closing the gap from the theoretical side of the equation. In contrast, the consulting approach seeks to understand more about deficiencies in the practice observed, and examines the costs and benefits of the design of management accounting tools/systems to provide better information for decision making.

Note that while a lot of care and attention has been taken to ensure that all the details in this book are up to date and accurate, there is still the possibility of errors or omissions. Therefore, one should seek professional advice before acting on any of this information.

Acknowledgements

I have received a lot of encouragement and assistance in writing this book. First, I acknowledge the support of the Teaching Development Unit and Department of Accountancy at the City University of Hong Kong and the LLE Courseware Development Project at Lingnan University. At McGraw-Hill Asia I would like to thank Pauline Chua, Angela Chew, Christine Chua and the anonymous reviewers of early drafts of the book.

I wish to thank the numerous colleagues for advice and feedback. These include many past and current colleagues, whose assistance was of great value in developing the original idea for the book: Robert Inglis, Kim Watty, Brian Andrew, Alan Davis, Margaret Fidow, Stephen Lynn, Maris Martinsons, Bin Sirindhi and Ronald Zhao. I also thank Ken Merchant for his insightful advice and encouragement.

I acknowledge the assistance of many students who were directly involved in gathering data for the case studies reported in this book: Wong Yiu Kwong, Pandora Lau, Mandy Lee Sui Man, William Yau, Ranco Chung Man Kit, Thomas Kwok Yick Hung, Elaine Feng, Ray Siaw, Cliff Tse, Meisy Wong, Sam Chan P.K., Lawrence Lee Yuk Lam, Sandy Lo Yun Mui and Alex Kwok. I also thank all of the students who studied the international management accounting course during the period 1999 through to 2004. You all inspired me to learn more about management accounting practice in China.

I thank Barbara Burns, Mike Poole, Jovi Leung, Katrina Lam, Gobi Lam, Olivia Mak, Shirley Kong and Carmen Kong for their editorial assistance. I accept all responsibility for errors or omissions in the text, and would be pleased to hear from readers who have any suggestions on how the book may be improved.

Finally, I thank my wife, Stephanie, and family (in Hong Kong and Australia) who, in many ways, have supported my work which has led to the writing of this book.

About the Author

Neale G. O'Connor, FCPA (*Aust.*) BBus (*Ballarat*), PGAcc (*Melb*), Ph.D. (*Griffith*)

Neale O'Connor is an Associate Professor in the Department of Accountancy at the City University of Hong Kong. In addition, he is the Programme Director of the City University of Hong Kong Master of Arts in International Accounting. He has a Ph.D. in Accounting from Griffith University, Australia. Before that, he held the positions of a lecturer at RMIT University and a tutor at the University of Melbourne. He also worked for Mann Judd Chartered Accountants, Australia.

Dr. O'Connor has been an active researcher and teacher in Hong Kong for the past eight years. He is a member of the CPA Australia (Hong Kong Branch) Business Management Cell and has conducted professional development seminars for CIMA, CPA Australia and HKICPA. Dr. O'Connor has personally researched and documented the nature of management accounting practice across many countries in the Asia-Pacific region, including, Singapore, South Korea, Australia, Hong Kong and China. His most recent research examined the use of management controls in international joint ventures in China and the adoption of formal management control mechanisms in Chinese SOEs. He is currently involved in researching the adoption of performance measures and their linkage to manager compensation in a public-listed firm in China. His publications on business and management accounting in China have appeared in several international journals: *Accounting, Organisations and Society*, *Journal of International Accounting Research*, *Journal of Business Research*, *Asian Pacific Journal of Management*, *Journal of Applied Management Studies* and *Advances in Management Accounting*.

Abbreviations

APA	Advance pricing agreement
BSC	Balanced scorecard
CCA	Cost contribution agreement
CIMA	Chartered Institute of Management Accountants
COGS	Cost of goods sold
COS	Cost of sales
CPM	Comparable profit method
EBIT	Earnings before interest and tax
EBT	Earning before tax
EDI	Electronic data interchange
EVA	Economic value added
FDI	Foreign direct investment
FEIT	Foreign enterprise income tax
GMAT	Graduate management admission test
GM	Gross margin
GP	Gross profit
HKIRD	Hong Kong Inland Revenue Department
HKSAR	Hong Kong Special Administration Region
IAS	International accounting standards
ICRG	International country risk guide
IRC	Internal revenue code
IRS	Internal revenue service
JIT	Just in time
MNE	Multinational enterprise
MOFTEC	Ministry of Foreign Trade and Economic Cooperation
MOLSS	Ministry of Labour and Social Security
OECD	Organisation for Economic Cooperation and Development
OLI	Ownership, location and internalisation
PBOC	People's Bank of China
PCT	Patent cooperation treaty
PLC	Product life cycle
PRC	People's Republic of China
PRS	Political risk services
RMB	Renminbi
ROA	Return on assets

ROI	Return on investment
SAFE	State Administration of Foreign Exchange
SAT	State Administration of Taxation
SEZ	Special Economic Zone
SME	Small- and medium-size enterprise
Tiprs	Trade-related intellectual property rights
TNC	Transnational corporation
TNMM	Transactional net margin method
UNCTAD	United Nations Conference on Trade and Development
USD	United States dollar
VAT	Value-added tax
WACC	Weighted average cost of capital
WTO	World Trade Organisation

CHAPTER

1

The International Business Environment and Information Needs

LEARNING OBJECTIVES

- Understand the strategic motives for multinational enterprise activity.
- Learn three main theories that help explain the reason for international expansion.
- Understand the different types of risk that MNEs face.
- Understand that cultural differences can impact the way businesses are conducted across countries.
- Understand the basic regulatory and business factors in China's business environment.

INTRODUCTION

International business involves the interaction of companies, consumers, financial institutions and governments in the global economy. Companies that have operations in more than one country through foreign direct investment (FDI) are called multinational enterprises (MNEs). FDI refers to the investment by a person or an entity from one country in an entity in another country that is of a long-term nature and involves some control of the entity in the host country. According to the United Nations Conference on Trade and Development (UNCTAD) more than 60,000 MNEs control over 800,000 foreign affiliates worldwide (World Investment Report, 2004). The largest of these have assets that eclipse the gross domestic product of many countries in the developing world. These enterprises provide an alternative, and in many cases, a much needed source of capital and technology for developing countries around the world.

When an organisation considers international expansion, management needs to consider the best mode of entry. For example, when companies expand internationally, they need to consider the external contract (mode of entry) that best fits their, 1) comparative advantage and strategic rationale for going international, and 2) assessment of economic and political risks that are associated with the location of their international expansion. Managers also need information on the informal rules or cultural dictates of the country to manage the operations once a particular mode of entry has been decided upon. The first half of this chapter provides an overview of these important areas of planning for international expansion.

In the second half of the chapter we consider these issues within the context of the China business environment since it is now the largest recipient of foreign direct investment (FDI). FDI in China has grown dramatically in the past decade, reaching US$52.7 billion in 2002 (*People's Daily*, 2003). Given China's recent entry into the World Trade Organisation (WTO), FDI will increase to an anticipated 15 to 20% annually in the future (*People's Daily*, 2004).

STRATEGIC MOTIVES FOR MULTINATIONAL ENTERPRISE ACTIVITY

MNEs expand their operations internationally for a variety of reasons ranging from the overall global strategy, the type of production technology (i.e., scale economies) and particular country risks and resource endowments. Therefore, in order to understand how MNEs contract for international expansion we first need to determine the *motivation* for establishing initial operations (e.g., distribution offices) or larger investments (e.g., wholly owned subsidiaries or joint ventures). This section introduces a variety of reasons/strategies as to why MNEs expand abroad, which is followed by an introduction to the theories that have helped to explain the global expansion of MNEs.

Practical Reasons Why Companies Go International

The practical reasons for going abroad range from exploiting the resources of another country to seeking new markets or even protecting home markets through the strategic positioning of overseas offices/operations. The most common of these reasons are as follows:

Resource seekers. Resource seekers include companies that seek physical resources including labour and intangible resources. They also search for lower production costs in other countries. Differences in resource costs across countries exist because of market imperfections in labour (e.g., minimum wage rates and labour mobility) and knowledge (i.e., technical and professional skills). Differences in resource costs also exist because of different natural resource endowments. These market imperfections translate into opportunities for the MNEs. Examples of such MNEs that deal in electrical products are Toshiba, Sony and Pioneer, and those that deal in sportswear and accessories are Fila, Nike and Adidas.

Market seekers. Market seekers include those companies that seek to sustain and protect existing markets, and exploit and promote new markets. Such companies are likely to enter new markets in an effort to follow their suppliers and customers. Their physical presence is important to the support strategy, which can include obtaining host government concessions and circumventing trade barriers. Examples of market exploiters in the soft drink industry are Coca-Cola and Pepsi, and in mobile phone production are Nokia, Motorola and Samsung.

Efficiency seekers. Efficiency seekers aim to rationalise the structure of established resource-based or market-seeking investments in such a way that the investing company can gain from the common governance of geographically dispersed activities. There are two types of efficiency seeking enterprises: those with activities spread across developed and undeveloped nations according to the division of labour, and those with activities spread across nations with similar economic structures and income levels. Traditional factor endowments play less of a role in this reason for going international. Such companies may also seek to enjoy economies of scale through the division of labour. Examples of these companies in automobile manufacturing are Mercedes Benz, Toyota and Yamaha, and IBM and Epson in computer hardware.

Strategic asset seekers. Strategic asset seekers are associated with efficiency seeking. Such companies are likely to pursue an integrated global or regional strategy. There are two main types of strategic asset seekers: protective and expansionary. Protective type strategic asset seekers are those MNEs which locate operations in another country in order to protect their domestic customer base. Good examples of such MNEs are the large accounting firms. During the 1990s each of the big five (now big four) accounting firms entered China with the express purpose of following their customer (MNEs) expansionary strategies, thus, allowing them to maintain their customer base. The second type of strategic asset seeker – the expansionary MNE – includes companies that are expanding for the first time by seeking to buy competitive strength in unfamiliar markets. Examples in the clothing industry include Polo Ralph Lauren, Burberry and DKNY, while examples in toy manufacturing include Bandai and Mattel.

Other motives for MNE activity. Other motives for entry include a) escape investments to circumvent restrictions on the share of domestic production that MNEs might attain, b) support investments, whereby an affiliate or branch office activity is a first step towards setting up a market- or resource-seeking production facility, c) passive investments, d) portfolio type investments (10–25% share), e) financially motivated investments, which are associated with investments in property, and f) reputation- and recognition-gaining motives. Examples of companies with the latter motive include professional associations such as the Association of Chartered Certified Accountants, the Chartered Institute of Management Accountants and standard-setting bodies such as the Test of English as a Foreign Language and the Graduate Management Admission Test.

Theoretical Reasons for Going International

Several theories exist for understanding the motives for MNE activity. The early theories (e.g., classical trade and factor proportions theories) focused on the production cost side of the equation (the nation and its inherent, natural or endowment characteristics). Several theories acknowledged the demand side of the equation. For example, Linder's product range theory states that unlike natural-resource-based industries, trade in manufactured goods is dictated by similarity in product demand across nations (Czinkota, Ronkainen and Moffett, 1996). International investment theory recognises that the country of comparative advantage changes as the technology of a product's manufacture matures. Product life cycle (PLC) theory recognises the wave of demand of the same products from developed to developing countries that shifts as the products mature and become available at more attractive prices. These later theories are more appropriate in describing trends in the internationalisation of technology-based products, because resource-based and service-based products are not so easily characterised by stages of maturity. Finally, Michael Porter's competitive advantage of nation's theory recognises the multiplicity of determinants of national competitive advantage. More recent theories of international business include the ownership, location and internalisation determinants (OLI) model, transaction theory and the bargaining power and resource dependence theories. These theories are discussed in the next section.

THEORY IN ACTION

Biscuit Ltd's Market Entry Strategy

Investment environment and mode of entry using the Porter framework

Biscuit Ltd started business in 1985 by promoting and selling biscuit production lines to its clients in China. The production lines that it sells are mainly used for the production of high-quality European-style biscuits. The company is also familiar with the leading biscuit manufacturers in China.

In the last few years, many equipment suppliers have terminated their agreements with Hong Kong agents due to the ability of foreign suppliers to do business directly with the Chinese. Therefore, to maintain profit and diversify the company business, Biscuit Ltd, is examining the possibility of establishing a new biscuit factory in China. The factory is designed to produce high-quality European-style biscuits to be sold in urban areas with relatively higher income levels. The overall objective is to improve the company's competitive position and better serve the needs of customers. The specific objectives include increased sales, improved market share and enhanced company image and reputation.

Factor conditions. The factory is located in Dongguan for easy transportation, cheap labour, reasonable land costs, good relationships with local officials and proximity to Hong Kong for easy access to financial, communication and import and export trading facilities.

Demand conditions. The income per capita in the southern provinces has increased sharply during the last few years. Consequently, the consumption of high-quality imported products has increased.

Related and supporting industries: The Garden Company, Nabisco and United

Biscuits are the major biscuit suppliers in Asia. These three companies have established their own joint venture factory in China to increase their market share and maximise their profits. To cope with increasing market demand, the companies are now expanding their production capacity by installing new biscuit lines or relocating their old plants to China.

Identification of a joint venture partner. After studying the various forms of investment available for foreign investors, the company found that an equity joint venture would be the most suitable for the new biscuit factory. The company expects that the joint venture partner will have a relationship with the local government and preferably have sales outlets.

Dongguan Sugar Cigarette and Wine Company is considered to be the suitable partner. The company is managed by the Commercial Bureau of Dongguan City. It has sales outlets and is familiar with consumer behaviour. As the construction and initial equipment costs will be the major costs in setting up the factory, the company, Biscuit Ltd will hold 60% of the capital share in the new factory. Dongguan's good relations with the local government and sales outlets will be an asset as the biscuit factory promotes its products and develops the market.

THE INTERNATIONAL BUSINESS ENVIRONMENT

In determining how to go global, managers must understand the *international business environment* in which they intend to operate, especially in terms of the economic, political and cultural factors that will be likely to affect MNEs. For example, the major challenge for market entry is the lack of information about end users. Thus, managers need to use secondary information such as hearsay, educated guesses and the opinions of intermediaries. Input or product sourcing, quality and the lack of convertible currency and protection of intellectual property rights are other challenges facing international managers.

Issues of government regulation pose difficult and complex problems, for they place managers in the position of having to choose between home country regulations and foreign business practices. Firms must also consider boycotts, trade embargoes and sanctions that are imposed by the parent company's country, antitrust laws and the Foreign Corrupt Practices Act (1977). General standards of behaviour and ethics should not be viewed in terms of what is legally possible in the pursuit of profit. Firms that adapt above-average standards and assert leadership should benefit in the long term through customer goodwill and avoidance of later recriminations. This challenge is made even more difficult because diverging standards of behaviour are applied to businesses in different countries. These issues can be summarised in terms of two basic questions. What formal rules must I follow? What informal rules must I follow? These two questions are summarised in Figure 1.1.

Figure 1.1 Basic Questions for the Global Manager

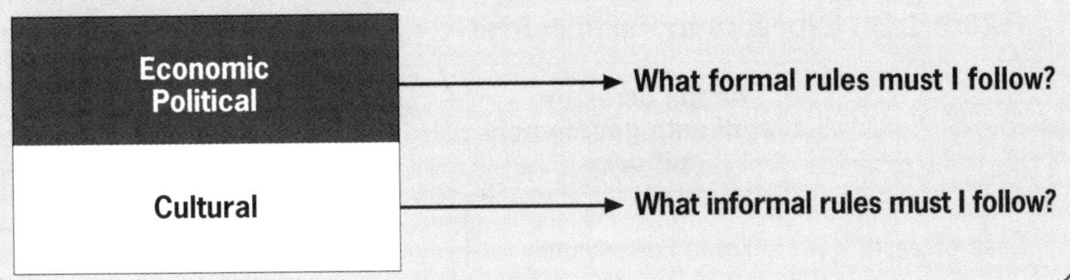

The Economic and Political Challenge

Political risk. From the host country's perspective, managers need to factor in the risk that is associated with the political environment. Executives of MNEs have found political events to be one of the most important factors in the foreign investment decision. Political risk refers to the risk that political events and processes within the host country and changing relationships between the host and the home country, as well as between the host country and other countries, will influence the economic well-being of the parent firm. Political risk is defined as unexpected changes in future cash flows due to political events in the host country (Feils and Sabac, 2000; Howell and Chaddick, 1994). Lessard (2000) defines political risk as the "the risk of political discontinuities resulting in losses through expropriation or major policy shifts". Harms (2000) defines political risk in terms of three sub-indices of the International Country Risk Guide (ICRG) index of financial risk: the likelihood of a "repudiation of contracts by governments", of the "expropriation of private investment" and of "losses from exchange controls". Kobrin (1982) noted that in assessing the level of political risk, changes could arise because of routine policymaking, in addition to those changes that arise from regular or irregular transfers of power.

Political risk may thus lead to unexpected increases or decreases in future cash flows. Rights and control over assets and the transfer of capital can change as a result of anti-US capitalism, anti-industry, or anti-Western/colonial motives of terrorists and new governments. Figure 1.2 shows the two types of risk factors that may affect either the loss of assets or loss of profits. Typically, the nationalistic motives of governments result in the loss of assets and/or profits. Government actions range from direct confiscation (with no compensation, such as what is currently happening in Zimbabwe), expropriation (with compensation, but usually unsatisfactory) and domestication (a more subtle form of control, where the government demands the transfer of ownership and management responsibility or more local content – either in inputs or profit retention).

Figure 1.2 Exposure to Political Risk

	Action taken by a legitimate government authority	Factors outside the government
Loss of assets	Forced divestiture	War, revolution
Loss of profits	Restrictions on inputs and outputs	Nationalistic buyers and suppliers

Export and exchange controls. As long as regulations are not harmonised internationally, firms need to be highly sensitive to different and perhaps rapidly changing export control regimes. Export control problems exist in four basic areas: determining what constitutes civilian, military and dual-use products; addressing the lack of national consensus on dual-use products; the difficulty in controlling knowledge-based products; and the different national economic interests that are being safeguarded (Czinkota, Ronkainen and Moffett, 1996). The changed environment of exchange controls makes it more difficult to police exports to and from non-friendly countries.

Government measures such as exchange controls to protect developing nations against high imports, tax policy and price controls pose a level of economic risk that must be accounted for in international business. The international executive may be forced to choose between shutting down the operation or continuing production at a loss in the hope of recouping profits when the government loosens or removes its price restrictions. For example, Harms (2000) shows that recent policy measures which have hurt foreign investors are Brazil's restrictions on hard currency remittances in 1989 and the exchange controls that were imposed by Venezuela in 1994 and by Malaysia in 1998. In Brazil, the policy was introduced in the wake of presidential elections, in Venezuela it followed the election of a president who partly reversed the reform-oriented policy of his predecessor, and in Malaysia an incumbent government imposed the restrictions.

Managing political risk. There are three basic ways in which an MNE can manage political risk. First, it should understand the legal differences and constraints (such as common law or code law, litigation propensity and laws on advertising) in the following areas:

- International bilateral and multilateral agreements that aim to ensure the equal treatment of local and foreign firms.
- International acceptable economic practices as defined by the World Trade Organisation (WTO) for its member nations.
- Intellectual property rights – including rights to inventions, patents, trademarks and industrial designs, and copyright on literature, music, art and photography. For example: 1) the Paris Convention, which provides the protection of industrial property for 96 national signatories, offers minimum standards of protection and 2) the Patent Cooperation Treaty (PCT), which provides procedures for filing one international application that designates the nations in which a patent is sought.

There are several examples of how the law can affect MNE operations: 1) domestic content requirements may force a firm to purchase its supplies and parts locally, thus resulting in higher costs and reduced efficiency and lower-quality products, 2) export requirements can hamper international distribution plans and force changes to or the closure of operations in third world countries, 3) a weakening of intellectual property right protection, which can undermine a company's core competitive edge, and 4) shielded industries in the MNE's home country can affect the long-term international competitiveness of operations abroad. Ultimately, knowledge is often the firm's most precious competitive advantage, and the violation of laws that protect such knowledge can have significant financial repercussions. Moreover, the MNE must closely monitor political developments and take out risk insurance, which may be offered by industrialised nations.

Second, the MNE can enter into partnerships with local firms in the countries in which they operate. These partnerships are typically formed under the guise of a cooperative or contractual (equity) joint venture. Such forms of partnership are discussed in further detail in Chapter 2. Generally, this is a cooperative strategy aimed at sharing different resources that are specific to each partner's factor advantages. This helps to reduce the dependencies of each partner, and over time promotes greater communication and trust between the MNE and the partner/government of the host country. Such ventures are, however, not without their complications (see Chapter 4 for further discussion).

Third, the MNE can increase its local responsiveness through local hiring, better pay or contributions to society (e.g., charities) (see Figure 1.3). One possible drawback is that if a firm is forced to hire nationals, this may result in poor cooperation and communication. For example, operations may have to be headed by poorly trained and inexperienced local managers (this issue is discussed in further detail in Chapter 3).

Figure 1.3 Management of Political Risk

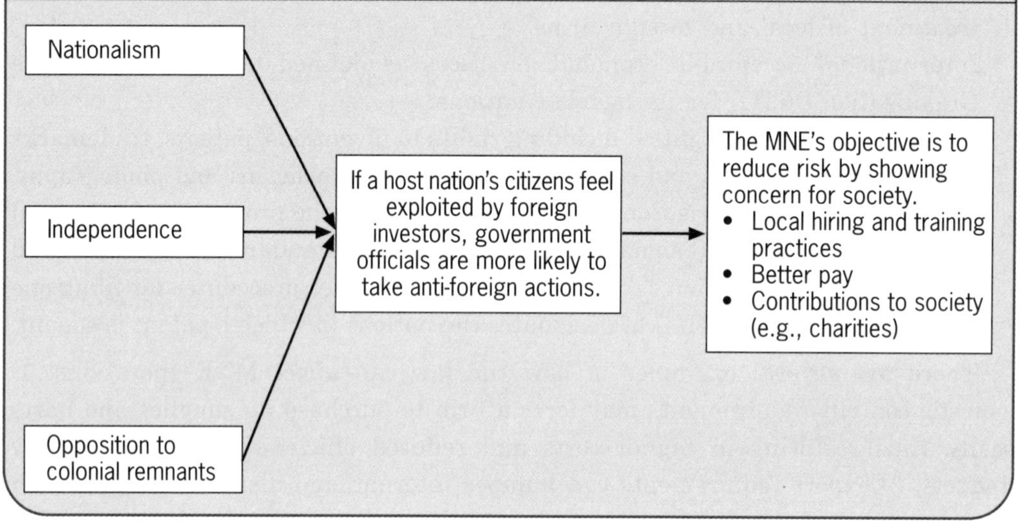

Measurement of political risk. The measurement of political risk is important. If an organisation wrongly assesses the political risk of a particular country in terms of the perceived risk being greater than the real risk, then it is likely that less investment will be made, thus resulting in lost chances to make profits. However, if the perceived risk is assessed to be less than the real risk, then it is likely that too much investment will be made, which can result in the loss of profit, or returns that are below expectations. As a result of the potential loss of profit or assets (or foregone opportunities), MNEs invest huge amounts in political and economic risk consultants to help them understand the firm's potential exposure to such risk when considering a particular investment. Several political and economic risk consultants have developed country ranking indices based on particular political and economic risk measures. Some of the more popular indices are as follows:

- Political Stability Index http://gsb.uchicago.edu/fac/marvin.zonis/ or www.marvinzonis.com
- Business Environment Risk Intelligence (BERI) www.beri.com
- Political Risk Services (PRS) www.prsgroup.com
- The Economist Intelligence Unit (EIU) www.eiu.com
- Dun and Bradstreet Information Services www.express.dnbsearch.com

In considering the best index to use, it is important to note that the country-ranking measures tend to be an aggregate of numerous unrelated factors that bear on political and economic risk. Some of these factors may not be relevant for a particular MNE investment. For example, from the viewpoint of the MNE, stability of the environment and human resource capability are two of the key factors in deciding whether to invest in a country. The Political Stability Index, developed by Marvin Zonis, a professor of International Political Economy at the University of Chicago, was one of the first quantitative models of political risk to incorporate these dimensions (see Table 1.1). Stability is a theme that runs through indicators one, three, four, seven and nine. The greater a country ranks in terms of stability, the

Table 1.1 Components of the Political Stability Index

1) Prosperity	Measured by the level of GDP. This measure is most important and is indicative of whether a return will be made for investment in a country.
2) Work ethic	Level of rental income received by a country. Rental income is non-work income such as royalties for oil and other natural resources. Greater rental income reduces the incentive to work. This measure is important because it is desirable to have an economic structure to induce people to work hard.
3) Equality	Measured in terms of the infant mortality rate. This is an indicator of stability based on the ideal that poor people should receive an acceptable level of benefits in a country.
4) Stability and predictability	Measured in terms of a low rate of inflation and a low rate of change in inflation over time. A strong legal system also contributes to this indicator. Overall, this measures the extent to which investing is predictable.
5) Rural lobbies	The presence of rural lobbies is a negative indicator of the work ethic because those countries with no rural industry (such as Hong Kong and Singapore) typically have to work harder to develop their economies.
6) Traumas	Survival causes countries to change successfully. This is another indicator of capability and work ethic.
7) Democracies	Which are characterised by the peaceful transfer of power, are crucial because a legitimate government provides stability to the country.
8) Competition	An indicator of work ethic and the ability of the workforce to meet a world-class standard of production.
9) Quality of life	Measured by the length of human life. As the country's life cycle increases, there is greater stability.
10) Human capital	Measured by the level of literacy of the workforce. This provides another indication of the capability of the workforce in the country.

lower is the risk premium needed in forecasting future returns from a planned investment. In contrast, capability is a theme that runs through indicators two, five, six, eight and ten. This group of indicators provides information to the MNE about the potential capability of the workforce of another country. This can help the MNE assess the efficiency of operations beyond a simple knowledge of wage rates, living costs and housing. Overall it is important to note that such indices serve as a guide for further examination of the risk factors that are likely to affect MNE investment.

The Cultural Challenge

Culture refers to the collective sharing of norms and values by a group of people that generally live in particular geographical regions or countries. Elements of culture include language, religion, values and attitudes. These elements have been characterised in the following terms:

- Context – For example, high-context cultures (such as Japan and Saudi Arabia, in which communication depends more on the context of the spoken word) versus low-context cultures (such as the US, in which the meaning of the spoken word has greater applicability across many contexts).
- Homogeneity – Japan and South Korea versus Southeast Asian countries.
- Cultural imperialism – For example, Brazil, Canada, France and Indonesia protect their cultural industries such as music and motion pictures.
- Economic development – Deeply ingrained systematic differences between the emerging democracies and Western firms continue. Highly prized, fully accepted fundamentals of the market economy, such as the reliance on competition, support of the profit motive and the willingness to live with risk on a corporate and personal level might not yet be fully accepted.

The cultural challenge is a significant factor in international business to the extent that different cultures affect international business processes both within the MNE and between the MNE and other people or entities. The norms and values that are collectively held by a group of people have been found to influence the way international business is transacted especially in the areas of contract negotiation, incentive orientation and the sharing of information.

Contract negotiation. The more central values and attitudes (such as religion) are, the more cautiously the international business manager has to move in terms of manners and customs. Negotiators must be prepared for different ways of thinking, such as the importance of "saving face" and roles of personal relations and personalities in the decision-making process, leaving sufficient time for negotiation. The following cultural elements should be considered in contract negotiation:

- Material elements – Economic, social, financial and marketing infrastructure
- Aesthetics – Good taste in terms of the arts and the symbolism of colours, form and music
- Education
- Social institutions – These affect the ways in which people relate to each other.

As a result, people with different cultural backgrounds often do not share the same basic assumptions and this has an influence at several levels of business negotiations (Usunier, 1996). For example, it is common for Chinese to use the expression "to lose 'face' (or *mianzi*) to justify a bargaining position or staying in an unprofitable business arrangement (Chen and Godkin, 2001) (see Highlights).

Incentive orientation of people. Different cultures have different approaches to risk and time and these factors are likely to impact on the effectiveness of various human resource policies (e.g., selection, socialisation, career development and

HIGHLIGHTS

Simple Steps for Successful Contract Negotiations in China

Choosing a negotiator. Choose a negotiator who does not single out people for accountability but who can win the trust and confidence of those you are trying to negotiate with.

Respect the Chinese culture. Due respect for the country's culture is crucial so that trust can be won quicker. Understanding the culture can enhance one's knowledge of Chinese negotiation tactics, which may help the negotiation process. At the very least this will help you to be more patient in negotiations.

Patience. The aim is to win the Chinese heart and trust, and this takes great patience, tolerance, calmness, persistence and honest dealings with the Chinese (Fang, 1999). The Chinese are likely to distrust salesman-type negotiators who want to make a quick deal.

Establishing and consolidating the relationship. Successful negotiations are likely to result from a long process of formal (company visits) and informal (socialising over meals, drinks, etc.) meetings. This is a process of relationship building during which differences in business styles and practices are resolved and a state of "old friends" bonded by trust appears (Fang, 1999).

compensation). The challenge for supervisors is how to develop the productivity and commitment of employees given their different economic orientation, philosophies and practices. For example, in training to be effective, it must be seen to lead to actual changes in behaviour such as enhanced productivity or commitment (reduced turnover). Compensation policies need to be flexible to fit the context in terms of the nature of rewards. For example, in some places in China it is still important to reward outstanding staff in non-monetary terms such as an award that is presented to the employee in front of his family.

Sharing of information. The traditional Western emphasis on the benefits of two-way information sharing does not naturally transfer to Eastern cultures, where greater emphasis is placed on one-way sharing and the saving of "face". This latter emphasis is institutionalised through the formal layers of hierarchy that exist in East Asian business systems (Whitley, 1994). In these organisations, strategic and, in most cases, operational decisions are centralised. People at the operations level are generally controlled via formal rules and procedures. The business system tends to reflect the hierarchical nature of the family in which elder family members command the highest respect. These business and social conditions tend to discourage the sharing of information upwards in the organisation. For example, Chow, Deng and Ho (2000) find that the People's Republic of China (PRC) nationals are significantly less likely than their US counterparts to share information files with co-workers that are not part of their "in-group". As a result, for the MNE wholly owned subsidiary that employs local staff, learning about problems may take longer, and seeking feedback about how to improve operations and avoiding potential problems is more difficult, thus adding to the costs of decision making and controlling people in the subsidiary.

THE CHALLENGE FOR INTERNATIONAL BUSINESS IN CHINA

China is now the largest FDI recipient in the world. In achieving this position and developing a market-oriented economy, the country had to overcome inadequate social overhead capital, a lack of business entrepreneurs and managers, conflict with the US and other Western countries and conflict with Taiwan. Now that China is a member of the WTO, the amount of FDI will continue to increase. However, the WTO deadlines are scheduled gradually, hence several regulatory barriers remain. Regardless of the advancement in regulatory openness accorded to the WTO, the uncertain business environment remains one of the main deterrents of FDI.

The China WTO Regulatory Environment

Compliance with regulations is an important consideration in any country. What makes China special in this regard is the location of regulatory authority with certain government officials and the constant change or lack of transparency in the regulations that are in place at any one time. The recent entry of China into the WTO will increase this transparency and will open many previously protected industries and markets to FDI and trade.

In the pre-WTO period, certain industries were prohibited from entry and minimum investment requirements were stipulated depending on whether the entry mode was a wholly foreign-owned subsidiary (WFOS) or a joint venture (see Table 1.2 for the general requirements). In certain industries however, the Chinese government does not encourage companies to form wholly foreign-owned subsidiaries (such as property development). In this case only equity or cooperative joint ventures are allowed.

As a result of the WTO agreement, most industries are now open to FDI of entry mode of WFOSs or joint ventures. The recent WTO agreement opened the way for access to a broad range of industries particularly the service sector. Table 1.3 provides a detailed timeframe of access for most of the service sectors in the China economy. While the WTO agreement has increased both access and transparency of FDI, it is still important that MNEs manage the non-regulatory factors and maintain good communications and relationships with the relevant government officials and focus on business, and not political, issues.

The China Business Environment

Once an MNE has chosen to enter China, within the regulatory guidelines there are several key factors that need to be considered, which can influence both the nature of contract choice and the way in which business is undertaken once a contractual agreement has been signed. These are: early timing, the nature and size of contributions (such as technology transfers and financing), *guanxi* (see page 21), human resources management, intellectual property rights and information technology.

Early entry and size of contributions. The benefit of early entry was best shown by Volkswagen's entry to China in 1985. For several years the firm made huge losses, but it prevailed and now commands over one third of the world's fastest-growing car market. In a longitudinal analysis of industry-wide, firm-specific data on FDI timing and foreign venture performance, Luo (1998) found that timing has a significant influence on overall, as well as individual, aspects of venture performance. Early entrants outperform late movers in terms of local market expansion and asset

Table 1.2 Chinese Policy Towards Foreign Investment in Selected Sectors

Sector	01/01/1998 WFOS	01/01/1998 Joint venture	11/12/2004 WFOS	11/12/2004 Joint venture
Accounting, auditing services	P	R	E	E
Legal consultancy services	P	R	R	R
Agency services	P	R	P	R
Airport management	P	E	P	E
Automotive	P	R,C	P	R(50%)
Aviation	P	R,C(35%)	P	R,C(49%)
Commercial retailing	P	PE,C	PE	PE
Education	P	R	P	E
Foreign trade	P	PE,C	PE	PE
Golf courses	P	R	P	R
Highway construction	E	E	E	E
Hotels	P	R	R	E,R
Leasing	R	R	PE	PE
Media	P	P	P	R,C
Medical institutes	P	PE,C	P	PE
Non-ferrous metal industry (including mining)	P	R	P	E
Non-metallic ores	P	R	E	E
Ports, piers	P	E,C	P	E
Power generation equipment	P	R	E	E
Railways	P	E	P	E
Real estate (high-grade villas and office)	P	R	P	R
Road transport	P	R	R	R
Travel agency	P	R	P	R

Code:

E Encouraged
R Restricted
PE Permitted
P Prohibited
C Chinese partner must have controlling stake
(%) % cap on foreign ownership
WFOS Wholly foreign-owned subsidiary

Source: Ministry of Commerce, PRC, Catalogue for the Guidance of Foreign Investment Industries. Amended in 2004. Accessed from http://www.fdi.gov.cn/itlaw/labinfodisp.jsp?id=ABC00000000000104539appld=1 on 3 February 2005.

Table 1.3 China and the WTO Commitments on Services

Sector	Market access commitment	Progress
Professional services		
Legal	Establish representative offices with no geographic or quantitative restrictions	Done
Accounting, auditing and bookkeeping	CPA licences issued on a national treatment by Chinese authorities can establish partnership or incorporated firms	Done
Advertising	Establish JV with majority ownership. Establish WFOS	Done 11/12/2005
Management Consulting	Establish JV with majority ownership. Establish WFOS	Done 11/12/2007
Telecom		
Value-added services and paging services	Establish JV with 50% ownership with no geographic restrictions	Done
Mobile voice and data services	Establish JV with 49% ownership	Done (in most major cities)
Domestic (fixed-line) services	Establish JV with 25% ownership in Shanghai, Guangzhou and Beijing Establish JV with 35% ownership in expanded areas Establish JV with 49% ownership with no geographic restrictions	Done 11/12/2006 11/12/2007
Distribution services		
Commission agents and wholesale (salt and tobacco is prohibited)	All business except chemical fertilisers, processed oil and crude oil Chemical fertilisers, processed oil and crude oil	Done 11/12/2006
Retail (tobacco is prohibited)	All business except chemical fertilisers Chemical fertilisers	Done 11/12/2006
Education services	Establish JV schools with majority ownership	Done
Insurance	Establish JV for life insurance with 50% ownership with geographic restrictions Establish JV for non-life insurance with 51% ownership with geographic restrictions Establish WFOS for non-life insurance No geographic restrictions	Done Done Done Done
Banking	Foreign currency business Local currency business No geographical restrictions	Done Done 11/12/2006

Table 1.3 China and the WTO Commitments on Services (Cont'd)

Securities	Representative offices Establish fund management JV with 33% ownership Establish fund management JV with 49% ownership and establish JV with 33% ownership to underwrite A shares and to underwrite and trade B and H shares and government and corporate debts	Done Done Done
Tourism		
Hotels and restaurants	Establish JV with majority ownership to construct, renovate and operate hotel and restaurants. No restrictions	Done 11/12/2005
Travel agency and tour operators	Establish restricted WFOS No geographic restrictions	Done 11/12/2007
Transport services		
Maritime transport	Establish JV under the Chinese flag with 49% ownership	Done
Air transport	Establish JV aircraft repair and maintenance enterprises The Chinese side shall hold controlling shares or be in a dominant position	Done
Rail transport	Establish JV with majority ownership Establish WFOS	Done 11/12/2007
Road transport	Establish JV with majority ownership Establish WFOS	Done Done

Code:
WFOS Wholly foreign-owned subsidiary
JV Joint venture
Source: Ministry of Commerce, PRC, Catalogue for the Guidance of Foreign Investment Industries. Amended in 2004.

turnover. Size is another important factor in venture success in China. The size of the MNE investment communicates commitment, and capability supports the investment in the long term. Size also implies an ability to benefit more from economies of scale and scope and invest in advanced equipment and technology (Luo, 1997). In a study of 127 randomly selected foreign-invested enterprises (FIEs) that operated in Jiangsu Province from 1989 to 1991, Luo (1997) found that in addition to the early timing of entry and *guanxi*, venture size is likely to have a positive effect on performance. Vanhonacker (1997) noted that companies must be prepared to bring something of value to China, usually jobs or new technology that can help the country develop.

THEORY IN ACTION

What Can We Learn from Coca-Cola? The Soft Drink Industry in China since 1979

Like many other industries in China, the soft drink industry is still controlled by the government. The Chinese government has been imposing serious *trade barriers* to protect the industry since its initiation of the Open Door policy in 1979. Before 1979, no foreign-branded soft drinks were available in China. Every bottle of soft drink was a local product of a state-owned enterprise. This situation started to change in 1979, but it was not until 1981 that Coca-Cola set up its first bottling plant in Beijing.

Even though the advent of foreign production was a great step in the opening of the Chinese soft drink market, different types of restrictions followed, including restrictions on the mode of entry and choosing of partners. In 1979, the only mode of entry for foreign soft drink investors was the cooperative joint venture, and there was no freedom in choosing partners. Partners were assigned by central government from amongst state-owned bottlers. Meanwhile, bottling plants had to be under the supervision of China National Cereals, Oils and Foodstuffs Import Export Corporation. In addition, the central government imposed an administrative policy that restricted the investment of foreign investors. This included the number of bottling plants and the share of the joint venture that a foreign investor could have. The following quotation from a Chinese official regarding China's attitude towards soft drink joint ventures with foreign partners vividly described the situation: "One part for you and three parts for us."

The soft drink market in China has experienced drastic changes since 1979. The share of foreign-branded soft drinks has gone up from 0% before 1979 to more than 80% in 1997. Coca-Cola occupies 40% of the soft drink market and 75% of carbonated drink market. However, this trend has started to reverse since Jianlibao (a large local producer) has entered the market. The reversal is also a result of the increasing Chinese concern about health (instead of taste alone). This has created a huge non-carbonated drinks market in which the sales growth has been rapid. It now accounts for 60% of the non-alcoholic beverage market in China.

Guidelines for Foreign Players in China

Controlled distribution. No matter how good the product is, it cannot be successful if you cannot reach the customer. The effect of controlled distribution can be seen on the contrasting experiences of Coca-Cola and Pepsi in China. Coca-Cola is using its directly controlled bottling plants and direct sales forces such as neighbourhood committees to distribute its products, whereas Pepsi is relying on independent wholesalers and its restaurant coverage to distribute its products. This significantly reduces the responsiveness of Pepsi to customer demand. Hence, the degree of control in distribution should be well considered.

Go native. This is a way of solving distribution and supply bottlenecks, and having to deal with unhelpful bureaucrats and develop local connections. It can be achieved by cooperation with local power establishments such as reformed state-owned soft drinks enterprises or semi-official enterprises. The other way of going native is to establish a localised product with a local image. This is important in increasing acceptance by the Chinese government and customers.

Correctly name the company and the product. This helps customers recognise the company and its product. It also can avoid trouble from the nuances of language and cultural differences. The Chinese translation of Pepsi is "Hundred Things Happiness", which sped up the company's market recognition. In Taiwan, the slogan of "Come alive with the Pepsi generation" was translated as "Pepsi will bring your ancestors back from the dead", which was obviously unacceptable.

Be willing to be a contributor. China is a developing country, so it is most welcoming to those companies that can bring in what it wants, such as new technology and economic development. Any company that is valuable to China will likely receive favourable treatment from Chinese officials. When Coca-Cola agreed to develop special new products for the Chinese market and transferred its production technology to its local partner, Chinese officials granted Coca-Cola the right to expand into ten new provinces.

Be adaptive to the industry and market environment. Like other developing countries, China does not have many well-developed provisions to regulate its political, economic, social and trade policies and environment. Any strategy that leads a firm to fortune today may put it in a harsh position tomorrow. As the *open door* policy further allows the Chinese to get in touch with the outside world, they will learn from the advanced technology and management experience of developed countries, and consumer tastes will change. If any company wants to have or keep a place in the Chinese market, then it should always consider its own adaptation to the ever-changing environment.

Guanxi. *Guanxi* refers to the informal network of relationships that permeates a business culture. As such it is one of the most researched factors in doing business in China because it pervades the business world in Chinese society (Luo, 1997). Vanhonacker (1997) notes that in addition to having a source of *guanxi* or social or political connections, companies need to take steps to avoid trampling on China's cultural or economic sovereignty. Good relationships with municipal governments and tax bureaus are very important. This will smoothen the approval procedures that are necessary in both the start-up and ongoing phases of doing business. Tse, Pan and Au (1997) found that in addition to the location of operation, levels of government interaction and *guanxi* affect entry-mode strategies. Nair and Stafford (1998) agree that *guanxi* is very important in China, because "*guanxi* facilitates working through the system".

One of the recent practices adopted by large MNEs is to contract for *guanxi* by recruiting ex-government officials. Since these officials understand the Chinese bureaucracy and speak the bureaucratic language, they are in a better position to simulate bureaucratic thinking, and thus are in a more advantageous situation to sell the MNE to the Chinese government. However, some ex-government officials have also admitted that there are situations in which *guanxi* does not work, especially when policy changes are mandated by the Government. To a certain extent, this may illustrate that *guanxi* could be contracted rather than acquired through cooperation with a local partner (as in equity joint venture partnerships).

Human resources management. China's vast population of relatively cheap labour provides an important rationale for much of the FDI China receives each year. The sourcing of cheap labour is particularly apparent in the footwear and light electrical industries. However, there are several challenges in managing this resource. First, the movement of labour is often unpredictable. Often firms will require one month's wages in advance as security for each worker to remain with the firm, but this security declines in value over time and eventually workers tend to leave for a chance to work at other firms or move to other locations closer to their families. Moreover, when workers move they often move as a team, thus if a supervisor leaves his job, it is often the case that several of his best workers will follow him.

Second, there is a shortage of skilled labour both at the professional and non-professional levels which heightens the costs of managing such operations either by investing more into human resource activities such as training and career development, or by relying on more expensive expatriates to ensure that operations run smoothly. The shortage of skilled labour is exacerbated by a high level of staff turnover, which varies widely by region, industry and type of enterprise. For example, a recent survey found that the average turnover rate for all types of foreign-invested enterprises in China was 13.3%, nearly unchanged from 13.4% the year before (Watson Wyatt, 2004).

Finally, the wages in China continue to rise especially in the Special Economic Zones (SEZs). This has forced many foreign firms to locate their investments towards the west of China where wage rates are lower by more than 50%. Minimum wages are also set at a level that is not less than half of the average wage in each province. According to Pun (2004), as of August 2004, the top five SEZs have the highest minimum monthly wage; RMB660 in Guangzhou, RMB635 in Shanghai, RMB620 in Nanjing, RMB610 in Shenzhen and RMB520 in Hangzhou.

Intellectual property rights. Under the agreement on trade-related intellectual property rights (TIPRs), WTO members must adopt and enforce strong and non-discriminatory minimum standards of protection for intellectual property. Many developed countries are extending strong protection to controversial areas, including biotechnology and electronic databases. Despite some reform, intellectual property rights remain a serious problem for MNEs in China. For example, several US companies (e.g., Heinz, SC Johnson, Procter & Gamble) have found that their local joint venture partners or people whom they have contracted have pirated aspects of their product design (Weldon and Vanhonacker, 1999). Foreign partners are also frustrated by the lack of power to enforce damages obtained through the court system. While not all measures are effective in reducing such pirating, MNEs have attempted to mitigate this problem by limiting technology and product design transfer to older generation technologies and by employing expatriates to control areas where such sensitive information exists in the foreign-invested venture.

Information technology. Up until the beginning of the century, most of the FDI in China was directed towards mass manufacturing of retail and intermediate goods. The reliance on technology was limited to the manufacturing technology and most firms employed expatriates to monitor and train locals to use such technology. But with the opening up of China to a broad range of services, the reliance on technology is likely to be more critical both internally, and in the distribution of the service to the market. One example is the banking industry where the People's Bank of China (PBOC) requires foreign banks to use the PBOC system in addition to the foreign bank's own system. The PBOC system is not as sophisticated to support the multitude of banking services offered by the foreign banks and repairs to the system often take days to complete due to the limited supply of skilled technicians. Another example is the limited expansion of the Internet in China, at present covering less than 10% of the population. In addition the use of credit cards in China especially

THEORY IN ACTION

The Challenges Facing Two Hong Kong Manufacturers in China

The two interviews were held with a clothes manufacturer (Company A) and a toy manufacturer (Company B), both of which had invested in Guangdong Province. Both companies located their manufacturing operations in China in order to take advantage of the lower labour, rental and transportation costs. The directors of both companies commented that political topics are sensitive in China. Hence, the interviews concentrated on business development, in which factors such as government policy changes, *guanxi*, changes of government officials and the legal system were more important.

Company A commented on employee problems. It had about 150 employees in Guangdong, and the director was worried about the potential risk of employees taking industrial action or the power of the trade union increasing. The director claimed that there was a cultural difference between Hong Kong and mainland Chinese employees. Hong Kong workers worked harder, and it was difficult to ask them not to work overtime. In contrast, money was the major motivation of mainland Chinese workers.

Another major factor for both companies was *guanxi*. They commented that *guanxi* was very important in China. It could help them to collect useful information rapidly. Good *guanxi* with government officials, suppliers and clients was extremely important. Although *guanxi* is theoretically different from corruption, the directors of both companies said that the distinction is difficult to make. The maintenance of good relationships with government officials requires many gifts and business meals. Sometimes the officials request extra services for their families. Hence, when government officials change, companies lose their "investments". Company A gave the example of a former Beijing mayor who was dismissed for corruption. Foreign enterprises in Beijing then lost the *guanxi* investments they had made in the mayor.

Keen competition and pirated products were also two major factors that concerned the companies. Company B said that pirated products were a great problem – some local factories copied its toys.

on-line has not yet gained acceptance. While the later example is part of the development process that China is going through, the limits of information technology is quite evident when it comes to the expansion of sales channels on-line or the move into new service areas that requires the support of more sophisticated information technology.

THEORY IN ACTION

Banking on China – Global Bank Ltd

Global Bank Ltd (GBL) is one of the largest commercial banks in the US. It is a well-known competitor in wholesale non-credit activities, providing a broad range of cash management services, cheque-clearing and collection services, fund transfer and information-based services. It has an extensive international presence, evidenced by its more than 100 overseas operations and 15,000 overseas employees. GBL has built an information-based business system which allows the bank to access the information of their customers immediately. It enables the bank to know about customers including all the products and services they use and how they like to use them. This integrated system, along with other kinds of information, now drive targeted marketing campaigns and provide analytical tools to identify new customers and create real benefits for the bank. However, the operation of GBL's business in China uses different strategies since the technological level of the banking industry in China is comparatively low and their processing system is far from automated.

GBL established their operations in Shanghai Pudong in 1996 after the bank industry of China was opened to foreign participants. Although the Chinese government permits the foreign investor to participate in the bank industry, only limited financial markets are opened to them. The licence to operate renminbi business was not granted to foreign banks until 1997. Therefore, GBL's business initially focused on the several types of corporate banking services, like foreign currency deposits and loans, foreign exchange, letters of credit, fund transfers and derivatives.

China Banking System

Based on the automation plan of the PBOC, all commercial banks are linked up by a system developed by the Central government. GBL has to maintain a software system provided by PBOC for reporting purpose. But the system is not compatible with the international bank system, so GBL needs to maintain another system integrated with their foreign operations. Two systems are running separately in GBL to meet the different reporting requirements of PBOC and the bank itself. A challenge posed by the local bank system is mapping and auditing. The capability of the local system is also insufficient for the large volume of transactions, therefore, the processing procedures are not fully automated and tracing a particular transaction is very difficult. The system is feasible only if the customer base is narrow. To overcome this problem, GBL has downloaded the data from the system for further processing by additional PC software applications. The technology now adopted by GBL in their China operations includes Windows, the intranet, the Internet, e-commerce and accounting programmes. GBL has also developed imaging which is the most recent technology in the banking industry.

Human Resources

Except for the incompatibility of the local system, GBL has been faced with the problem of human resources. Owing to the under-development of both hardware and software engineering in China, the local server supporting service is so poor that when machines break down it is a few days later before the engineers come. The technical know-how of the local engineers is also poor; GBL has assigned the technical experts in Hong Kong or other Asian regions to work in China. However, some local staff have also been trained to do some routine network administration work. Further to the gradual reformation of the financial sector in China, GBL can foresee that information technology will become a major subject in the universities and more expertise will be available.

Competition and Future Strategy

From experience, GBL found that there is a large gap of technology between foreign and local banks in China. The restriction on the activities of foreign banks has prevented them from investing large amounts of capital for technology innovation in China. Their systems are developed in foreign countries and adopted in China at a later date. While the local banks are using the system provided by the central bank without modification, their work is paper intensive and their products are still standardised with little choices. The product and services offered by foreign banks are more personalised and customer oriented, this is the major factor contributing to high competitive power of the foreign banks.

GBL continues to maintain their operation in China at a minimum capital investment because of the existing political obstacles. When China becomes a strategically important market for large global companies, the banking sector in China will be a battleground for competition. GBL is still waiting for the opening of the remaining business areas that may appear in the near future.

SUMMARY

With increasing globalisation, the complexities and opportunities of managing an international business has become a critical knowledge area that every manager must understand. MNEs in their pursuit of their strategic objectives undertake international expansion for various reasons. MNEs typically have various locations in mind for expansion. Thus it is important to understand the reasons for expansion and the information required to assess the costs and benefits of the various alternatives.

The first part of this chapter provides a framework for understanding two important areas of planning for international expansion: the strategic rationale for MNE expansion and the international business environment. Global managers should be familiar with the economic and political rules of the country in which they are planning to expand. They should also be familiar with the informal rules or cultural dictates of the country. Both of these areas of concern must also be considered in the light of the strategic rationale for international expansion. After considering these factors, they will be in a better position to understand the reasons for particular contracting and management control choices.

The second part of this chapter highlights the WTO regulatory and business environment issues facing MNEs that enter China. While political issues were not the most important consideration, other factors such as *guanxi*, employee problems and protection of intellectual property were considered to be more crucial in decision making. And while the planned changes to the rules governing the various industries are likely to enhance the transparency of the environment, it remains important that MNEs maintain good communication and relationships with the relevant government officials and focus on business issues.

QUESTIONS

1) What are the different motivations for MNEs to expand internationally? Provide examples.
2) List two main questions that MNE managers should ask when looking to invest in developing countries.
3) Define political risk.
4) In what ways can MNEs attempt to manage political risk?
5) Name three types of political risk indicators.
6) What are the disadvantages of using political risk indicators to measure the political risk of a particular country?

7) What are two main characteristics that MNEs seek when investing abroad?
8) In what ways do differences in national culture affect MNE operations?
9) Find an example of a company that fits into each of the following categories for going international (be sure to note the country to which its business motive relates, and the nature of the product or service provided).
    a) Resource seekers
    b) Market seekers
    c) Efficiency seekers
    d) Strategic asset seekers
    e) Other motives for MNE activity
10) What are the main reasons for an MNE expansion into China? Provide examples.
11) What are the main influences on doing business in China?
12) What is *guanxi*?
13) What are the various alternatives in contracting for *guanxi*?
14) To what extent has China opened up as a result of her entry into the WTO?
15) Find an article on business failure in China. Explain what factors led to the failure and what measures could be taken to minimise the risks of failure?
16) China's entry into the WTO is viewed by some (along with the rule of law) as a magic wand to protect foreign business investment. Do you agree? Discuss.

CASE STUDY 1

A Ltd – *Guanxi* and Agency Problems in China

INTRODUCTION AND MOTIVATION

"Corruption, bribes and kickbacks have almost become part of the system in China, just like the old days before the communist revolution. Somebody that you have to bribe is not going to be a good business partner" (Barth, 1997). In a culture where *guanxi* has always been more important than laws, establishment of the legal framework has been futile without increased enforcement of existing laws. Foreign businesses are not the only ones frustrated by the problems that remain in China today. Nevertheless, *guanxi* is still regarded as one of the important determinants in the success of wholly owned foreign enterprises and joint venture businesses in China. The problem is that many Hong Kong investors have benefited from *guanxi* on the mainland. Will they be in a worse position in the coming years? What are the implications of agency theory for joint ventures in China? What strategies do foreign-invested enterprises need to implement in order to cope with such changes? The assessment of the case of A Ltd demonstrates that *guanxi* is still very important, though not without adverse effects.

Cost factors such as lower labour and capital costs and lower rent and land prices are still the dominant motivation behind investing in China. Geographical and cultural proximities, FDI and tax incentives and the attraction of the large Chinese market are also important investment motivations. Moreover, the high levels of *guanxi* that are maintained between Hong Kong investors and Chinese officials make Hong Kong FDI in China easier for Hong Kong investors than those from other countries. As will be shown in the case of A Ltd, there is an agency problem in Hong Kong–China joint ventures. Most of the non-owner managers of these joint ventures act in their own interests or with their personal welfare as a priority.

I wish to acknowledge the assistance of Wong Yiu Kwong in the preparation of this case study. This case was developed as a basis for class discussion rather than to illustrate either effective or ineffective handling of an administrative situation.

THE BACKGROUND OF A LTD

A Ltd has been operating a trading business in Hong Kong for more than ten years with an annual turnover of over HK$200 million and a total asset value of more than HK$2 billion in recent years. The company also operates other businesses in Hong Kong, such as securities dealing, wholesaling and retailing. Among these, the company's main business is manufacturing plastic products such as toys, stationery and household products, and selling them to overseas markets in the US, Canada and other western European countries. Mr Chan is the major shareholder and managing director of the company. In view of the low profit margin of the company's trading business, he planned to set up manufacturing plants in China. Hence, in 1994, he set up a factory in Dongguan, Guangdong. The factory was owned by A Ltd and the Chinese government by way of an equity joint venture. A Ltd provided funds, machinery, managers and skilled workers, and the Chinese side provided land, buildings, unskilled and semi-skilled labour.

In the course of forming the joint venture, Mr Chan knew that the effect of *guanxi* was very important to business in China. Without good local connections it would be almost impossible to set up a joint venture in Dongguan within a year. When forming and operating the joint venture business, A Ltd had to pay "management fees", even when applying for telephone and electricity connections. These fees ranged from RMB1,000 to RMB100,000.

Mr Chan was not personally involved in the joint venture. Instead, he employed an experienced general manager, Mr Wang, to oversee the operations, and periodically sent accountants to audit the joint venture. In 1996, he set up similar joint venture in Shantou, another city in Guangdong.

AGENCY PROBLEMS FACED BY A LTD

After operating for four years, Mr Chan found that there was an agency problem between the general manager and himself. The problem surfaced in three types of requests made by the agent.

Requesting more money and time for building up and maintaining *guanxi*. Mr Wang, the general manager in Dongguan, continually asked Mr Chan for more money to establish and maintain *guanxi* which he did by paying various types of management fees, and for gifts, entertainment and so on. Sometimes, the entertainment expenses were more than RMB100,000 per month. Mr Wang recognised that he spent much time in nightclubs, karaoke bars and restaurants, which sometimes meant that he had no time to monitor the performance of the factory. Major decisions were often delayed. Nevertheless, Mr Wang insisted that it was necessary for the business to maintain good *guanxi*, and when Mr Chan questioned the legality of the payments, Mr Wang replied that regardless of legal concerns they were necessary in the maintenance of operations. Hence, even though the *guanxi* was a liability to the company, it was an asset to Mr Wang, because it meant that he as the focus of the *guanxi* could not be dismissed. This also led Mr Wang to ask Mr Chan to increase his monthly salary and bonus every year.

Agent requesting the principal to expand its operation. Mr Wang continually asked Mr Chan to expand the operation in Dongguan because he received a 5% share of annual profits in addition to his monthly salary. Despite this personal motive, he claimed that any increase in the size of the business would mean that a local bank would lend it larger sums of money. Mr Chan eventually doubled the size of the business, but a loan application was not approved. Mr Wang said that the bank had claimed that the business was still not large enough, and asked Mr Chan to invest more because the bank manager would only "give face" to a larger company.

Agent requesting the principal to engage in other businesses. Mr Wang often asked Mr Chan to engage in other businesses in Dongguan, such as restaurants and karaoke bars, as suggested by local government officials. In most cases, Mr Chan rejected the proposals, and Mr Wang countered that the government officials would be unhappy if their suggestions were always rejected, and that the *guanxi* he had built up would be negatively affected. Soon after, Mr Chan also discovered that Mr Wang had invested a small sum in a karaoke bar in Dongguan, which was made possible by the good connections he had established with local government officials. Mr Wang was continually looking for other investment opportunities, which Mr Chan considered to be a distraction from the joint venture operations.

Currently, most of Mr Wang's production duties have been delegated to his assistant managers, and he is only responsible for maintaining *guanxi* with local government officials and bankers.

CONCLUSION

In view of the above agency problems, Mr Chan is planning to modify his human resources management policy and his investment strategy in China to minimise the costs and effects of the current situation.

CASE STUDY QUESTIONS

1) According to the agency model: What are the costs and benefits of doing business in China?
2) Which aspects of agency theory can be applied to A Ltd's problem? Which aspects cannot? Provide examples.
3) How can A Ltd possibly solve this problem with the use of performance evaluation and compensation practices?
4) Is *guanxi* a Chinese business practice or a universal phenomenon? Discuss.

CASE STUDY 2

SK Group – Selecting Capital Investment in China versus South Korea

COMPANY BACKGROUND AND DECISION FRAMEWORK

SK Group Inc, a US company, is engaged in the semi-conductor business, including microchips and high-tech products, in the US and Europe (see Figure 1), with over 6,000 employees worldwide. SK Group's management targeted Asia for expansion in consideration of the fast growth of its semi-conductor market. That market comprised nearly one-half (48%) of SK Group's $16.87 billion global revenues in 2000. SK Group's most competitive strategy is its unique product with advanced technology and design, so the management wanted to select a high-control mode for entry into the Asian market. It decided to establish a wholly owned subsidiary in one Asian country. The subsidiary would have dual roles as a manufacturing plant and a marketing channel of the SK Group in Asia (see Figure 1).

The SK Group management selected the subsidiary location in line with its two global strategies of being a market seeker and a resource seeker. The regional choice had to bring the benefits of the Asian market share and low production cost to SK Group. Because of this, South Korea and China were taken into consideration. South Korea possessed leading-edge technology and market position in the global semi-conductor industry. It was ranked as the third largest global market leader, and its exports had 40% of the world's market. South Korea had a high-quality labour pool and stable semi-conductor market growth. In contrast, the development of the

I wish to acknowledge the assistance of Wong Yiu Kwong in the preparation of this case study. This case was developed as a basis for class discussion rather than to illustrate either effective or ineffective handling of an administrative situation.

Figure 1 Organisation Structure of SK Group

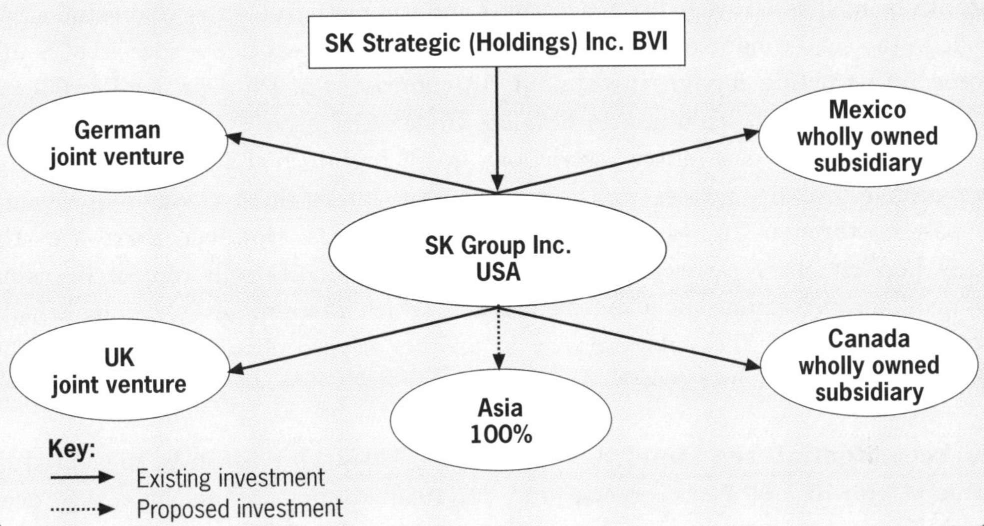

Chinese semi-conductor industry was far behind that of South Korea. However, China was expected to experience immense market growth after its accession to the WTO. (Based on current economic growth trends and semi-conductor development, it is believed that by 2010 China would become the world's second largest market for semi-conductors). In addition, China had a competitive incentive with a cheap labour pool.

This case study assesses the determinants of selecting capital investment in China versus South Korea. The OLI model and resource-based theory are used to assess the two investment alternatives. Information that is related to economic statistics, literature and an interview with the SK Group management are collected and applied to the analysis.

LOCATION ADVANTAGE COMPARISON

The comparison of the location advantages of China and South Korea focuses on three perspectives: political and government policies, market potential and economic factors of the host country. According to the criteria in Table 1, South Korea beats China in 12 areas, compared to the nine areas in China's favour. Each of these perspectives is discussed in turn.

Political environment (see Panel A, Table 1). Government, legal, taxation, trade and FDI entry policy are all favourable in South Korea. Generous investment incentives such as ten-year tax concessions and complete free entry and established trade in the semi-conductor industry are undoubtedly critical to the success of South Korea in attracting foreign investment. In contrast, the Chinese semi-conductor industry is only just beginning to develop. Under China's WTO commitments, the government has to ease entry restrictions in all high-tech industries by allowing foreign investors direct access to the market, thus lifting the previous requirement on passing through Chinese partners or intermediaries. However, there are still many implicit entry restrictions. For example bureaucrats still control licensing approval for protecting the Chinese market, which discourages entry by wholly owned subsidiaries. Technology piracy is another severe obstacle for FDI in the Chinese semi-conductor market.

Market potential (see Panel B, Table 1). Market potential can be measured in terms of growth and size (Terpstra and Yu, 1988). China has an advantage over South Korea in this respect. What most distinguishes the Chinese market is its high economic growth. China's GDP is currently growing at 7.3% per annum, and is expected to continue at this rate in the coming years (BBC Monitoring Asia Pacific, 2002). This rapid economic growth will cause a boom in the vast consumer markets, especially those of consumer electronics, telecom and wireless communications, further driving the need for increasing chip content and the growth of the semi-conductor market. As a result, China is expected to be the fastest growing semi-conductor consuming country and the world's second largest market for semi-conductors in the next decade. Although South Korea is now in a leading position, its niche market is too remote when compared to the Chinese giant market. From the investor's standpoint, the size and high potential of the Chinese market make it a superior choice.

Other economic factors (see Panel C, Table 1). The countries have equal scores in this area. Among all of the factors in panel C (see Table 1), wages have the most influence on FDI. Low wages lure many MNEs to move their investment bases from other Asian countries to China, South Korean semi-conductor manufacturers included (*Korea Herald*, 2001). The average monthly wage in China is only 40% (US$60) of that in South Korea (US$150). Moreover, strong labour union protection against minimum pay in South Korea is considered to be a demerit from the foreign investor's point of view.

The comparison indicates that the overall location advantages of South Korea are slightly superior to those of China, especially the investment risk in terms of

Table 1 Comparison of Location Advantages

	China	South Korea	Location advantages (√ = better) China	South Korea
Panel A: Political environment				
1) Legal system	Code law	Common law (following the US in recent years)		
a) Contract enforcement	International commercial contract based on Chinese laws	International commercial contract based on international laws		√
b) Intellectual property right protection	Low	High		√
c) Corruption	High	Low		√
2) Sovereign credit rating	BBB stable outlook	BBB+		√
3) Tax policy on FDI	33%	15% to 27% – 15% if profit < 100 m – 27% for excess > 100 m		
a) Corporate income tax	Maximum eight years' concession	Maximum ten years' tax tax concession		√
b) Incentives to high-tech FDI	Full exemption for the first two years and 50% tax exemption for the next six years	Full exemption for the first seven years and 50% tax exemption for the next three years		√
4) Entry restriction on high-tech industries	Restrictions eased in 2002 under WTO commitments, but a complete phase-out period will take several years	None		√
5) Trade restriction on high-tech products/materials				
a) Import	Restrictions eased in 2002 under WTO commitments, but a complete phase-out period will take several years	None		√
b) Export	None	None	–	–
6) Capital and exchange flow	Free	Free	–	–
7) Government subsidisation of local suppliers	Yes	Yes	–	–
8) Government expropriation	None	None	–	–
Sub-total			**0**	**8**

Table 1 Comparison of Location Advantages (Cont'd)

	China	South Korea	Location advantages (√ = better) China	South Korea
Panel B: Market potential				
1) Economic growth				
a) GDP growth (2001)	7.3%	3%	√	
b) Inflation (2001)	0%	4.1%	√	
c) Population	1,200 million	45 million	√	
d) GDP growth per capita (2001)	10%	–10%	√	
2) Semi-conductor market				
a) Global market position	Not ranked within the top ten	The third market leader with 40% of global market revenues		√
b) Regional market suppliers	Diffused	Dominated by few giant suppliers	√	
c) Potential market growth	Extremely high, 20% in the next five years	Moderate, less than 3% in the next five years	√	
Sub-total			**6**	**1**
Panel C: Other economic factors				
1) Labour force				
a) Education and quality	Low (82% literacy rate)	High (98% literacy rate)		√
b) Wages (based on average monthly)	Around US$60 (RMB500)	Around US$150,000 (200,000 won)	√	
c) Trade union protection	None	Yes, minimum wage level	√	
2) High-tech development and infrastructure	Infant stage	Well established with government subsidisation of R&D		√
3) Exchange risk	High, floating rate and great fluctuation on RMB	High, floating rate and great fluctuation on won	–	–
4) Stock and financial markets				
a) System and fluctuation	Speculative	Well established		√
b) Growth	Extremely high, ranked as first among global stock markets in 2001	Moderate, ranked fourth among global stock markets in 2001	√	
Sub-total			**3**	**3**
Total score (1 for each √)			**9**	**12**

political and government policies. Nevertheless, China is attractive for its giant market potential, in terms of market size, growth and cheap labour. However, location advantage is interdependent on ownership and internalisation for foreign investment decisions. In this respect, the next section will review SK Group's entry mode and its ownership advantage, and how these factors affected the location advantage results.

OWNERSHIP AND INTERNALISATION ANALYSIS

To compete in the host country market, SK Group has to possess superior competitive resources. The firm's competitive assets are reflected by its size and multinational experience, and its skills are reflected by its ability to develop differentiated products. Table 2 shows the most and least competitive of the firm's core resources. SK Group possesses supreme technological capabilities and can produce differentiated products with pioneering technology and design. It may be risky for SK Group to expand into a country that has low intellectual property rights protection and immature high-tech infrastructure, however, the firm's substantial size will allow it access to a country with high market potential through a high-context entry mode (i.e., a wholly owned subsidiary). As SK Group has already decided to enter the Asian market through a wholly owned subsidiary, the worry about technological and quality control risk is reduced. Intellectual property risk and potential market benefits come hand-in-hand, but the latter seems to be the most important. Overall the ownership and internalisation factors more than outweigh the potential problems associated with locating the new operation in China. Thus, SK Group finally decided to invest in China.

Table 2 SK Group's Core Resources

Most competitive core resources	Least competitive core resources
1) Supreme technological capabilities	1) Lack of knowledge and experience in the Asian market
2) Substantial firm size	2) High production cost
3) Excellent exployee know-how	3) Immobile workforce
4) Product reputation	

CASE STUDY QUESTIONS

1) What are the advantages and disadvantages of the OLI model?
2) How does SK Group reconcile the choice to enter China in terms of the OLI model? Compare the two assessments and explain.
3) Which factors appear to carry more weight for the decision by SK Group to invest in China?

CASE STUDY 3

Hotel Kunming Ltd – An Evaluation of a Hotel Investment in China

THE HOTEL INDUSTRY IN CHINA

Competition in China's hotel industry has become much more intensive since the adoption of the Open Door policy in 1979. Furthermore, China is predicted to become the number one tourist destination by 2020, so the opportunities and demand for mid-market hotels in China is very good.

Traditionally, hotels have been viewed as a collection of different businesses under one roof. Rooms, conference and banquet areas, restaurants, bars and other services all generate different revenue streams. In a typical hotel, the room department includes the front office (reception and reservations). The food and beverage department includes banqueting, restaurants, bars and room service. Other services include telephones, guest laundry and fitness club. Each business has specific attributable costs and constitutes a profit centre in its own right.

Internationally, the number of affluent, double-income families is increasing and transportation becomes quicker, easier and less expensive. Hence, the travel industry has seen an increase in pleasure travel, and this trend is likely to continue with resort areas receiving the greatest benefit.

INVESTOR COMPANY'S BACKGROUND

Hong Kong Company (HKCO) is a multinational enterprise with its head office in Hong Kong. It is listed on the Hong Kong Stock Exchange. Its main line of business

---

I wish to acknowledge the assistance of Wan Ho Yuen in the preparation of this case study. This case was developed as a basis for class discussion rather than to illustrate either effective or ineffective handling of an administrative situation.

is investment in various types of construction projects in Asian countries, and mainly in China. One of its business objectives is to achieve growth through strategic acquisitions and further diversification into different lines of business, with a stronger presence in the Chinese market.

As the keen competition and high cost of land in Hong Kong required large capital injections, HKCO began to invest in China, where there were many more investment opportunities. In line with the key concern about profit maximisation, other factors that were taken into consideration by HKCO were project size, nature and location. The diversification of business risk by investing in different types of business was HKCO's strategy. To summarise, HKCO's stated objectives were:

- maintenance and improvement of profit performance,
- increase in market share,
- achievement of a balanced portfolio, and
- growth by diversification.

The target project was located in China and would be the company's first capital investment project in the construction and operation of a hotel. The project was to construct a four-star hotel in Kunming, an important tourist area, which would be owned by a company with a local government background (see Table 1). The HKCO management thought that hotel investment was a valuable long-term strategic capital investment. The proposed investment structure is presented in Figure 1. The proposed timeline of construction to delivery is presented in Figure 2.

ANALYSIS OF THE PROJECT

SWOT (strengths, weaknesses, opportunities and threats) analysis is applied in this appraisal to determine core competencies and a structured/functional approach. HKCO needed to take the following five steps.

1) Identify strategic factors and value-creating activities.
2) Compare factors and activities with historical information and internal standards of excellence.
3) Compare the strengths and weaknesses with the capabilities and resources that are associated with key competitors.
4) Compare the strengths and weaknesses with the key requirements for success.
5) Use the results as input for formulating the appropriate strategies.

The SWOT analysis is shown in Figure 3.

Table 1 Details of Target Project

Motivation	Invited by local government of Kunming
Location	Kunming in Yunnan Province (has the largest amount of tropical forest reserves in China)
Trigger event	1999 International Horticultural Exposition • First time organised by a developing country • Supported by local and central government, e.g., Yunnan planned to invest RMB10 billion in Kunming • Infrastructure construction • Held from 1 May to 31 October 1999 • 61 countries and 19 international organisations involved • Organisers planned to attract more than 10 million visitors • The local and central governments planned to inject funding into the project so it could become a permanent attraction
Investment	Construction (estimated cost RMB70 million) and operation of a four-star hotel with • 185 rooms • Car parks • Restaurants • Entertainment centres, e.g., karaoke
Ongoing costs	Maintenance estimated at 4% of the construction cost per year. Inflation is assumed to be 5% per year
Time of offer	Mid-1997
Form of investment	Joint venture in the build, operate and transfer (BOT) mode
Period	15 years
Equity contribution	RMB100 million (80% of total)
Return	All of the profit except the payment of RMB2 million per year to the Chinese government
Risk	Bear all risk (financial and non-financial)

Figure 1 Proposed Investment Structure of Hotel Kunming Ltd

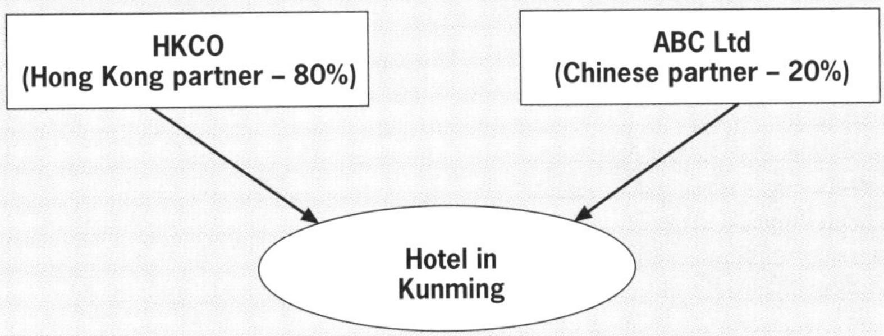

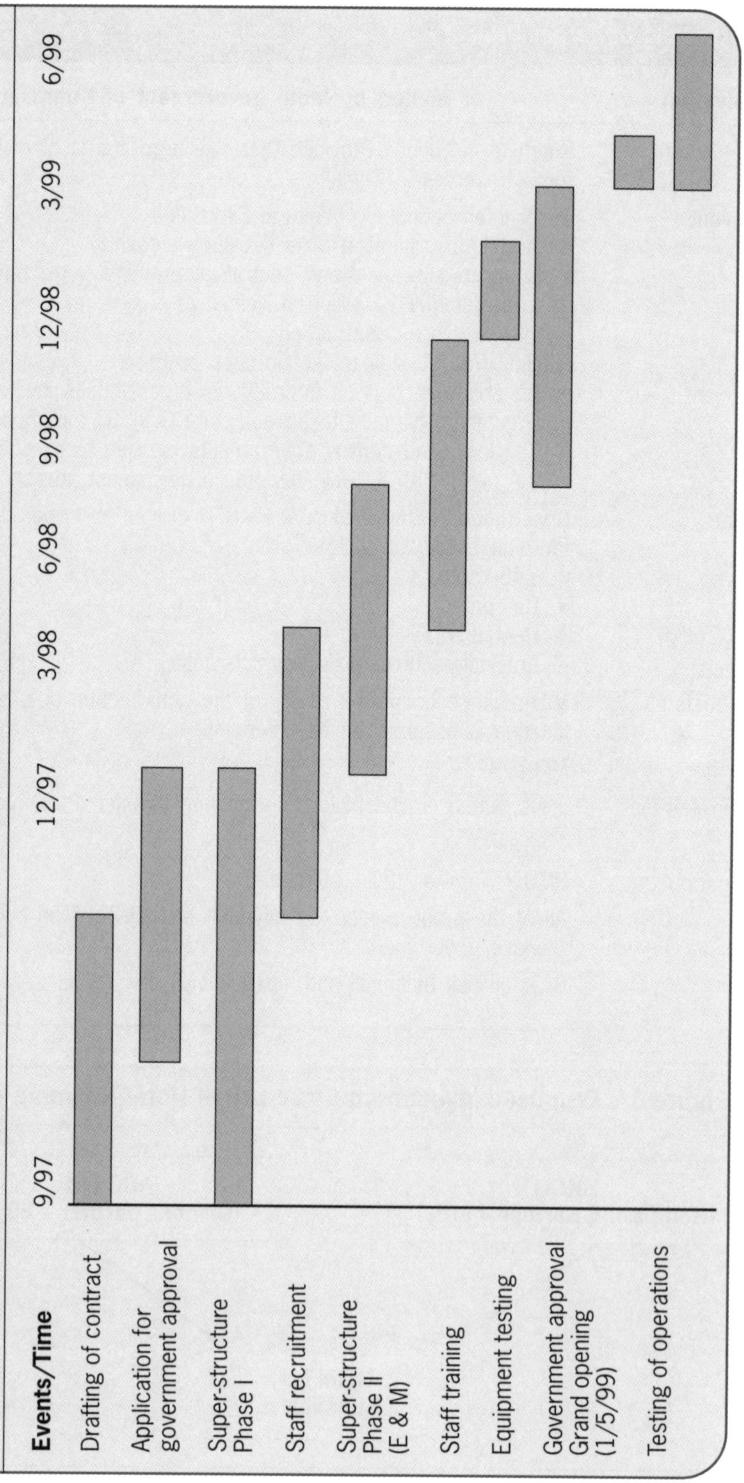

Figure 2 Proposed Timeline of Construction and Delivery of the Project

Figure 3 SWOT Analysis

	Strengths	Weaknesses
Internal	• Adequate finance for investment, which reduces the interest cost (the debt equity) • Connections in China (being invited to invest)	• Management calibre, lack of professional experience in the hotel industry • Relatively higher risk
	Opportunities	**Threats**
External	• Work out a marketing strategy in conjunction with domestic inbound travel agencies to attract group tourists from all regions in China • By horizontal expansion, that is, investing in hotels in different locations in China • By vertical expansion, for example, travel agency business	• Political risk in China may influence government policy in the hotel industry or the tourism business, which will in turn influence the revenue source • Potential lack of success for the exposition

FINANCIAL CONCERNS

Four commonly adopted capital investment evaluation techniques are net present value, internal rate of return, payback and accounting rate of return. Even though net present value and internal rate of return using discounted cash flow are more sophisticated than the other two tools, they are the most appropriate because the time value of money needs to be taken into account. However, an investment in a new project (which is also a new line of business) is comparatively more risky than the replacement or expansion of existing projects. Therefore, further modelling of cash flow, such as sensitivity analysis, can be prepared. Table 2 shows the details of the financial risk analysis undertaken. Tables 3 and 4 show the consolidate balance sheet plus profit and loss account for the Chinese partner (ABC Ltd), respectively.

NON-FINANCIAL CONCERNS

Because the timely completion of the hotel is absolutely critical to the profitability of this project, a critical path analysis performed by HKCO is fundamental. Further consideration should be given to human resources, in particular the calibre of management. The company's decision is to assign existing staff to manage the project. However, expertise and professional experience in the hotel industry should also be considered. One possible solution is the use of management contracts, which

Table 2 Financial Risk Analysis Undertaken

Panel A: Financial risk

Feasibility study performed	Data available	Result
Review latest financial statements for the joint venture partner and perform ratio analysis	• Balance sheet • Profit and loss account • Ratio analysis (included in Tables 3 and 4)	Sound financial background for a good business partner
Site visit to Kunming	Revenue estimation, i.e., room occupancy rate	
Perform cash flow analysis	15 years of cash flow	Net cash inflow reported from 2007
Based on internal cost of capital to calculate NPV	Discounted cash flow	IRR – Project 12.92% IRR – Investor 11.77%
Match time of completion and budget of expenditure	Gantt chart (included in Figure 2)	Could catch the exposition opening

Panel B: Non-financial risk

Management's concern	Decision on key factor	
Changes in market factor in tourism • The attractiveness of the exposition • Future tourism	Room charges and revenue from the restaurants	Favourable
Investment risk in China	Difficulty in withdrawal of capital	High
Human resources in hotel management – daily operation	Retain control and maintain quality services	Undertaken by existing HKCO staff

emerged in the US hotel industry during the 1980s. Under this type of agreement, a hotel company takes over the day-to-day operation of a hotel. The hotel management entity generally has no ownership interest in the hotel and is not responsible for funding any operating losses.

First, HKCO will have relatively less bargaining power in relation to the terms of the contract with joint venture partners who have local government backgrounds. Second, if the hotel is not opened before the exposition, six months of peak revenue period will be lost. The most important concern is that the company could miss the opportunity to build up and promote the hotel image to visitors from around the world. Third, HKCO did not have hotel professionals at the evaluation stage of the

Table 3 ABC Ltd Consolidated Balance Sheet

ABC Ltd
Consolidated Balance Sheet as at 31 December 1998

RMB,000			*Increase/(Decrease)*	
	1998	*1997*	*By value*	*By %*
EMPLOYMENT OF CAPITAL				
Fixed assets	12,257	13,288	(1,031)	(7.76)
Intangible assets	652	1,199	(547)	(45.62)
Long-term investments	42,624	41,656	968	2.32
	55,533	56,143	(610)	(1.09)
Current assets				
Short-term investments	2,283	4,283	(2,000)	(46.70)
Inventories	3,174	3,027	147	4.86
Trade receivables	1,227	(629)	1,856	(295.07)
Other receivables and prepayments	1,124	1,124	0	0.00
Cash and bank balances	10,852	7,659	3,193	41.69
	18,660	15,464	3,196	20.67
	74,193	71,607	2,586	3.61
Capital employed				
Share capital	80,000	80,000	0	0.00
Reserves	10,000	10,000	0	0.00
Retained earnings	(17,203)	(20,405)	3,202	(15.69)
Total capital and reserves	72,797	69,595	3,202	4.60
Minority interests	0	0	0	0.00
Current liabilities				
Trade payables	1,557	1,436	121	8.43
Other creditors and accrued Liabilities	91	828	(737)	(89.01)
Tax payable	(252)	(252)	0	0.00
	1,396	2,012	(616)	(30.62)
	74,193	71,607	2,586	3.61

Table 4 ABC Ltd Consolidated Profit and Loss Account

ABC Ltd
Consolidated Profit and Loss Account for the year ended 31 December 1998

RMB,000	*1998*	*1997*	*Increase/(Decrease) By value*	*By %*
Turnover	5,855	4,852	1,003	20.67
Operating profit	3,201	2,894	307	10.61
Exceptional items	0	332	(332)	(100.00)
	3,201	3,226	(25)	(0.77)
Share of profits less losses of associated companies	0	0	0	0.00
Ordinary profit before taxes	3,201	3,226	(25)	(0.77)
Taxation	0	0	0	0.00
Profit after taxation	3,201	3,226	(25)	(0.77)
Interests of minority shareholders	0	0	0	0.00
Profit attributable to the members	3,201	3,226	(25)	(0.77)

ABC Ltd
Ratio Analysis

Liquidity ratios[1]				
1) Current ratio	13.37	7.69	5.68	73.91
2) Quick ratio	10.29	5.62	4.67	82.97
Solvency ratios[2]				
1) Debt ratio	1.88%	2.81%	(0.0093)	(33.0347)

[1] Liquidity ratios

1) Current ratio: 13.37. A popular rule of thumb for this ratio is 2 (2:1). In this case, the ratio indicates that ABC Ltd had sufficient financial resources to put current assets to work.
2) Quick ratio: 10.29. A quick ratio between one-half and one is considered satisfactory. In this case, the ratio indicates that ABC Ltd could convert its assets to cash in a very short time. Again, the company had strong potential to expand its business.

[2] Solvency ratios

Debt ratio: nearly 2%. This ratio indicates that the company's risk of being unable to repay its debts was very low because its investments were wholly financed by share capital. The ratio also indicates that the company had the ability to raise funds from the outside, such as through individual investors (which is very popular in China), financial institutions or bankers.

project. Hotels are unique real estate investments because they contain many elements, which in turn affect the associated risk and benefits. Hotel professionals would have been able to evaluate, for instance, the total cost of furniture, fixtures and equipment, which can account for up to 25% of the total property value.

CASE STUDY QUESTIONS

1) What are the various factors that affect the decision to invest in the hotel property in China?
2) Evaluate these factors in terms of the level of business risk faced by HKCO.
3) What would you advise HKCO on this hotel investment opportunity? Provide reasons to support your recommendation.

CHAPTER

2

International Expansion and External Contracting

LEARNING OBJECTIVES

- Understand the different modes of entry available to MNEs.
- Understand the theoretical reasons for contract (mode of entry) choice.
- Understand the various independencies among theories in the OLI model.
- Understand the different foreign investment alternatives that are available in China and the advantages of each.

INTRODUCTION

Once the strategic, country location and risk factors are known, the next key decision is to determine the appropriate external contracting arrangement or mode of entry. Given a particular strategy, the multinational enterprise (MNE) manager must understand the external contracting arrangements that are required to organise the sale or provision of services in a particular country. This is the external contract choice with the common alternatives ranging from market-oriented type contracts, such as licensing and franchising, to hierarchical-based contracts, like joint ventures and wholly owned subsidiaries.

There are two basic decision steps in contracting for the MNE. The first step is to select the appropriate mode of entry. A mode of entry is the structuring of an external contract for a foreign direct investment (FDI) transaction. Mode of entry types include wholly owned subsidiaries, joint ventures and franchise and licence (sub-contracting) agreements. Different companies have different needs, and the decision requires information for planning, negotiating and writing the contract. What is of most interest is the information that enables the company to get the contract right (see Figure 2.1). In other words, the emphasis at this stage is on minimising errors with respect to the external contract choice decision, because management controls have limited power to substitute for a poorly worded contract or wrong contract as they can only be exercised within the confines of the agreement.

Figure 2.1 Contract Choice

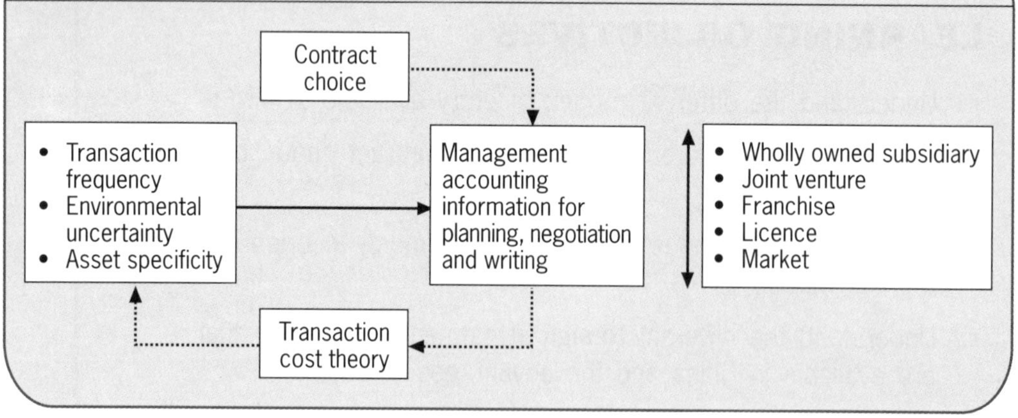

Although in pure contracting theory terms there are no more costs involved, there is a second managerial step (the costs of which are already factored into the original contracting costs), and that is to manage the contract. The information that enables the company to manage the contract (see Figure 2.2) includes the contracting party's performance. For example, both licensing and franchising involve contracts that set out the rights and obligations of the parties. The control of each is left mainly to the market price (licensing) and the stipulation of minimum quality standards (franchising). Controlling hierarchical forms of contracts such as joint ventures and subsidiaries requires information to facilitate effective planning and control.

Figure 2.2 Managing the Contract

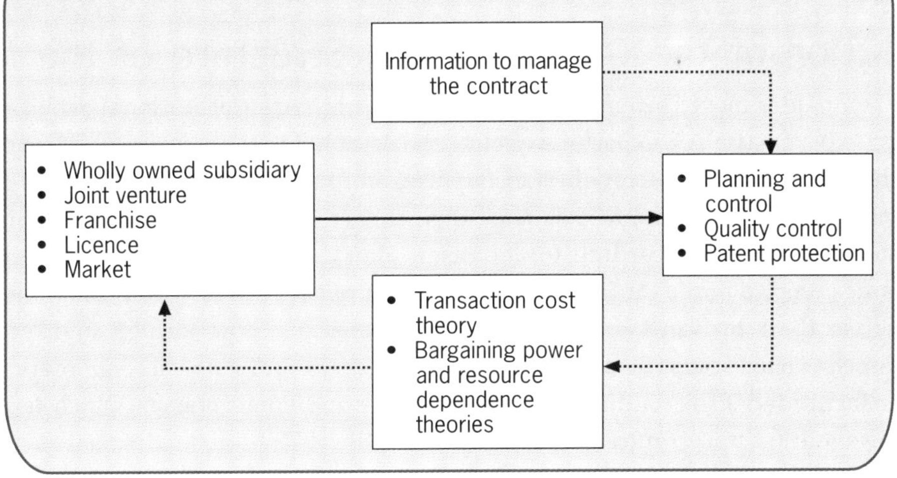

This chapter specifically considers the MNE mode of entry choice (the planning and control issues associated with joint ventures and subsidiaries are covered in Chapters 3 to 5). It is divided into four parts. The first part outlines the basic alternative contractual forms available to MNEs and the typical steps taken towards international expansion. The second part reviews several theories that help explain the determinants of entry mode choice. The third part introduces an encompassing framework that helps to explain the MNE mode of entry choice. The final part reviews the mode of entry choice in the China context.

MODE OF ENTRY (CONTRACTING CHOICE)

There are four major modes of entry for the MNE to consider for international expansion: franchising, licensing, a joint venture and a wholly owned subsidiary. Franchising differs from the other modes in that a company's final or intermediate product is manufactured outside of the target country and subsequently transferred to it. Licensing is a non-equity and contractual mode with one or more local partners. A company transfers to a foreign organisation the right to use some or all of the following property: patents, trademarks, company name, technology or business methods. Joint ventures and wholly owned subsidiaries entail direct investment in business sites in the target country. Joint ventures involve two or more organisations that share the ownership, management, risks and rewards of the newly formed entity. Each partner contributes equity, which can take the form of money, plant and equipment or technology. Wholly owned subsidiaries are an entry in which the parent company has full ownership and sole responsibility for management.

Evolution of the Organisational Structure of the MNE

Many companies move through distinctive stages in their multinational evolution: no regular export activities, export via agents, the establishment of overseas sales offices and the establishment of production facilities abroad as a fully integrated, global enterprise. This is also known as the stage theory of MNE evolution or company internationalisation. According to Johanson and Vahlne (1977), large resourceful companies tend to pursue internationalisation more aggressively, and companies can generalise their previous experience when entering a new foreign market with familiar characteristics. The acquisition of knowledge about a new foreign market can also be facilitated if the conditions are more stable and homogeneous, which serves to minimise market uncertainties (Stopford and Wells, 1972).

Each of the stages has its share of problems and opportunities. In the initial stages, having international exposure in terms of export or a foreign sales office offers lower risk, but this comes with little control or coordination over the international operations. For example, many of the disputes over production allocation, scheduling, product adaptations and transfer pricing are between the foreign sales office and the domestic production facility.

The international and global structure stages involve the establishment of foreign production facilities (e.g., licensing agreements, joint ventures and subsidiaries). With the international structure, new problems of responsibility and control develop because changes occur in at least two operating environments, namely domestic and foreign. In addition, the growing diversity of international operations requires an international division to replace an export division, with substantial autonomy because foreign sales are a small part of total sales. As foreign sales grow, the international division must exercise tighter control over the numerous operations and activities by adding staff. This creates more complexity and competition for resources with the domestic operations. Such forces make it necessary to undertake a major reorganisation.

Finally, the global structure typically involves companies that have diverse or complex products which are subject to rapid technological change. Here, product knowledge and expertise is most important. The global structure is needed when there is a greater need for production and logistical coordination, as in vertically integrated companies or those in global business, that require international production rationalisation to obtain scale economies of production. This structure is also suited to companies with simple and stable product lines that require local adaptations or local expertise about consumption practices and government policies.

To coordinate further growth of either structure, the global grid/matrix structure has emerged as a way of reconciling the conflicts between the geographical and product divisions. However, dual reporting leads to conflict and confusion; information overload is created out of the proliferation of committees and reports. Overlapping responsibilities create turf battles and lower accountability. Barriers of distance, language, time and culture exacerbate the confusion and conflicts.

THEORETICAL BASIS FOR CONTRACT CHOICE

Selecting an institutional arrangement – a mode of entering and expanding in a foreign market – is one of the most crucial strategic decisions that an MNE has to make (Root, 1994). The theoretical basis for determining an entry mode is primarily derived from two perspectives that have dominated the attention of international business research. First, the transaction cost perspective, which postulates that the strategic choice is the function of the costs and benefits of full ownership in comparison to those of shared ownership. The entry mode that an investor adopts will be that which minimises transaction costs.

The second line of research falls under the general category of control and bargaining power (resource dependence) and centres on the capability and bargaining power of MNEs and host governments (Zhao and Zhu, 1998). There are also a number of other theories that help us to explain the linkage between various factors and modes of entry, such as resource-based theory, game (agency) theory and organisational learning theory. The following discussion focuses on the two main theories that have dominated the mode of entry literature.

Transaction Cost Theory

A rich theoretical tradition in the international business literature can be drawn on to explain the choice of mode of entry. Buckley and Casson (1976) used transaction cost theory to explain FDI. In their theory of internalisation they proposed that an MNE would internalise its activities in a foreign country if the cost of internalisation was less than exporting or other contractual agreements. Research in this area has drawn heavily on the transaction cost literature (Anderson and Gatignon, 1986; Kogut and Singh, 1988; Kim and Hwang, 1992). The transaction cost approach postulates that the strategic choice between full and partial ownership is the function of the costs and benefits of full ownership in relation to those of shared ownership. The entry mode that a company will choose is that which results in the lowest transaction cost. Three research questions are raised by transactions cost theory:

1. What are the costs associated with transacting a business in different ways?
2. How do circumstances cause these costs to vary?
3. Given the choice of governance structure (mode of entry), what *ex post* governance mechanisms are put in place to complete the contract, in the mind of the contracting parties?

Transaction cost principles. Transaction costs are the costs of information, measuring, negotiating, monitoring and ensuring the settlement of a contract. Transaction cost economics is mainly concerned with the governance of contractual relations. Economising on transaction costs is mainly responsible for the choice of one form of capitalist organisation over another. Transaction cost theory raises the basic question of vertical integration: when should a company make rather than buy a good or service? Or, in the international arena, what determines the mode of entry?

Transaction cost theory raises the secondary question of farsighted and incomplete contracting. *Farsighted contracting* assumes that economic actors have the ability to look ahead, discern problems and prospects, and factor these back into the organisational/contractual design. Plausible farsightedness will suffice. *Incomplete contracting* implies that all complex contracts are unavoidably incomplete, and hence there is an opportunity for *ex post* governance. The following conditions are generally observed: 1) parties cannot anticipate all possible contingencies that may affect their costs or ability to perform as promised, 2) often it is more economical to respond to foreseeable events when the need arises rather than to plan in advance for every foreseeable contingency, 3) writing unambiguous contracts is difficult because of natural languages, and 4) enforceable contracts can be made contingent only on information that the parties share and that courts can verify.

Transaction cost determinants. The transaction is the basic unit of analysis. Therefore, the choice of governance can be explained by the frequency of transactions (transaction frequency), the knowledge of the environment and contracting party (environmental uncertainty) with which one is contracting and the degree of uniqueness of the assets contributed to the contract (asset specificity). One way to view the three determinants of transaction costs is in terms of linkages between each as a system. When a company first contracts for international expansion, the risk that is associated with bringing the company's assets into a new environment is likely to be a function of all three determinants. However, over time the nature of assets and environment are more strongly connected by the frequency with which the company wishes to contract (see Figure 2.3). For example, the higher the transaction frequency, the greater the chances are that the company will become more experienced, have a greater understanding of contracting parties and the strength of institutional enforcement mechanisms in place (i.e., reduced environmental uncertainty). Similarly, more frequent transactions help in the communication of their value, and reduce a company's dependence on any one asset (i.e., reduced asset specificity). Alternatively, across industries, the nature of specific assets may dictate the level of transaction frequency and, in turn, environmental uncertainty. For example, pharmaceutical and motor vehicle industries that require large investments in specific machinery and research and development assets.

Figure 2.3 Linkages between the Transaction Cost Determinants

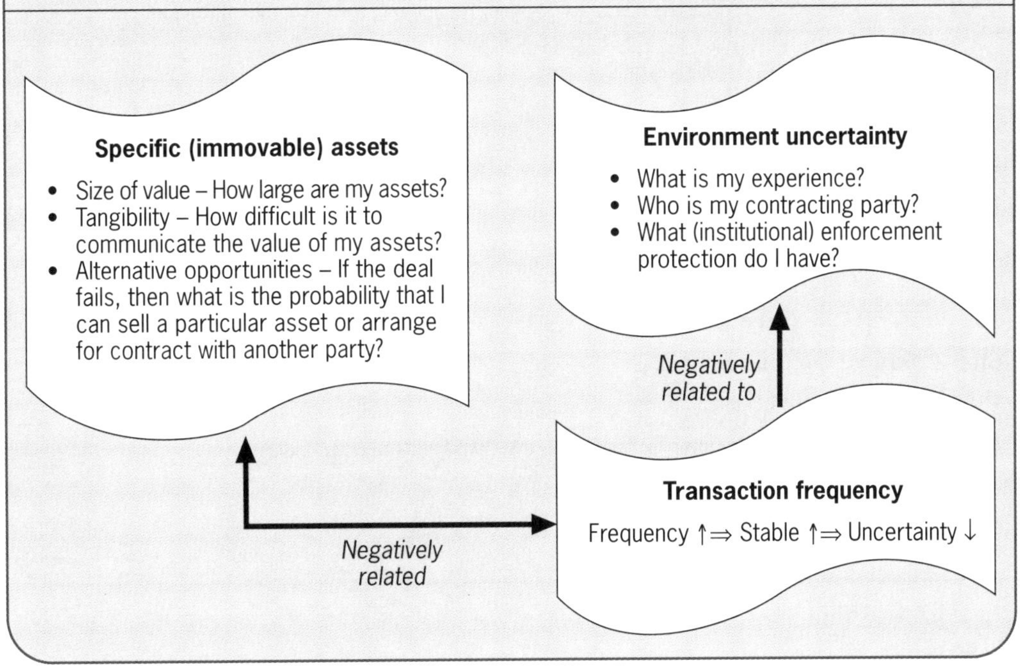

Transaction cost components. There are three basic components of transactions costs: 1) thinking and planning ahead, 2) negotiating and agreeing to terms, and

3) writing terms and conditions. There is also a fourth transaction cost (enforcement and litigation), but under the principle of farsighted contracting, the costs that are associated with enforcement and litigation are factored into thinking and planning ahead. In other words, the post-contracting enforcement costs (legal enforcement and court costs) are considered to be expensive and are assumed to be a second best solution to designing a better contract (see Step 1 in Figure 2.4). Figure 2.4 shows the simple steps that are involved in connecting the components of transaction costs with the type of contract (external or internal).

Figure 2.4 Simple Framework for Comparison

External (A) versus internal (B) contract mode of governance

Step 1: Components of transaction costs

A Transaction Costs – Sub-contracting/Licensing
1) Planning
2) Negotiating
3) Writing
4) Enforcement

Enforcement through litigation is considered costly – the probability of which is factored into the planning cost of contracting.

B Transaction Costs – Hierarchy
1) Organising
   • Decision making and planning
2) Monitoring
   • Control

Step 2: Structuring the contract

A > **B** = Hierarchy (internal contract), e.g., wholly owned subsidiary

B > **A** = External contract, e.g., licensing/franchise

To compare the transaction costs of the external contract we need to understand the components of those transaction costs that are associated with internal (hierarchy) contracts (also see Step 1 in Figure 2.4). The transaction costs that are associated with a hierarchy are planning and control costs. These costs are often referred to as agency costs by researchers who employ agency theory to understand organisations. Both the agency and transaction cost theories have similar assumptions, with the exception that transaction cost theory assumes bounded rationality. Once the costs components that are associated with each contract alternative is known, we can proceed to comparing the two contract alternatives to ascertain which has lower transactions costs (see Step 2 in Figure 2.4). In applying transaction cost theory, companies will choose the contract that has the lowest transaction costs.

Negotiation considerations. For arm's-length buyers in a market to pay for value, they first must be able to see value in the product being transacted. For tangible products (e.g., cars and non-specialised manufacturing equipment) it is possible for the buyer to ascertain the value of the asset without significant loss to the seller. For example, the buyer can test drive such assets to determine the value without significantly diminishing the value of the asset. However, for products of an intangible nature – with higher information content (e.g., computer softwares) – it is more difficult for the buyer to to determine the value without significant loss to the seller. For example, computer software can lose its value as a result of buyer opportunism (a buyer makes a copy of the product and decides not to buy it). In such case, the seller is less willing to show the full product details to the buyer, in which case the buyer is less willing to pay for the real value of the product (see Figure 2.5).

Figure 2.5 Paradox of Information and Asset Valuation

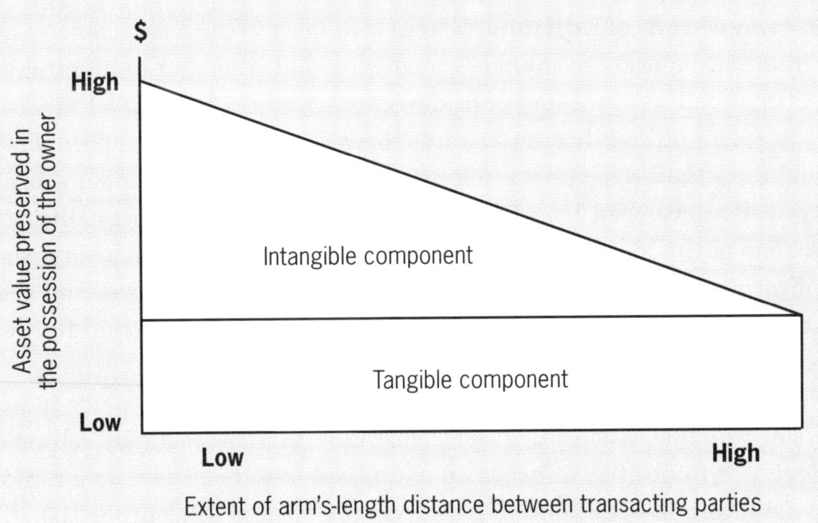

Laws that provide patent and copyright protection are therefore an important part of securing asset values in arm's-length transactions. When MNEs enter markets in developing nations, the contribution of know-how to overseas joint ventures or subsidiaries is likely to be a critical value component. This, in turn, makes legal protection a more important determinant of how market entry is contracted for. Figure 2.6 depicts a basic framework that compares the transaction costs which are associated with different combinations of 1) the amount of asset specific contributions, and 2) the degree of legal protection in a country. By classifying countries in terms of the strength of law over property rights (e.g., patent and trademark protection), the transaction costs that are associated with a given amount of asset specificity are likely to vary accordingly.

Figure 2.6 Transaction Costs – Negotiation (Enforcement) Considerations

Asset specific contributions – know-how	**Strength of law over property rights (e.g., patents/trademarks)**	
Value	*Low*	*High*
High	Transaction costs very high	–
Low	–	Transaction costs very low

Writing terms and conditions. There are many contract choices available, ranging from pure market exchange, franchising and licensing to hierarchical forms of contracting (joint venture and subsidiary). Each of these contract forms requires different terms and conditions to aid successful fulfilment. *Franchising* is a contractual form that involves the selling of goods and services under a brand name that is typically developed based on the maintenance of certain quality standards. Therefore, one of the most important terms associated with franchising contracts is the specification of quality standards and terms for the inspection and monitoring of these standards over time. It only takes one bad franchise to ruin the reputation and the value of the brand name that is associated with the franchise.

Licensing is a contractual agreement between one or more parties to use a good for a fee. For example, when Microsoft sells office XP it is basically selling a licence to the purchaser to use the software on a single computer or multiple computers, in the case of a multiple-site licence. The important term of a licence is the stipulation of any patents or registered designs that are incorporated into the goods that are subject to the licence. Therefore, when MNEs seek to licence in other countries, patent and trademark protection is an important consideration.

The joint venture contract involves an agreement between two or more partners, and typically includes a profit (based on equity contributions) sharing arrangement. A joint venture agreement legally creates a joint venture through a contract, and identifies the major rights, duties and obligations of the participants. The agreement typically identifies the provisions for management and the performance of joint venture obligations, such as provisions for the transfer of knowledge. However, given contract limitations, the weak enforcement regimes in developing countries and the need to nurture inter-party cooperation, joint venture partners typically rely on various controls to influence behaviour in areas that could not be or were not included in the joint venture agreement, and ensure the fulfilment of those parts of the agreement that are difficult to legally enforce. Thus, various control mechanisms are used to help plan and control the joint venture operations; for example, the appointment of expatriates, training routines, the allocation of decision authority, meetings and informal communications, and performance measurement and incentives (see Chapter 4). These planning and control mechanisms are also prevalent in wholly owned subsidiaries (see Chapter 3).

Figure 2.7 provides a simple outline of the main contracting forms that are available, along with the main type of information this is needed to manage the contract. The figure also displays the three types of transaction costs and the different types of transaction cost drivers.

Figure 2.7 Determinants of Transaction Costs and Various Contracting Terms and Conditions

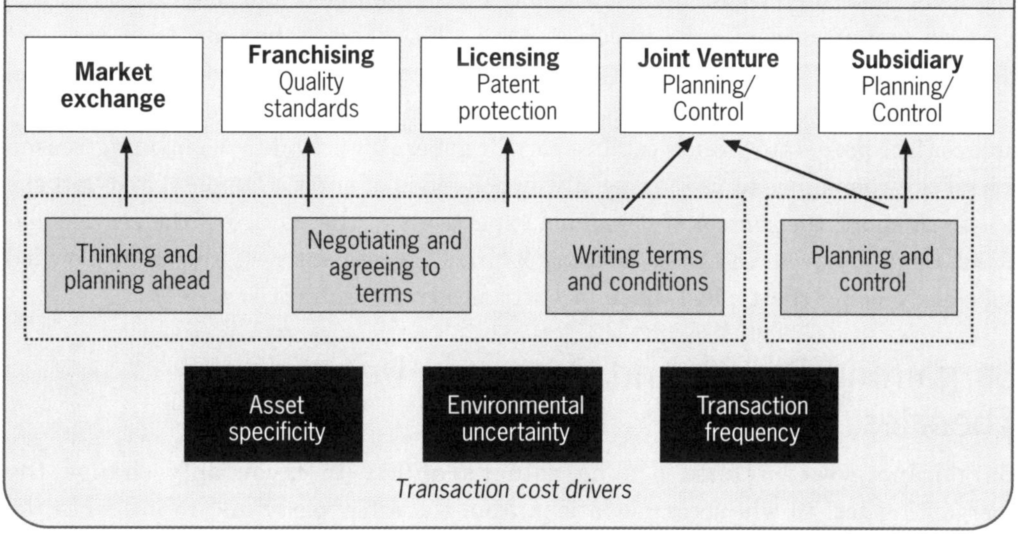

Transaction costs in service companies. There are several distinguishing characteristics of service companies that highlight aspects of transactions costs not typically found in manufacturing companies. First, a notable difference between services and manufacturing is that a service company seldom requires large-scale investments in physical assets such as capital equipment and facilities to establish a presence in foreign markets. The value-creating assets of a service company rests more in its human capital than its physical infrastructure (Campbell and Verbeke, 1994). According to Erramilli and Rao (1993), the production/delivery of services typically relies on a high intensity of human capital – the skills, talent and knowledge of a company's employees that are not easily transferred to different organisational or social contexts.

Second, the degree of idiosyncrasy that characterises a service is another key factor to consider when discussing the internationalisation of service companies. Because many services are labour intensive or people centred, the marked difference between employees in terms of skills, education or specialised know-how create considerable variance in performance at the service production or delivery stages. Companies can reduce this risk by substituting physical resources for the human element or through the extensive education and training of employees. When training is extensive and employees have a high level of skills when joining a company, the degree of human capital is greater. Finally, Zeithaml, Parasuraman and Berry (1985) showed that inseparability of the service personnel and the customer is also a feature that distinguishes many service companies from manufacturers. When inseparability is high, the performance of employees who deal directly with customers is important for the maintenance of a company's quality standards.

As a result of these factors, several scholars have suggested that service providers tend to prefer higher control and lower resource commitment entry modes than do manufacturing companies (Sarathy 1994). This is because local partners have lower quality standards such as maintaining consistency in different processes, which Carman and Langeard (1980) suggest can be overcome with detailed contracts and control procedures. Such conditions will generally provide a compelling reason for service companies to use the wholly owned mode of entry (Campbell and Verbeke 1994). In short, the control of personnel expertise and the nature of the service and client relations drive the basis of foreign direct investment with the wholly owned subsidiary being the typical mode of entry in service enterprises.

Bargaining Power and Resource Dependence Theories

Bargaining power refers to a bargainer's ability to favourably change the "bargaining set" to win accommodations from the other party and to influence the outcome of a negotiation (Yan and Gray, 1994). During the negotiation of the equity joint venture, the outcome is dependent upon the relative bargaining power of the partners. Bargaining power is a dynamic rather than static concept. That is, at a certain point in time, it can be weakened or strengthened on either side by the local government of the host country (being the key stakeholder, particularly if the prospective local partner is a state-owned enterprise) or the foreign investor. Following the bargaining power approach, the contractual terms of an MNE's involvement in the local business of another country are considered to be continually subject to negotiation – an assumption that is particularly relevant in explaining contracting behaviour in developing countries where the rule of law is not complete.

Bargaining resources grid. The assets that each partner possesses are elements of the bargaining power set. Based on resource dependency theory (Pfeffer and Salancik, 1978), if an MNE is resourceful, then it is less dependent upon the local partner for resources. Hence, when bargaining power refers to a set of key bargaining resources (Brouthers and Bamossy, 1997), a 2×2 grid (see Figure 2.8) can be used to explain the observed trend towards wholly owned subsidiaries or majority-owned foreign enterprises. From a macro perspective, the choice of entry mode into another country can be exemplified by the 2×2 grid, with the vertical axis representing the bargaining power of the local partner, and the horizontal axis representing the bargaining power of the foreign investors (see Figure 2.8).

Figure 2.8 Bargaining Resources Grid

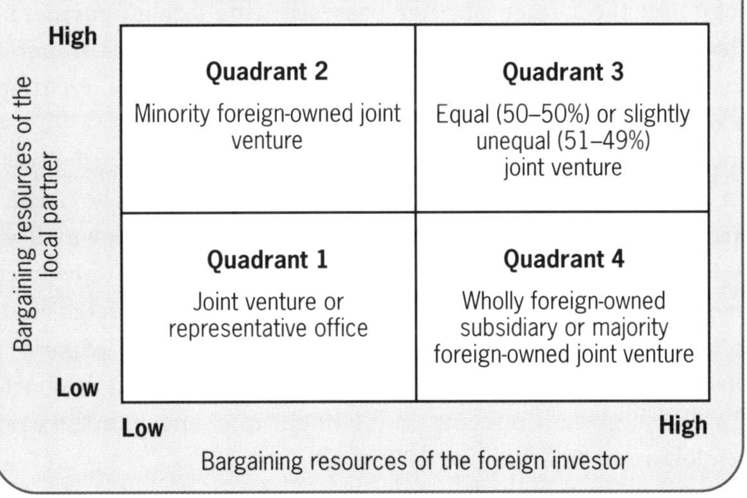

The grid hypothesises that there is a positive relationship between bargaining power and the level of commitment by the foreign investor (Quadrant 1 denotes the lowest level of commitment, whereas Quadrant 4 denotes the highest). The level of commitment can, in turn, be measured by the amount of capital resources that are invested by the foreign investor, spanning a spectrum from a representative office (minimum capital investment), minority shareholding, equal or slightly unequal shareholding and majority shareholding to wholly foreign owned (maximum capital investment). Except for a representative office (and perhaps also non-equity contractual joint ventures), the foreign investor's percentage equity shareholding in the equity joint venture can be treated as a proxy for the level of commitment. Hence, it is expected that the more resourceful (bargaining power) a foreign investor is relative to the local partner, the higher the equity shareholding in the equity joint venture that the foreign investor will hold.

Quadrants 1 and 3 seem self-contradictory because they suggest that the foreign investors and local partners have similar bargaining powers, which results in radically different situations. Quadrant 3 demonstrates the reciprocal interdependence or cooperative ethos (Buckley and Casson, 1988), in the sense that cooperation is built upon mutual forbearance and that the parties are mutually dependent on each other to accomplish activities and achieve desired goals. Both parties in return have to relinquish certain controls and play roles of both principals and agents (Blodgett, 1991). One of the distinguishing characteristics is that each partner owns some assets, tangible or intangible, of which the other partner lacks and seeks access to. A typical example is oil and gas exploration, wherein the local partner owns the field (the local partner's bargaining resource) but lacks the capital and technology that the foreign partner possesses (the foreign partner's bargaining resource). The foreign partner has no access to the field unless through cooperation with the local partner. The cooperation itself represents the creation of a new product market for both partners.

Quadrant 1 can be approximated by the contract manufacturing that is prevalent in industries such as garment manufacturing. The local partner is probably interested in creating employment or filling under-utilised capacity, whereas the foreign partner is attracted by the relatively low labour costs. Either partner's need for an equity joint venture is not urgent. The foreign investor is still at the early internationalisation stage, moving from passive exports to overseas production as suggested by the staged development model that is characterised by incremental, risk-averse and reluctant adjustment to changes in the company or its environment (Johanson and Vahlne, 1977).

Quandrant 2 can represent the early stages of opening of a protected industry to foreign investment. For example, telecommunications, whereby the local partner seeks new technology and know-how to expand/upgrade the infrastructure, but is reluctant to subsume control owing to the more sensitive nature of the industry. Foreign partners view this initial access as a positive step towards greater long-term investment in the newly opened industry.

Equity joint ventures represent the crystallisation of intense bargaining among prospective partners. From a more macro perspective, the host country partners can include the stakeholders of the host country (Brouthers and Bamossy, 1997). This is especially true in China, where a foreign investor will soon find during an equity joint venture negotiation that it is also negotiating with various government authorities, especially if the intended project is of significance to the local municipality or will involve a state-owned enterprise.

In short, the bargaining power perspective provides a greater in-depth coverage of the dynamics behind shifts in MNE mode of entry over time. The dynamics boil down to one or more of the following scenarios: a weakening of the relative foreigner dependence on the local partner (e.g., market knowledge and access to distribution networks) leads to a dynamic shift in the balance of bargaining power and increases the likelihood of foreign investors choosing wholly owned subsidiaries as their entry mode. A weakening of the relative local partner's dependence on the foreign partner (e.g., learning new technology) leads to a dynamic shift in the opposite direction and increases the likelihood of the local partner setting up competing ventures independent of the venture with the foreign partner.

Resource-dependence model. The resource-dependence model (Pfeffer and Salancik, 1978) states that the possession of key resources by one partner in the equity joint venture could make the other partner(s) dependent on that partner. This is similar to "partial interdependence" (Inkpen and Beamish, 1997), which states that a company's objective might be better served by cooperation with another party. The model can be seen as an extension of bargaining power theory, because control over key equity joint venture resources creates a basis for bargaining power (Inkpen and Beamish, 1997). An entity that has the option of contributing or withholding a key resource or input could therefore utilise that option as bargaining leverage (Pfeffer, 1981). This is especially important if the key resource is irreplaceable or non-substitutable and a dependency situation develops. The partner that controls the key resource will also have more potential partners to choose from than will the partner without that control (Yan and Gray, 1994). Alternatively, the partner that lacks bargaining power over strategic key resource will have lesser dominance in the inter-partner equity joint venture negotiation, and will not be able to gain dominant control over the equity joint venture. Equity ownership is unlikely to be symmetric in the event of a dominating partner.

Hybrid modes of entry. Joint ventures are generally motivated by the need to share risk and uncertainty. The underlying rationale for a joint venture is likely to include goal congruence, asset inseparability or government requirements. In most cases where joint ventures are not a required form of entry, partners come together to share assets or competencies (asset inseparability) that they find to be necessary to do business. To a lesser extent, joint ventures are formed solely for goal congruence. The high instability among joint ventures has shown that partner goals, especially in international joint ventures (between partners from developed and developing countries) are more likely to be divergent. According to Tallman and Shenkar (1994), joint ventures can be viewed as resulting from either market failure or hierarchical failure. Joint ventures become a more viable alternative to market-based transacting due to asset specificity, opportunism and the tacitness of resources. Joint ventures become a more viable alternative to hierarchies due to the existence of non-core business, resource preservation, the need for complementary assets and government policy (see Figure 2.9).

Figure 2.9 Rationale for Joint Ventures

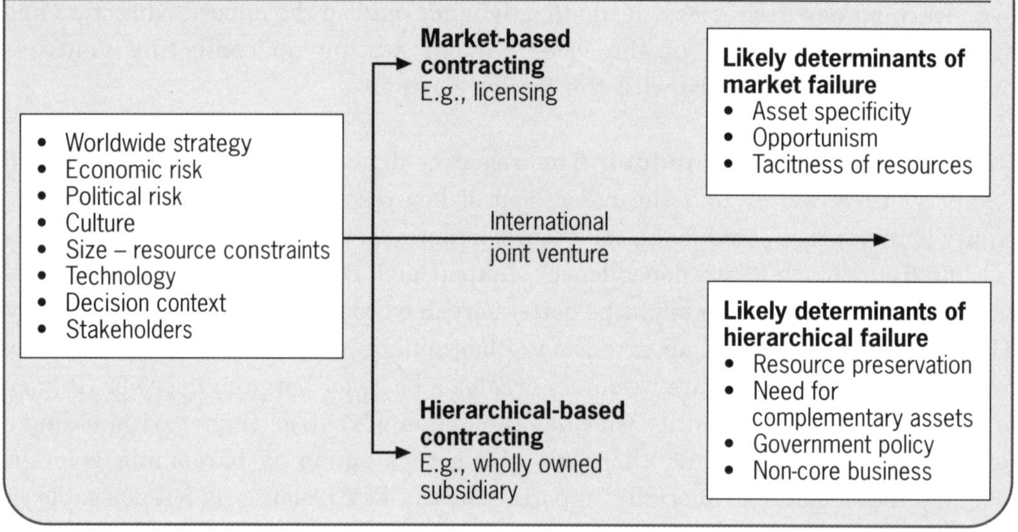

INTEGRATING MODE OF ENTRY FRAMEWORK

Dunning's (1988 and 1999) OLI model has emerged as the most prominent theory for framing the complexity of factors that affect a company's decision to go international and how to go international over the past two decades. OLI refers to ownership advantages ("O"), location advantages ("L") and internalisation ("I"). The model blends together elements from several theories of the firm that are used to explain FDI such as transactions costs and resource dependency. The OLI model is explained in the next part and this is followed by a brief review of the mode of entry literature.

The OLI Model

The OLI model bridges early theories and transactions costs theory by incorporating transaction costs into the internalisation part of the model. The paradigm comprises several theories on international business. The model has three parts. The first component is organisation advantage, which derives from Porter's (1985) theory of competitive advantage: What specific core competences does an organisation have to offer when it goes international? The second component is location advantage, which derives from early theories of Adam Smith's advantages of trade. It relates to the reason for going international. The third component (internationalisation advantage) derives from transaction costs theory and helps us to understand the way in which international expansion is contracted for.

The OLI model is useful in helping us understand the components and the sequence of influences of each of these components on the international business formation. For example, Dunning (1999) emphasised that the growing importance of intangible assets, the mobility of location-bound assets and the international allocation of economic activity affect where the foreign investments will be made. According to Anand and Delios (1997), location-specific disadvantages are caused by the non-transferability of parent resources and capabilities to host countries. Agarwal and Ramaswami (1992) found evidence to support the interdependence of the three factors that comprise the OLI model. In particular, they found that company size, multinational experience, product differentiation and market potential directly affected the investment modes.

Although the OLI model appears to be encompassing, it has had its share of criticism. For example, some notable researchers did not support Dunning's suggestion of internalisation as the primacy determinant and deemed that location advantage was the most significant factor. For example, Gastanaga, Nugent, and Pashamova's (1998) survey of 49 developing countries from 1970 to 1995 indicated that location advantages had a greater effect on FDI than did internalisation and ownership advantages. Casson (1987) argued that the failure of international immediate product markets was both a necessary and sufficient condition to ensure the existence of MNEs. The distinction between ownership and internalisation advantages seems irrelevant if there are no differentiated external markets.

Researchers are also divided on the exact nature of the influence of location factors. For example, some researchers have deemed that the host country's political and government policies, including legal, tax, trade and entry restriction policies, are primacy determinants of foreign investment (Doz and Prahalad, 1986; Gastanaga, Nugent, and Pashamova, 1998). Others have pointed out that the fast economic development in Asian countries makes government policies on foreign investment more competitive and comparable, which means that the host country's market potential is the key consideration in FDI (Terpstra and Yu, 1988).

"Actually, not all MNEs consider their OLI advantages before investment in foreign countries. They may decide to invest by chance, or they could just be following a trend. O'Farrell, Wood and Zheng (1998) found that 75 out of 90 small- and medium-sized enterprises (SMEs) could not recall the detailed decision-making processes when they decided upon an entry mode ten years previously. Sixty (67%) SMEs did not have alternatives in choosing entry modes, while 36 (40%) of the 90 SMEs indicated that the initial entry decision was due to a contract or request to tender for a one-off project abroad. Only 20% of companies actively considered alternative entry modes. In short, critics of the OLI model claim that the OLI model only points out why MNEs go abroad, and not why they decide on particular market entry modes."

Mode of Entry Empirical Literature

Although many papers have studied the different modes of foreign entry that are used by MNEs to enter foreign markets, it is not clear which factors are the most important in influencing this decision. A number of country-level, company-level and industry-level factors have been analysed. Bhattacharya (1999) consolidated the modes of foreign entry literature in the international business area through a quantitative meta-analysis, and compared the relative importance of various categories of factors in influencing the market-entry decision. Country-level and company-level factors have stronger effects than do industry-level factors, though all are significant. Study findings also reveal that the consolidated effect size of all categories of factors is small, thus leaving a large amount of unexplained variation.

The following summary classifies extant research into four categories – entry mode studied, theory used, source of data and the factors that were hypothesised to affect the mode of entry choice (see Table 2.1). These studies reveal that a variety of entry modes have been compared in the literature. Moreover, a large number of factors have been hypothesised to explain mode of entry choice.

Table 2.1 Mode of Entry Empirical Literature

Study	Focus of study	Theory used and source of data(s)	Factors hypothesised to affect choice of mode of entry
Sharma (2002)	International trade and foreign direct investment	Transaction cost theory and OLI model	US companies have a favourable cultural and proximity position to invest in big Latin American emerging markets. Makes a case for US companies choosing high resource commitment entry modes due to enhancement of global market position, matching resources of host country competitors, complete control over product offerings and becoming insiders in these markets.
Chen and Hu (2002)	Equity joint venture, contractual joint venture and wholly owned subsidiary	Transaction cost theory	MNEs investing in marketing skills, brand names and in projects with long durations are more likely to select the high control mode of subsidiary. Wholly owned subsidiary commands the highest level of advertising intensity and the longest duration, followed by equity and contractual joint ventures. Wholly owned subsidiaries are mostly formed in industries with high growth rates.
Chen and Hu (2002)	An analysis of the determinants of contractual joint ventures, equity joint ventures and wholly owned subsidiaries	Transaction cost theory	When the investments involve proprietary products, or cultural distance is large between home and host countries, the wholly owned subsidiaries are more likely to be chosen than contractual joint ventures.
Chung and Enderwick (2001)	Exporting and foreign direct investment	OLI model	International experience, type of products and immigrant effect significantly influence the entry mode choice.

Table 2.1 Mode of Entry Empirical Literature (Cont'd)

Study	Focus of study	Theory used and source of data(s)	Factors hypothesised to affect choice of mode of entry
Meyer (2000)	Wholly owned subsidiary, joint venture, international trade and contractual arrangements	Institutional and transaction cost theories	Wholly owned operations are more feasible in nearby and familiar locations. Companies with extensive worldwide experience prefer wholly owned subsidiaries because that experience reduces the costs of and thus facilitates internal organisation. Company size favours wholly owned subsidiaries only vis-à-vis contracts, thus indicating that small companies often use contracts.
Palenzuela and Bobillo (1999)	Wholly owned subsidiary, distribution and joint venture	Bargaining power theory and transaction cost theory	The automatic choice of entry-shared modes by companies with low-specificity assets is real world form of behaviour. Resource commitment and government restrictions could play a decisive role in the choice of entry mode.
Aulakh and Kotabe (1997)	Degree and performance consequences of channel integration in foreign markets (service companies)	OLI model	Companies prefer "market" mode to an intermediate mode when the level of asset specificity increases. They prefer flexibility over control when faced with country risk due to economic and political uncertainties. The degree of channel integration is not related to performance.
Tse, Pan and Au (1997)	Choice of entry modes and alliances between foreign companies in China	OLI model	Companies are motivated to form alliances with other foreign companies to reduce the investment risks, to capture growing markets or to facilitate their operations in China.

Table 2.1 Mode of Entry Empirical Literature (Cont'd)

Study	Focus of study	Theory used and source of data(s)	Factors hypothesised to affect choice of mode of entry
Kwon and Konopa (1993)	Foreign production versus exporting	Transaction cost theory 134 companies selling the same product in two foreign markets	Levels of tariff barriers, levels of expropriation, levels of foreign ownership restrictions, local currency convertibility, levels of local content requirements, levels of unionisation, language similarity, size of target market, economic growth/performance.
Erramilli and Rao (1993)	International entry-mode choice of service companies	Transaction cost theory 175 service companies	Service companies tend to favour shared-control modes more when asset specificity is low than when it is high. This intensifies when services are inseparable, with increasing country risk, and as companies become smaller.
Agarwal and Ramaswami (1992)	Effect of inter-relationship among a company's ownership, location and internalisation advantages on the choice of entry mode	OLI model	The size and multinational experience constrains companies to choose the direct investment model.
Kim and Hwang (1992)	Licensing, joint venture and wholly owned subsidiary	Perlmutter's orientation of firms and OLI 629 US-based MNEs	Global concentration, global synergies, global strategic motivations, country risk, location unfamiliarity, demand uncertainty, competition intensity, value of company specific know-how, environmental uncertainty, asset specificity and the influence of global strategic variables used to provide a greater scope for explaining entry mode choice than is provided by transaction cost analysis.

Table 2.1 Mode of Entry Empirical Literature (Cont'd)

Study	Focus of study	Theory used and source of data(s)	Factors hypothesised to affect choice of mode of entry
Gomes-Casseres (1990)	Joint venture and wholly owned subsidiary	Bargaining power Secondary data	MNEs in the industry, GDP growth of host country, research and development expenses, number of foreign manufacturing subsidiaries, amount of sales, type of product, familiarity within the host, parent and subsidiary asset size.
Kogut and Singh (1988)	Acquisitions, joint ventures, greenfield investment	Transaction cost theory Secondary data	Diversification, country experience, multinational experience, asset size, research and development spending, advertising spending, cultural distance and uncertainty avoidance.

FOREIGN DIRECT INVESTMENT ALTERNATIVES IN CHINA

In China, foreign investment is basically divided into direct investment and other means of investment. The direct investment, which is widely adopted, includes wholly owned subsidiaries, equity joint ventures, cooperative joint ventures and foreign-funded shareholding companies. The other means of investment generally include licensing, joint exploration, processing and assembly arrangements and counter trade.

Main Forms of Foreign Direct Investment

In China, foreign companies are generally free to choose entry modes. Wholly owned subsidiaries and equity joint ventures dominate the various entry modes; together they account for approximately 80% of the total foreign capital inflow into China. Cooperative joint ventures are the next common form of market entry.

Wholly owned subsidiaries. A wholly owned subsidiary is a legal entity that is directed either to introduce advanced technology or export its products. While there is no minimum investment amount, the regulations stipulate that the cash amount must not be less than 80% of the total capital contributed by the investor and registered with the Chinese authorities at the date of establishment (registered capital) and that the registered capital cannot be reduced during the term of operation.

Equity joint ventures. An equity joint venture is a separate legal entity with limited liability. Authority resides in a board of directors led by a chairman and the profits, risks and losses are shared by the parties involved in the joint venture in proportion to their capital contributions. The proportion of the investment that is contributed by the foreign participants is generally no less than 25%. And while there is no minimum investment requirement, the ratio of total registered capital to total allowable investment by all partners over time decreases with the size of the initial investment. This gives greater flexibility for larger joint ventures. For example, for small investments (US$3 million or less), registered capital must account for at least 70%, whereas for large investments (US$36 million or more), registered capital must account for at least 33.3%. Consistent with the laws governing wholly owned subsidiaries there are restrictions on the non-cash component of the partner contributions. For example, the value of property and technology contributed by the foreign investor must not exceed 20% of the registered capital or 50% of the foreign partners total capital contribution. As with the wholly owned subsidiary, the joint venture's registered capital cannot be reduced during the term of operation. The recent law that governs equity joint ventures allows an unlimited life for joint ventures, and also provides foreign investors with greater flexibility in joint venture management and foreign exchange control. For example, it relaxes the foreign exchange supervision by permitting banks other than the Bank of China to oversee foreign exchange transactions.

Cooperative joint ventures. Cooperative joint ventures offer greater flexibility than equity joint ventures in terms of the form of organisation, capital contribution and profit distribution. A cooperative joint venture can be either a legal entity or a non-legal entity. The law allows the contracting parties to determine the distribution of profits or products and to share losses in the proportion agreed, rather than in proportion to their capital investment as required under the equity joint venture law. While the cooperative joint venture law imposes the same restrictions (as with the equity joint venture law) on the amount of non-cash component of partner contributions, the law does allow the foreign participant to recover its investment within the contractual period. The main advantage of a cooperative joint venture is its flexibility, especially the ability to distribute profits in accordance with pre-agreed percentage splits instead of equity shareholdings. The main disadvantage is the lack of regulation of cooperative joint ventures (e.g., there are no implementing regulations).

Other means of investment. Apart from the three main modes of entry, there exist several other forms of investment. *Licensing* is often involved in joint ventures and compensation trade. A front-end payment is made to cover the establishment cost of the technology, followed by 5 to 20 years of royalty payments. *Joint exploration* investment is mainly in the form of the joint exploration of offshore petroleum. It can be divided into two stages. In the first stage, foreign investors bear all the costs of geographical exploration. In the second stage, Chinese participants join the foreign investors to make their contribution. The profit is shared between the two parties in set proportions. *Processing and assembly* agreements occur when the foreign company supplies raw materials or parts that the Chinese partner then processes and assembles according to design specifications. The Chinese partner receives a processing and assembling fee in return. In the case of machinery, equipment or technology that is supplied by the foreign party, the fee is discounted. All the resulting products are usually re-exported. Finally, *counter trade* is used to cover any type of non-cash transaction such as barter, counter purchase and compensation trade.

Mode of Entry Trends in China

Transaction cost theory predicts that joint ventures will be the dominant mode of entry into a specific industry in a specific country if 1) the government mandates the formation of joint ventures, 2) there is asset inseparability between the partners, and 3) there is partner goal alignment. The first factor is especially relevant in China, where only the government gives permission for the formation of joint ventures in specific industries. This will continue in accordance with the central government's plan to control such industries (e.g., telecommunications). The second factor, asset inseparability, exists in the form of *guanxi* with government and parties in the value chain (suppliers and distributors). Finally, partner goal alignment, rarely exists. Exploratory theoretical research into Chinese joint venture partners indicates that there are differences in each partner's strategic objectives (Shenkar, 1990; Yan and Gray, 1994).

In the early stages of economic reform, foreign partners established equity joint ventures as an expedient alternative to wholly owned subsidiaries (Beamish, 1993; Child, 1994). However, the dominant form of entry has changed over time. Since 2000, the number of wholly owned subsidiaries established has exceeded that of joint ventures. By 2003, the number of newly established wholly owned subsidiaries was double their joint venture counterparts. The reasons for this trend are as follows:

HIGHLIGHTS

Setting Up a Joint Venture in China

When setting up a joint venture in China, your potential partner can obtain the paper work that is required. The following points need to be considered carefully.

1) **Choose the right partner.** What is it exactly that you perceive your current contractor (potential partner) as providing to the joint venture? Government access? Market access?
2) What are the objectives (**benefits**) of going into a joint venture? For example, if you want to sell products in China, then you need to determine the scope of the market value of this opportunity.
3) What are the **costs** associated with the joint venture?
   a) Partner's share of profits
   b) Different objectives – Your Chinese partner may receive merit from local government for initiating the joint venture, and after the joint venture is in operation they may not care too much about whether it makes any profit.
4) What **safeguards** do you intend to put in place to protect your assets?
   a) Negotiate for the supply of raw materials or exclusive marketing rights
   b) Maintenance of working capital
   c) Regular board meetings
5) **Breach of contract clauses.** Are you prepared to include breach of contract clauses that allow you to sue your partner? Such breaches would include the partner:
   a) using the assets of the joint venture as collateral for financing their own investments,
   b) claiming excessive expenses, and
   c) charging the joint venture interest for any finance obtained.

Control and integration with global strategy. Although the foreign and Chinese partners in a joint venture ideally share interests and have equally strong resources to draw upon, the reality can be quite different. Furthermore, all decisions in a joint venture are, or could be, subject to review or revision by the Chinese partner. In the wholly owned subsidiary structure, the foreign investor is better able to integrate its local planning with its global strategy.

Ease of future equity injections. Many long-established joint ventures have matured to the point where at least one investor, often the foreign partner, feels that more equity must be invested in the venture. As a change in equity investment means that investors' equity stakes and arrangements for sharing profits and losses must be revised, equity injections can be a contentious issue that affects the ability of investors to work together. Moreover, the foreign partner may sometimes expect a zero-dividend policy because it wants to re-invest the venture's profits, but the Chinese partner may choose to declare dividends. Consequently, some foreign investors prefer to act alone.

Benefiting from China experience or changes in foreign investment policy. In the early years of foreign investment in China, many foreign investors found that having a Chinese partner was critical to understanding the operating environment. However, with the accumulation of operating experience many foreign investors have developed sufficient confidence in their abilities to work effectively in China, thus lessening the need for a local partner. Other foreign companies are now interested in re-positioning their Chinese operations and believe that remaining with their local partner would be counter-productive. In some cases, this issue is resolved by the foreign partner buying out the local partner's stake in the joint venture. Some foreign companies choose instead to establish wholly owned subsidiaries to complement their existing joint ventures. Companies that were initially required to adopt joint venture structures to invest in certain industries have found that with the relaxation of rules they are now able to set up wholly owned subsidiaries. Some foreign investors that are satisfied with the joint venture structure have discovered their local partners are unable to expand with them to other parts of China. Consequently, the foreign party must either act alone or establish a new alliance with yet another domestic company, the interests of which might not be fully aligned with those of the foreign party and/or the existing joint venture.

SUMMARY

The purpose of this chapter was to provide the foundation for understanding various forms of contracting by MNEs. That foundation lies in the contracting choice made by the MNE in its expansion strategy. The first part of the chapter introduced the two-stage process of contracting decision making. That is, companies first decide on the form of external contract, and after this decision has been made they decide on how to manage the contract. The emphasis is on minimising errors with respect to the external contract choice decision, because management controls have limited power to substitute for a poorly worded contract or the wrong contract as they can only be exercised within the confines of the contract agreement. The second part of the chapter provided the theoretical basis for understanding the determinants of mode of

THEORY IN ACTION

Early Wholly Owned Foreign Enterprise Entry into China – A Fortune 500 MNE Experience

IT Inc is an MNE engaged in the information technology industry. The Hong Kong branch was established in the late 1980s. IT Inc's first investment in China was in the form of a wholly owned subsidiary during the early 1990s.

According to IT Inc, its wholly owned subsidiary was the first of its kind in China. Obtaining approval was difficult because of the sensitive nature of the information technology industry. Even though it proposed a wholly owned subsidiary, Chinese officials forced IT Inc to hire specific employees. During the initial operating period, the Chinese were paranoid about the arrangement and kept the subsidiary under close surveillance.

The subsidiary was solely financed by IT Inc's US parent company. Most of the earnings made by the subsidiary were retained for a number of reasons.

1) Most of its clientele were local enterprises (state or collectively owned). Companies with FDI generally imported their own information technology through an overseas licence agreement signed directly with IT Inc instead of the subsidiary.
2) IT Inc had a separate entity (in the form of a representative office) in China to handle foreign currency transactions. Therefore, the subsidiary's retained earnings were in renminbi, which was not freely convertible.
3) IT Inc is a cash-rich company and rarely relies on local Chinese loans for the investment and expansion needs of its subsidiary in China.

Initially, IT Inc planned that the subsidiary would conduct independent research and development on information technology products. However, it was more cost effective to continue that research and development in the US parent company. The products developed were imported into China and sold to the local clients tailor-made. The subsidiary now acts more like an importer and sales agent.

A wholly owned subsidiary was chosen because IT Inc is a leader in information technology and felt that a subsidiary would best protect its intellectual property. The choice of exactly where the subsidiary would be located was based on the proximity to major local clients. Currently, the subsidiary has a total workforce of over 300. Ten to 20 of them are expatriates – mostly ethnic Chinese seconded from the head office and four other regional offices in China. IT Inc felt that the supply of good managers in

China was limited and that expatriates were essential for the diffusion of knowledge and creativity.

Interestingly, IT Inc did not regard management expertise as one of its bargaining strengths. During the initial years of the subsidiary's operations, it was managed by an ethnic Chinese expatriate in a manner very much like a Chinese family-owned firm. It was only more recently that a new manager was brought in to change the operations. The subsidiary is now managed in a manner similar to its overseas parent company.

When IT Inc first decided to invest in China, it did not place a high value on local knowledge (*guanxi*). However, this attitude has recently changed. Being in a business in which most sales are conducted via personal contacts instead of media promotion, IT Inc started to realise that *guanxi* was of more value than it had originally perceived. The company now knows that business is much slower in China without *guanxi*.

From its experience, IT Inc knows that joint venturing with a powerful and influential local Chinese partner (with support from the ministerial level) is a key to obtaining quick access to contract acceptance from local clients. The company also learnt that the local partner could act as a goalkeeper or opinion leader; to access end users a local partner is necessary, even if that means less profits. The incremental benefits of having a local partner exceed the costs because without a local partner, certain sales would be difficult if not impossible. The net contribution, as IT Inc put it, "depends on how powerful your partner is".

IT Inc felt that the choice of cooperating with a municipal government versus the central government in terms of local partner affiliation was largely dependent upon the market being targeted. A municipal government is desirable if the target market is the area governed by the municipality. However, if the company is targeting the national market or a market more geographically dispersed, either the provincial or central government would be a more ideal candidate. This is especially true if the local partner still enjoys effective control over its subsidiaries at the municipal level.

According to the company, entering a joint venture now might seem to be irrational on the basis of formal investment analysis, but is less so if considered in terms of the quasi-exclusivity that a local partner has over market access to its subsidiaries and affiliates. As one manager put it, "our focus is to invest and seek returns in the long term ... and in the long term a local Chinese partner is essential because it contributes more to enhance the value of the direct investment than it costs". IT Inc feels that the assets possessed by both partners are complementary, and that the final form of any equity joint venture that it undertakes will be an equal or slightly unequal ownership. Moreover, the joint venture should ideally be managed independently from the influence of both partners.

THEORY IN ACTION

Early Joint Venture Entry into China – A Hong Kong Investor Experience

A local company entered China via a processing agreement in late 1980. However, it cancelled the contract and formed a wholly owned subsidiary in 1994. The principal activity of the company is manufacturing aluminium gift products, and its major customers are from Europe and America. The reasons for changing the investment structure are as follows:

- The company had expanded very rapidly and could not take on extra orders. Thus it had to invest more to increase its production capacity. The company planned to construct a factory and purchase more machinery. Consequently, to better safeguard its assets, it decided to form a wholly owned subsidiary.
- Although the company originally invested via a processing agreement, there was much conflict, especially in relation to the management of workers. For example, when the company wanted to punish workers for their mistakes, the Chinese side did not agree. Because the Chinese party had the formal rights for all matters related to workers, no punishment took place.
- The company found that some of its customers, especially its European customers, were more confident of the quality of products made by a wholly owned subsidiary than by a joint venture with a Chinese partner. The perception was that managerial skills, control procedures and technology were poor in China.

entry choice. These include the transaction costs, bargaining power and resource dependence theories. The transaction cost approach serves to analyse the costs of having or not having a local partner. Bargaining power theory addresses the factors that affect the bargaining and negotiation processes before the equity joint venture formation, which among other things must stipulate the equity shareholdings of both the local and foreign partners. The resource dependence model explains the bargaining leverage that is inherent in the control over critical or strategic bargaining resources. The third part introduced the OLI model – an integrative framework of organisation capability, location and entry mode choice. This part also provided a review of the literature on mode of entry. The final part of the chapter provided a summary of the mode of entry issues facing MNEs with investments in China. The laws governing the various modes of entry were briefly described in terms of the restrictions on investment and the main trend towards the establishment of a wholly owned subsidiary was explained in terms of the MNE's need for control and flexibility and the greater level of experience in operating in China.

QUESTIONS

1) What are the two stages of the contracting decision and how are they related?
2) What are transaction costs?
3) What factors cause transaction costs to increase?
4) What is the fundamental paradox of information?
5) How do companies that manufacture and distribute products overcome the paradox of information?
6) What are three examples of difficult-to-trade assets?
7) How does transaction costs theory explain particular modes of entry?
8) What key role does the pricing system play in the market?
9) Under what conditions will markets for intermediate inputs be subject to high transaction costs such that hierarchical coordination is more efficient?
10) What is the transaction cost rationale for joint ventures? Provide three points.
11) What are the various modes of entry that are used to organise the manufacture, sale and distribution of products or services?
12) What key factors dictate the undertaking of each mode of entry?
13) What information needs are required in planning for and undertaking each mode of entry?
14) Can you think of any variable that influences the way in which you may contract for business expansion when attempting to contract for the manufacture of intermediate goods with special patented designs?
15) What forms of contracting require more extensive management accounting information?

EXERCISES

1) PCCX mobile company manufactures and distributes special mobile phones to the European and US markets. Its head office is in Hong Kong, and it has manufacturing subsidiaries in Germany, Ireland and the US. You are consulting for PCCX for the reengineering of the compensation system for its functional

managers in both its Hong Kong and overseas operations. You have also been asked to advise on PCCX's expansion into China. PCCX sees China as providing cheap labour resources for the manufacture of component parts. These component parts will be exported to its overseas subsidiaries. What is the most efficient way that PCCX can contract for this expansion? You have been asked to join the consulting team because you have excellent skills in asking the right questions to gather the essential information that is needed for providing a successful value-added recommendation.

a) List the questions that you should ask when advising PCCX how to contract for entry into China.
b) Explain the rationale for each question. Refer to one of the theories noted in this chapter where appropriate.

2) A US multinational company wants to set up business in mainland China. What factors affect the mode of entry?
3) List the questions that you should ask as a consultant when advising an MNE to enter a foreign country. Explain the rationale for each question. Refer to one of the theories noted in this chapter where appropriate.

CASE STUDY 4

Adams Corporation – Best Mode of Entry for Further Expansion into China

COMPANY BACKGROUND

Adams Corporation, a United States corporation founded 30 years ago, is engaged in printing graphic tags and labels (see Table 1 for a summary of the company's business). The major customers are large retailers in the US such as Wal-Mart, and garment and shoe manufacturers in the Asia-Pacific region, such as GAP, Nike and Reebok. These renowned retailers and manufacturers usually source hangtags and labels from Asia for attachment to their products in their production plants before delivery to the US market. Adams currently holds a 50% market share in this printing industry, with annual turnover of US$250 million.

With continuous expansion, Adams has established production plants in Shanghai, India, South Korea, Hong Kong and Singapore (see Table 2). The first two investments are in the form of equity joint ventures, and the last three are wholly owned subsidiaries. The number of total employees has increased to over 1,600. Adams Asia, one of the wholly owned subsidiaries, is responsible for coordinating the business activities in Asia. It receives orders from customers in the Asia-Pacific region and coordinates the production activities of various production plants. Adams' investments in Asia have growth tremendously and have become the predominant business activities of the group, accounting for about 75% of its profits. The performance of investments in Hong Kong and Shanghai are the most prominent, with 20% and 67% growth in sales, respectively, in 2002 (see Table 2). The growth of outputs from the Hong Kong and Shanghai plants in 2003 were estimated to be 18% and 69%, respectively. To cope with the rapid growth in demand, Adams is eager

I wish to acknowledge the assistance of Lawrence Lee Yuk Lam in the preparation of this case study. This case was developed as a basis for class discussion rather than to illustrate either effective or ineffective handling of an administrative situation.

Table 1 Summary of Company Business

Product	Graphic tags and labels
Company size	Market share: 50% Annual turnover: US$250 million Number of employees: 1,600
Market competition	Low level of competition with two major competitors: Universal Printing Corporation and National Tags & Labels Corporation
Major financial performance	ROS: 15% ROA: 55%
Customer profile	50% large retail stores 30% garment manufacturers 20% footwear manufacturers
Operations	Factories located in the US, Hong Kong, South Korea, Singapore, Shanghai and India. The US office is responsible for coordinating the overall corporate strategy, whereas the Hong Kong office is responsible for coordinating the business activities in Asia
Sources of income	25% generated from production plants in the US 75% generated from production plants in Asia
Form of decision making	Centralisation in corporate decision strategy and decentralisation in regional business decisions

Table 2 Adams Corporation's Existing Investments in Asia

Location	Investment mode	Proportion of corporate sales				Sales growth		
		Actual		*Forecasted*		*Actual*	*Forecasted*	
		2001	*2002*	*2003*	*2004*	*2002*	*2003*	*2004*
Hong Kong	Wholly owned subsidiary	63%	65%	66%	65%	20%	18%	20%
Singapore	Wholly owned subsidiary	18%	16%	14%	10%	2%	2%	2%
South Korea	Wholly owned subsidiary	11%	10%	9%	4%	1%	2%	2%
Shanghai	Equity joint venture	5%	7%	10%	20%	67%	69%	75%
India	Equity joint venture	3%	2%	1%	1%	–8%	1%	1%

to look for extra printing capacity, as management perceives that the production capacities will reach its maximum within three years.

The long-term economic opportunities in China are remarkable, particularly since China's accession to the WTO. Adams' management considers the continuous economic growth in China to be an opportunity for expansion, and forecasts that the sales in Hong Kong and Shanghai will increase by 20% and 75%, respectively, in 2004 (see Table 2). Adams had its initial entry in Shanghai by means of equity joint venture with a local enterprise (a former sub-contractor) in 1998. With the joint venture, Adams and the Chinese partner equally shared returns, equity and management controls. The success of the Shanghai investment has broadened Adams' knowledge about the legal system, economics and market system in China.

Adams' management plans to establish two additional printing plants in China over the next few years. The construction of the first will commence by 2005, and the second project will probably commence after the first plant begins production (see Figure 1). Adams is now considering whether to establish the first plant in Guangdong province or Shanghai, and deciding upon the appropriate mode of investment (see Figure 2 for Adams' options). Both Shanghai and Guangdong share a logistical advantage over inland provinces by their proximity to major international shipping routes, which provide easy access to the world markets.

Figure 1 Timeline for Proposed New Printing Plant

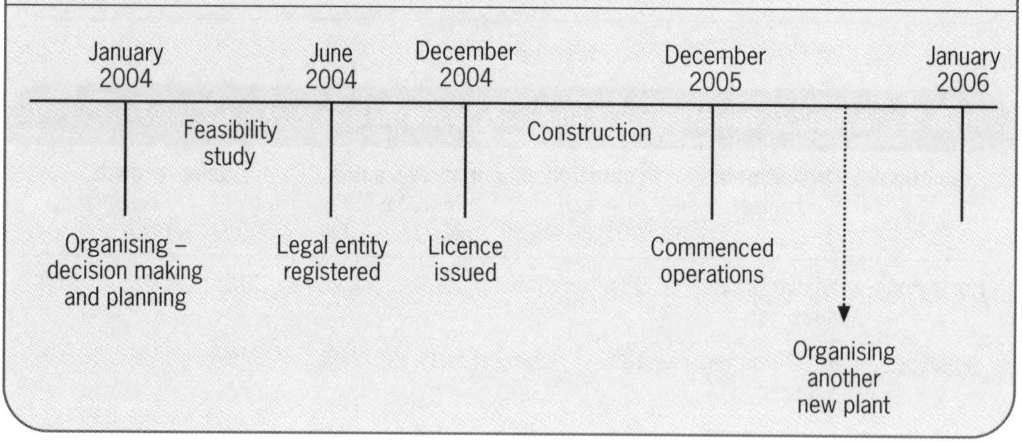

Figure 2 Decision Tree of Adams' Proposed Investment

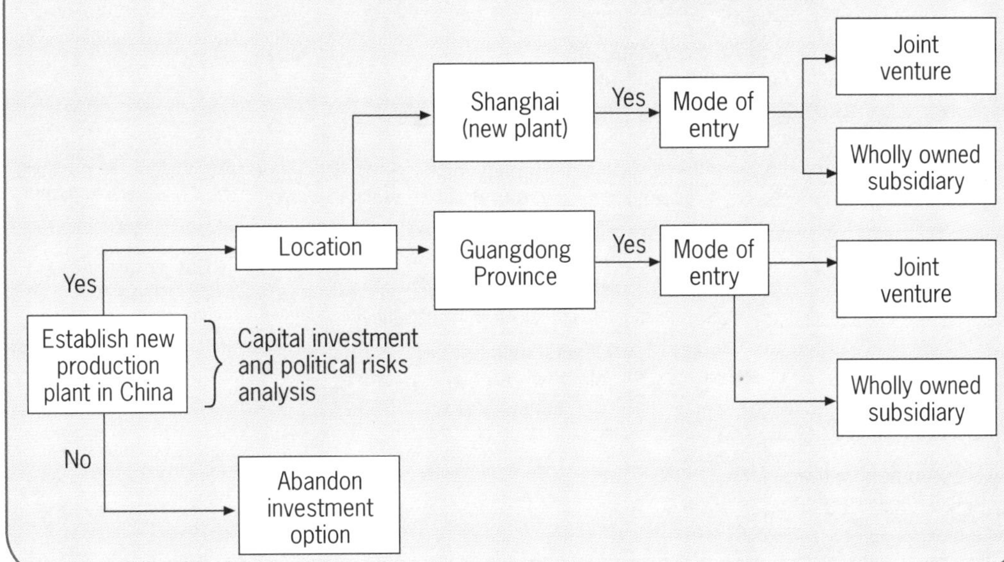

PROPOSED OPERATION STRUCTURE OF THE NEW PLANT

The operation of the new printing plant will be similar to that of the existing plant in Shanghai. Raw materials are mainly sourced by Adams Asia in Hong Kong and then shipped to China. The printing plants will ship the finished graphic tags and labels either directly to customers in China or to Adams Asia for trans-shipment to customers in the Asia-Pacific region (see Figure 3).

FACTORS DETERMINING ADAMS' DECISION TO ESTABLISH A NEW PRINTING PLANT

Location Factors

Shanghai. The existing situation in Shanghai does not seem entirely favourable because the industrial development policy has been shifting the priority of business promotion to high- and new tech industry (the city government has been pursuing stable growth in GDP). Shanghai is also keen on the development of large-scale

Figure 3 Proposed Operation of New Production Plant

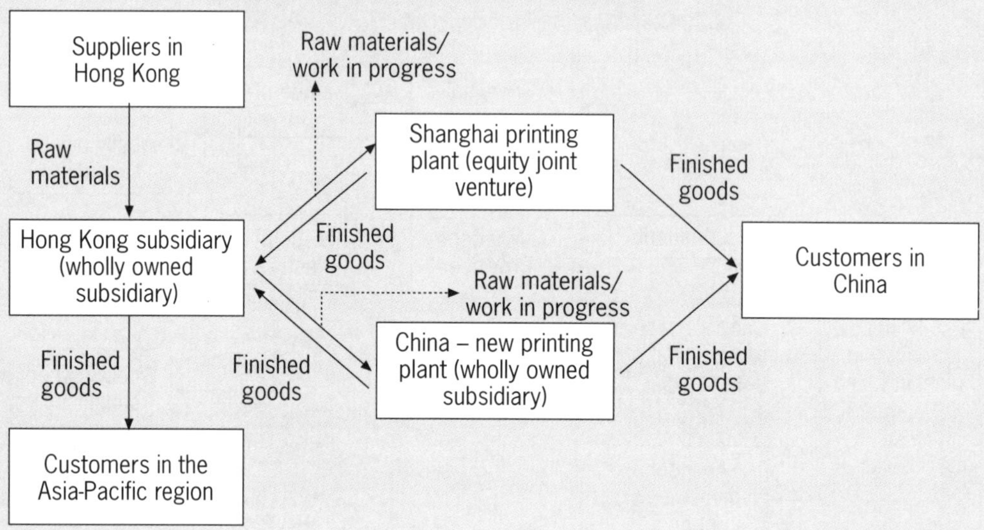

projects with foreign investment, such as the chemical industrial projects in Caojing Chemical Industrial Zone and the integrated circuit projects in Zhangjiang Development Zone, and the setting up of R&D centres to stimulate foreign investors to strengthen their R&D and technical innovation. This implies that the bargaining power of Adams in setting up a new manufacturing plant in Shanghai will not be as strong as it was when the first plant was established.

The cost of land and labour in Shanghai has also increased dramatically. This is mainly due to many late-coming MNEs scrambling for the rights to use land and other facilities, and offering more competitive remuneration to recruit experienced local workers. Hence, the turnover rate of the employees in Adams' Shanghai subsidiary has increased recently.

Guangdong. As the costs of running business operations in Shanghai are ever increasing, Adams should consider Guangdong as an alternative. Guangdong has low production costs, is closer to Adams' clients, close to ancillary firms and holds potential as a peripheral market. In Guangdong, FDI business activities are overwhelmingly concentrated in low-tech, labour-intensive outward processing industries. The dominant mode of cooperation has been processing and assembling operations, with Hong Kong companies providing construction plans, raw materials and primary products. Finished products are then typically distributed via the global distribution network established by the Hong Kong offices.

Guangdong has an inexhaustible supply of cheap labour, continually augmented by a permanent stream of migrant workers from the hinterland, and has, to a great extent, kept a lid on labour costs during the past few years despite the increasing demand. In the southern locations the availability of skilled workers such as engineers and technicians makes Guangdong particularly attractive.

Firm Specific Factors

With a long history in the printing industry, Adams has established its brand name in terms of good quality products, rapid response to customer needs and on-time delivery. The company has established a worldwide distribution and customer network, and enjoys comparative advantages in product costing with low-cost labour, the availability of raw material and economies of scale of production. Adams takes advantages of advanced information technology by engaging in electronic data interchange (EDI) – the inter-company exchange of computer-processable business information, with its suppliers and customers. The prerequisite for EDI is the forming of trading partner agreements among various organisations. EDI provides a means of directly linking stock systems to purchasing, payment and delivery systems, which enables the trading partners to coordinate sales and production operations and maintain an uninterrupted flow of raw materials. Adams' transaction cost of managing the supply chain is reduced by the use of EDI, and the potential for expanding its international business activities is increased as customers can place orders via EDI or a website anywhere at any time.

COST AND BENEFIT ANALYSIS

Adams' accumulated knowledge from its existing Shanghai joint venture will help it to increase local commitment, reduce operational uncertainty and enhance economic efficiency. Knowledge is typically accumulated through a process of learning by doing, which is a positive function of the length of presence in the host country. As Adams has experience and knowledge in setting up and running production operations in China, the reliance on the local partner will gradually decline, which means that a wholly owned subsidiary could be a preferable entry mode for the new plant.

In addition, by operating a wholly owned subsidiary, Adams could improve its ability to reduce risks associated with the market environment, including operation risks (the risk of price control and local content requirement), political risk, ownership/control risk, (the threat of expropriation and intervention) and transfer risk (such as currency inconvertibility and remittance control). This will enable Adams to increase its investment in China step by step.

Managing a joint venture is often more difficult than running a wholly owned subsidiary when special cooperation and trust between the partners are required. Adams has encountered problems with its local partner in Shanghai which can be traced back to the difference in culture, management styles and interests of the partners. This resulted in a more complex and destructively slow decision-making process. Adams is also concerned that under this option, the local partner will develop its own distribution channel and finally become a competitor.

Therefore, a wholly owned subsidiary would enhance Adams' organisational control over local operations, eradicate the costs of inter-partner mistrust and opportunism and protect the company's tacit knowledge and technology investment in China, where intellectual property right systems are not well established. Table 3 presents a summary of the costs and benefits of adopting either a joint venture or a wholly owned subsidiary as the new investment foundation.

Table 3 Cost and Benefit Analysis

Joint venture	
Costs	**Benefits**
• Problem of goal congruence – Chinese partners are more concerned about their own interests than the overall profit of the joint venture. • Poor coordination – culture difference will hinder cooperation between local and foreign managers and employees. • Conflicts between foreign managers and Chinese managers under decentralised decision making. • Loss of operation autonomy – the Chinese partner usually has more control than the MNE over the operation of the joint venture. • The Chinese partner's leverage is likely to be restricted to its own province. • Joint ventures create many areas of confusion between legal explanations and daily practice.	• Having a Chinese partner is the most effective means of gaining access to key resources and developing distribution channels in China. • Chinese partners can share and help reduce the economic and political risks of investment. • Lower resource commitment than in a wholly owned subsidiary. • Significant incentives have been granted, including tax holidays and import duty exemptions for essential production equipment and materials.

Table 3 Cost and Benefit Analysis (Cont'd)

Wholly owned subsidiary	
Costs	**Benefits**
• MNEs bear all risks involved in the investment. • Higher resources commitment than in a joint venture. • Takes time to establish customer relationships and distribution channels especially in China, which is a *guanxi*-dominated society. • As the Chinese generally do not want foreign companies to take advantage of China, questions about cultural and economic sovereignty may arise.	• Ensure goal congruence within the organisational hierarchy and the integration of the China expansion with the global strategy. • Better coordination and scale economies among various business units. • Full control over the subsidiary. • Ensure a reliable supply of resources. • Avoid search and negotiating costs in external contracting. • Reduce transaction costs when transfering resources within the group. • Maintain control over internal information and better safeguard assets. • Facilitate the maintenance of a firm's technological leadership. • Create internal markets and control market outlets.

CASE STUDY QUESTIONS

1) Which mode of entry best suits Adams Ltd? Why?
2) Which location is most appropriate for Adams' expansion plan in China? Why?
3) Which factors have the greatest influence on the attractiveness of each location for the Adams group?
4) Which transaction cost elements are most important in determining the best mode of entry? Explain.

CASE STUDY 5

Ace Style – Best Mode of Entry for Expanding Its Production in China

INTRODUCTION

Ace Style Intimate Apparel Limited was founded in 1985. The company has 1,750 employees and produces about 3,000 styles of lingerie per annum using computer-aided design systems. Headquartered in Hong Kong with subsidiaries in China, Malaysia and the UK, it specialises in manufacturing high-quality branded ladies lingerie, swimwear and sportswear around the world. Calvin Klein, Esprit and Gap are examples of its branded customers.

The company has a very strong presence in Europe, which accounts for more than 70% of its total sales, and has expanded gradually to the US, which accounts for another 25% of sales, and other Asia-Pacific countries, including China. In terms of sourcing, 60% of the company's products are manufactured in China, and the remaining 40% come from Malaysia. The sales turnover in 2001 was about US$112 million, and sales are expected to increase in the future. The company's objective is to improve production and market efficiency and increase market share and profit levels. To meet these ends, it is targeting the expansion of sales with greater market share, and embarking on a programme of cost control.

As a result of planned strategic business development, the company has forecasted a production capacity problem, and establishing a second production site is necessary. The company expects this new factory to be in northeastern China to complement its existing factory in southern China, and to increase overall production by 20%. Strategically, the proposed factory will mainly be used to produce lingerie items of relatively lower quality than the company's southern factory, which

I wish to acknowledge the assistance of Sandy Lo Yun Mui in the preparation of this case study. This case was developed as a basis for class discussion rather than to illustrate either effective or ineffective handling of an administrative situation.

produces higher-quality garments. The plan will enable the company to capitalise on the cheaper and affluent resources in the northeast.

There are many macro and micro factors together with the intangible asset of long experience in China to be considered when analysing the feasibility of establishing a new factory in China. Such a factory is certainly in line with the company's strategic objective of attaining a global market for its products and production efficiency, because it will gradually gain preferential treatment in terms of import duties and quotas from Europe and the US under WTO regulations. This will allow more room to promote and distribute Ace Style's products to different parts of the world by means of original equipment manufacturing (or original design manufacturing).

BACKGROUND OF EXISTING PLANT

The existing production site in southeastern China was established in 1992, and it has about 800 employees, of which the majority are local workers. This wholly owned subsidiary was initially operated as a joint venture for several reasons. First, China is a *guanxi*-dominated society, which signals the advantages of having Chinese partners/companies. Second, questions about cultural and economic sovereignty may arise, as the Chinese generally do not want foreign companies to take advantage of China. Third, although China's WTO accession demands an opening of distribution-rights for foreign companies, such companies may find it difficult to develop their own distribution channels.

In 1996, Ace Style took over the assets of the Chinese partners. This occurred because the joint venture performance depended greatly on qualitative factors such as individual personalities, organisational culture, administrative style and management philosophy. These factors did not encourage the development of the management system that Ace Style wanted. Table 1 provides details of the existing and proposed production sites in China.

DETERMINANTS OF THE MODE OF ENTRY CHOICE FOR THE NEW PLANT

The company's strategic need to centrally coordinate its global operations is likely to diminish the value of shared control mode of entry. However, there are two additional factors to consider. First, relating to the uncertain environment, Ace Style

Table 1 Existing and Proposed Production Site Details

Factors to be considered	Existing production site	New production site
Scale	8,000 sq metres with 800 staff	4,000 sq metres with 300 staff
Duration	10 years	To establish
Location	Southeast China	Northeast China
Market penetration	Market seeker	Intended to be a market seeker
R&D intensity	R&D centres located in New York and Europe	R&D centres located in New York and Europe
Skill intensity	Abundance of low-cost skilled labour	Relatively lower supply of skilled labour than in the southeast
Productivity	60% of total production	20% of total production
Cultural distance	High	High
Market potential	High market potential	Low market potential
Product	Premium-priced lingerie	Discount-priced lingerie
Distribution	Europe	US and Southeast Asia

established its first Chinese factory in 1992. This means that the management of the company has appreciated and experienced, to a certain degree, the cultural norms and regulations in the country. Such experience will greatly reduce the organising and monitoring costs in running the new factory. Therefore, Ace Style faces much less uncertainty than other foreign investors when considering capital investment in a production site in China.

Second, relating to the level of asset specificity, Ace Style is involved in producing ladies lingerie, and both tangible and intangible assets are involved. Computer-driven weaving machines and special automatic programmed-driven spare part cutting machines are the company's most significant tangible assets. They are not easily modified and transferred to other companies. In terms of intangible assets, the company's production management and labour skills are specific to its production process. Hence, Ace Style's asset specificity is high. Table 2 summarises the results of theory condition analysis.

Table 2 Determinants of Mode of Entry Choice for the New Plant

Theory conditions	Level of concern	Prediction
Global strategy	Centralised	Wholly owned subsidiary
Environmental uncertainty	Low	Wholly owned subsidiary
Asset specificity	High	Joint venture

MANAGEMENT CONCERNS

Other than the factors considered above, the experience gained from establishing its first factory in China is also important. Interviews with three management staff members allowed the determination of the level of concern about internal and external factors in the entry mode decision. Table 3 summarises the results.

Table 3 Management Perceptions of Various Mode of Entry Determinants

Risk factors	Level of concern
Target market factors	
• Political risk	Low
• Investment risk	Low
• Host government local content requirements	High
• Qualifications of local partners	Medium
Company factors	
• International experience	High
• Need for local knowledge	High
• Synergies among global operations	High
• Competitive position	High
• Need to protect technology	Medium

CASE STUDY QUESTIONS

1) Which factors have the greatest influence on the attractiveness of each mode of entry for Ace Style?
2) Which transaction cost element was most important in determining the best mode of entry? Explain.
3) Which mode of entry best suits Ace Style? Why?

CASE STUDY 6

XYZ (HK) Ltd – Using a Distributorship versus Retail Outlet Ownership as a Mode of Entry into China

INTRODUCTION

XYZ (HK) Ltd belongs to a group of companies that specialise in promoting and selling a line of branded accessory products such as handbags, backpacks, luggage and cosmetics/perfumes. Headquartered in Italy, the group has subsidiaries in Hong Kong, the US and Europe. The group uses major distributors for its sales and does not use manufacturing subsidiaries. All subsidiaries, with the exception of the Hong Kong subsidiary, deal exclusively with sales. XYZ takes care of the sales function in the Asia-Pacific region, as well as the sourcing function for the whole group.

With sufficient international experience, the Hong Kong subsidiary wants to explore the market in China, which has enormous potential. In the absence of any good business experience in China, the company is critically evaluating the best mode of entry. Several companies, both from China and Hong Kong, are showing keen interest in selling its products in China. The company is confident that its strong and world-famous brands will gain a sound foothold in the Chinese market. XYZ's existing annual turnover is approximately US$50 million, but the sluggish economy in its sales areas poses a threat to it. The company objective is to search for continuous sales growth with an average 20% return on stockholder equity, and China is viable target market. However, the company sold goods to a China-based company five years ago and incurred losses of around US$200,000. Hence, the company perceives the business risk to be great.

I wish to acknowledge the assistance of Sam Chan P.K. in the preparation of this case study. This case was developed as a basis for class discussion rather than to illustrate either effective or ineffective handling of an administrative situation.

The senior management of the company is considering either establishing its own retail outlets (a type of internal contracting) or appointing a distributor (a type of external contracting) as mode of entry to China. The different types of contracting have different management and business implication in terms of culture, legal ramifications, finance, risk, management and strategic development. It is important to carefully contemplate the two alternatives for an optimal solution to be adopted.

TRANSACTION COST DRIVERS

Transaction cost theory can be used to examine the decision on the mode of entry. In view of this analysis, a recommendation on the choice of either having retail outlets (e.g., wholly owned subsidiary) or using distributorship will be made. The primary data was collected mainly through an interview with the director of the company regarding its management philosophy and view of overseas investment in China. The focus of the interview was on those transaction cost factors that could mould the choice of entry mode.

Environmental uncertainty. Two environmental factors are specific to XYZ. First, running a retail outlet and appointing distributors have different degrees of risk. XYZ will not be able to avoid business risk, financial risk, operating risk and legal risk if it owns retail outlets, because it will be a legal entity registered under Chinese law. These risks can be substantially reduced if a distributorship mode of entry is used to explore the market. In legal terms, the appointed distributor will take on most of the risks. However, there is a chance that the cultural distance, which exists between the Italian headquarters and potential local distributors will result in higher transaction costs.

Knowledge dependence and asset specificity. XYZ has no direct business experience in China. To develop the sales function of the company in China, it has to rely substantially on third-party connections to explore the market. Thus, knowledge dependence will be high, particularly in the early stages of operations. This dependence will be the areas of securing a retail licence from government, establishing relationships with department stores or other distribution channels, decorating retail outlets in terms of local taste preferences, booking advertising space in the mass media such as television and newspapers, setting logistics arrangements and taking care of all relationship with the relevant government departments.

COST AND BENEFIT ANALYSIS

The management of XYZ has to weigh the trade-off of using its own retail outlets against a distributorship. Table 1 summarises the cost and benefit factors. In comparing the entry modes, the main difference is in the resources committed. The level of resources committed will be much greater if XYZ decides to establish its own company and run the retail outlets. In contrast, under the distributorship mode, XYZ will not have to commit as many resources. The greatest outlays will be in subsidising the distributor in decorating the retail outlets or by donating fixtures or contributing part of the advertising budget.

Table 1 Cost and Benefit Analysis

Costs	Benefits
Owning retail outlets	
• XYZ will directly be responsible for any kind of risks if it is judged to be negligent. Potential compliance costs. • Will incur huge fixed overheads in running the retail outlets, and thus high leverage beyond its operating capability.	• It is easier to use this mode of investment to approach the China market as it is allowed by law with China's WTO membership; less restriction. • It is easier to determine with more autonomy in respect to suitable business strategies in exploring the market potential; more power of control. • More direct control over the operations and the ability to conduct more training of sales personnel.
Distributorship	
• Substantial loss of control over the retail operation in China; less say in business strategy. • Resource commitment will be less as distributors will invest in this part of the market to promote the products. • XYZ's management will miss the chance of training in ways of expanding and setting up business networks in China.	• Less risk for XYZ as the distributor will take care of all supply and sales chain operations in China. The distributors carry most of the operating liability. • Less resource commitment, but XYZ will retain the usual mark-up when goods are supplied to the distributors. • Will allow capitalisation on the expertise and solid business network of the distributor to capture a bigger market share. XYZ can specialise in product design.

CASE STUDY QUESTIONS

1) Which factors have the greatest influence on the attractiveness of each mode of entry for XYZ Ltd?
2) Which transaction cost element is the most important in determining the best mode of entry? Explain.
3) Does prior experience in China influence this analysis in any way? Explain?
4) Which mode of entry best suits XYZ Ltd? Why?

CASE STUDY 7

MHK Ltd – Using a Distributorship versus Branch Office as a Mode of Entry into China

INTRODUCTION AND COMPANY BACKGROUND

MHK Company was founded in 1987, and specialises in the supply of respiratory products and the provision of after-sales service to individual patients and hospitals. MHK has gained more than 55% market share in Hong Kong, and management believes that the Hong Kong market has reached maturity. In contrast, the market in China is at an early stage. According to a survey, 2% of the population in China suffers from respiratory diseases, and the medical treatment for this field is still in its infancy. Doctors and hospitals generally have limited knowledge about tackling these diseases and may not have enough information to catch up with the technological trend.

MHK has obtained the distribution rights in China for a well-known brand name of respiratory products. The company currently operates in China through holding the management rights of a domestic company that sells and distributes the medical equipment. This management right allows MHK to fully control and monitor the whole operation, including the hiring of employees and profits sharing. The Chinese party is a silent partner and the management believes that the arrangement is the stepping stone for the company. MHK is planning to diversify into other medical equipment fields and foresees that China offers large potential for expansion. However, the prohibition of foreign direct investment in the medical

---

I wish to acknowledge the assistance of Caren Chow in the preparation of this case study. This case was developed as a basis for class discussion rather than to illustrate either effective or ineffective handling of an administrative situation.

equipment field limits the choice of entry mode. MHK has two options for expansion in China: 1) establishing a branch office for the existing domestic company, or 2) establishing a sub-distribution arrangement with a local Chinese company.

After several years of operation, the current arrangement has created the following problems: 1) slow sales growth and increased competition from the local suppliers, which have begun to catch up with it in terms of technology and produce similar products, 2) the restriction on the selling of medical equipment as each item requires a lengthy registration process with the state drug administration (SDA), and 3) the geographical dispersion of MHK outlets creates management control problems. MHK now operates in four main cities and finds it difficult to exercise tight control over the actions of staff. These problems are likely to be exacerbated with the introduction of more competition from 2003 onwards. Consequently, MHK management thinks that the company must try to enlarge its market share.

COST AND BENEFIT ANALYSIS

Country-specific Factors

Governmental intervention. The medical equipment industry is fully controlled and closely monitored by the Chinese government. Although the local company that is managed by MHK is allowed to operate in the industry, it is subject to more stringent rules and regulations than are in place in uncontrolled industries. Licences must be obtained from the State Administration for Industry and Commerce for selling and distributing medical equipment, and they are subject to annual renewal, which is often unpredictable. Different cities have different sets of regulations in handling the industry.

A related issue is the registration of new medical equipment. New medical equipment must have SDA approval before it can be launched into the market. The duration of the application process for this approval is unpredictable due to governmental bureaucracy and the different regulations in different provinces. Any delay in the process can provide room for competitors to take market share from MHK. Thus, governmental intervention is expected to be high.

Property rights systems. The property rights system in China is still under developed, and MNEs suffer from infringements and piracy by local firms. MHK acts as a distributor of a well-known brand and assumes responsibility for tackling piracy and maintaining brand recognition. Hence, there is greater emphasis on controls that can help MHK to safeguard the brand name.

Geographic dispersion. While China has a large market, the market prospects vary across different cities. This, along with the limited resources, has forced MHK to operate in only four major cities. This has allowed local players to enter the market by imitating MHK's products and take substantial market share in a short period. Moreover, the dissemination of new product knowledge is slow. Before the launch of a new product, extensive training must be provided to ensure correct usage.

Industry-specific Factors

Asset specificity. Service firms usually do not require high tangible asset intensity in comparison to manufacturing firms. However, the transfer of the intangible assets requires significant investments in skills, expertise and know-how that are uncommon and not easily transferable to other situations. As MHK requires high professional skills and specialised know-how, its asset specificity is presumed to be high.

Growth in the number of firms. MHK is now experiencing more vigorous competition than in previous years. Currently, MHK maintains a competitive advantage due to its close connection with overseas practitioners and the technological advancement in the products that it offers. However, the advent of more sophisticated products manufactured by local players is a threat to MHK.

Firm-specific Factors

Knowledge dependence. MHK's targeted customers are doctors, and the medical equipment industry is labour intensive and knowledge oriented. MHK staff members have to demonstrate their expertise in the industry to maintain the company's professional image. Hence, the company has high training costs and relies heavily on the transfer of knowledge.

Risk factors. MHK operates in a high-risk industry because suppliers are legally liable for the improper use of equipment. When choosing a mode of entry, the management must consider which mode offers them the minimum risk. In the full-control mode, MHK will be able to exert tight control over the actions of staff. However, if a sub-distribution arrangement is chosen, MHK may face contractual risk. The evaluation of the appropriate agent will take a long time, and contract enforcement may create other kinds of management-control problems.

Cost and Benefit Summary

Table 1 summarises the costs and benefits of establishing a branch office or a sub-distribution arrangement.

Table 1 Cost and Benefit Analysis

Costs	Benefits
Sub-distribution arrangement	*Sub-distribution arrangement*
• MHK may incur high negotiation, contract and monitoring costs for the enforcement of the contract with the agents. • MHK risks abuse of the brand by the agent.	• Partnering with local players may reduce the number of competitors in the market. • Increased market channels and sales opportunities will create barriers to further market entry. • Will improve the liquidity of MHK because the company will not be required to financially support the agent.
Branch office	*Branch office*
• Sales growth will be slow due to resource limitations. • More resources will be allocated to monitoring and training the staff.	• MHK can undertake better strategic marketing campaigns to monitor sales growth. • Will ensure the proper use of the brand. • Management is familiar with the business model and can easily transfer it to other locations.

CASE STUDY QUESTIONS

1) Which factors have the greatest influence on the attractiveness of each mode of entry for MHK Ltd?
2) Which transaction cost element is most important in determining the best mode of entry? Explain.
3) Which mode of entry best suits the expansion plans of MHK Ltd? Why?

CHAPTER

3

Management Control of Wholly Owned Subsidiaries

LEARNING OBJECTIVES

- Understand the basic management control framework including the difference between formal and informal controls.
- Understand the interdependencies between components of the management control framework.
- Understand the issues in the management control of subsidiaries with specific reference to the challenges posed by decentralisation, controllability and national culture.
- Understand some of the issues in human resource management and control in China.

INTRODUCTION

Wholly owned subsidiaries are the contract of choice for the MNE as they allow greater flexibility in controlling the MNEs' operations. For example, wholly owned subsidiaries allow the parent company to fully transfer its accounting and control system, which enhances comparability in performance evaluation. Wholly owned subsidiaries also provide a safeguard against the risk of appropriation of proprietary knowledge. However, the wholly owned subsidiary is not without its weakness. As will be explained in the following chapters, there are various costs associated with control such as managing risk and fitting in with another country's political and cultural dictates. It is for these reasons that joint ventures have been a popular alternative for managing foreign direct investment in developing countries in the past 20 years.

Once head office management has decided to structure the overseas investments through a wholly owned subsidiary or joint venture, the internal contracting and control mechanisms that are required to manage such a structure must be chosen. This chapter introduces a range of control mechanisms that are likely to be used and provides an overview of the management control issues that face the management of wholly owned subsidiaries (Chapter 4 considers similar issues in the management of joint ventures). The chapter is divided into two parts. The first part outlines the theoretical foundations and various mechanisms of control. The interrelationship between control mechanisms is also considered. The second part develops an integrative framework of MNE subsidiary control. Three areas in which control problems typically surface in the MNE are expanded upon. A brief reference to human resources control problems in China is also made.

MANAGEMENT CONTROL MECHANISMS

The purpose of control mechanisms is to ensure that the behaviour and decisions of people in the organisation are consistent with the organisation's objectives and strategies (Merchant, 1989). There are numerous ways in which control systems can be characterised. One useful classification is the object of control that was developed in part by Ouchi (1989) and Merchant (1989). Groot and Merchant (2000) provide several examples of control mechanisms that are classified in terms of the object of control that can be used in the subsidiary or joint venture context (see Table 3.1). Action controls include a range of mechanisms that directly influence the actions of people such as locks, security protocols, rules and procedures and contractual safeguards. Result

Table 3.1 Types of Control Mechanisms Classified by the Object of Control

Action controls	Result controls	Personnel/Cultural controls
• Require adherence to specific actions defined in legal contracts.	• Set performance targets and monitor performance reports, ask for explanations and give advice where appropriate (e.g., *participation in budget setting*).	• Select partner(s) who can be trusted (e.g., reliable history shared management philosophy).
• Require adherence to pre-specified policies and procedures (with checking by auditors and penalties for non-adherence) (e.g., *the use of legal safeguards*).	• Set performance targets and monitor performance reports. Intervene when necessary (e.g., *budget-based performance measures*).	• Place qualified, loyal personnel in key operating positions (e.g., *expatriates*).
• Review and approve certain planned decisions (e.g., *delegation of decision authority*).	• Set performance targets and promise and provide rewards for good performance (e.g., *performance-based bonus*).	• Require specified training (e.g., *socialisation*)

Source: Groot, T.L.C.M. and Merchant, K.A. (2000). Control of international joint ventures. *Accounting Organisations and Societies*, 5. Copyright 2000 by *Accounting Organisations and Society*. Reprinted by permission of Elsevier. Examples in italics added.

controls focus on the outcomes of people's efforts such as sales, performance evaluations based on cost management versus budget comparisons or performance bonuses that are attached to these and other outcomes. Behaviour controls (also referred to as personnel/cultural controls) focus on shaping people's behaviour and include mechanisms such as communication routines, meetings and training.

Formal Control Mechanisms

Control mechanisms have typically been classified along the formal–informal divide. Formal controls are those that are likely to be action- and result-oriented as their object of control. Such controls are more explicit in terms of being objective (free from bias) and/or verifiable. Formal control mechanisms can be divided into four categories: human resource selection, delegation of authority, performance measurement systems and reward systems. This list is obviously not exhaustive and it reflects the economic view that mechanisms are required to minimise knowledge transfer and agency costs. While knowledge transfer costs are associated with the delegation of authority, it is the agency costs that are first implicated during the selection process of human resources for the organisation. Once the right people are selected, then choices need to be made about the extent to which they are given decision authority (decision rights) commensurate with their job function. Along with this is the need to determine how to measure the performance of personnel and how to link this measurement to particular rewards.

Human resource selection procedures. Sourcing and employing the human resources capability occurs before the problem of control, and can have enormous implications for the effectiveness of other control mechanisms that are subsequently installed. There are two basic selection criteria: skill set and organisation fit. As a general rule the selection criteria for a position must be clear in terms of whether it is largely based on the applicant having a particular capability (skill set) or fit with the organisation culture, or a more equal combination of both. Correct human resource selection, like the choice of external contract, can lead to substantial cost savings in the long term. For example, retrenchment and turnover costs are likely to be higher if the wrong people are selected to begin with. These costs can also be higher due to costs that are incurred during a person's term with the company.

Human resource selection procedures are particularly critical for the MNE given the likely geographic and cultural distance that is associated with having a subsidiary in another country. Following the first (skill set) of the two criteria noted above, the capability of the subsidiary in a new country needs to be organised. A great deal of attention needs to be given to the selection of personnel. Does the MNE send in a team of expatriates? If they are available from another country, from where should expatriates be employed? If not, then how are suitably qualified managers selected in the host country? Host governments are eager for FDI to help ease the burden on unemployment. What is the extent to which the host country government will interfere in this employment process?

In terms of the second selection criteria (organisation fit), there are high contracting costs from selecting the wrong type of manager or employee. This is apart from expatriates, who may already be under the same contract terms as the home country head office. For example, Bruton (2000) recommends that companies hire new graduates as they can be moulded and developed with little resistance compared to their older counterparts. Contracting the wrong managers and employees can also bring with it high control costs if the firm has to provide further training and monitor more mundane procedures than first thought appropriate.

Selection processes are also related to other informal controls such as training and communication routines (discussed later). Together, these controls can have an impact on the retention of staff. For example, the controls can be combined such that there is a selection emphasis on skill set with subsequent socialisation or a selection emphasis on fit with subsequent skill training. In short, the role of selection activities acts as the first formal control over human resources in the subsidiary and should be considered as part of the formal and informal control package. Other controls are considered next.

Performance measurement and reward systems. Once human resources are selected, then the issue of controlling these resources becomes important. It is important that in designing a performance measurement and reward system that certain basic characteristics are met and that they fit in with the authority structure of the firm.

Basic characteristics. Performance measurement and reward systems generally aim at bridging the gap in information and objectives between the principal and the agent. The aim is to align the interests of parties and to share risk in a fair and appropriate way. To do this there are several basic characteristics of a good performance measurement and evaluation system.

- Organisational objectives are consistent with corporate objectives and clearly communicated to the agent.
- The scope of the performance measures matches the responsibilities (those factors that the agent has control over – controllability) of the agent.
- Performance metrics are measurable and verifiable (able to be contracted upon).
- Performance targets are perceived as fair, meaningful and comparable.
- There is an economic cost and benefit trade-off.

Table 3.2 provides examples of these characteristics in the MNE subsidiary environment. Examples are given for both budgetary and performance evaluation considerations.

Linkage with decision authority structure. Formal management controls have been modelled in terms of a typology of decision rights, performance measures and performance rewards. Senior management plays a major role in formulating the organisational structure, which includes decisions about how much authority to delegate to functional managers, and how to structure the performance evaluation and reward system so that qualified employees are attracted, retained and motivated (Brickley, Smith and Zimmerman, 1997) (see Figure 3.1). When delegated to managers in various profit or cost centres, authority rights – which are the rights to decide on and take action – can boost organisational adaptation and market responsiveness (Bushman, Indjejikian and Smith, 2000). Knowledge transfer costs

Table 3.2 International Performance Evaluation

	Basic conditions of a good performance evaluation system				
	Performance criteria • *Consistent with corporate objectives*	*Decision rights* • *Responsibility* • *Controllability*	*Performance criteria* • *Understandable* • *Measurable* • *Verifiable*	*Performance standards* • *Realistic* • *Meaningful* • *Comparable*	*Economic benefits > costs*
Budgeting considerations	1) Strategic differences in subsidiaries result in • different performance evaluation measures, and • use of budgeting 2) Budgets enable different performance benchmarks to be used in conjunction with the different strategic roles of subsidiaries	1) Budget participation 2) Line items are controllable 3) In which currency should the budget be prepared?		1) Use of budgets enables the parent to tailor separate performance goals for each subsidiary, for example, adjustment for foreign exchange	1) Culture and use of budgets 2) Transfer pricing 3) Uncertain economic environment (e.g., high inflation)
Performance evaluation issues of the MNE	1) What is the role of the subsidiary? 2) Strategic independencies need to be accounted for (adjusted transfer pricing)	1) Unit versus managerial performance 2) Foreign exchange – stable/unstable 3) Operating/financing/ taxation responsibility	1) Financial • ROI, ROA • include/exclude uncontrollable costs, tax, interest from the denominator • include/exclude uncontrollable assets from the denominator 2) Non-financial • external sources (e.g., customer surveys)	1) ROI adjusted for • country risk, and • specific objective of each foreign unit 2) How should the foreign currency element be dealt with?	Environment 1) Country risk government restrictions on • assets held, and • profits repatriated 2) Interdependencies of an MNE's operations performance problems in one affiliate may affect the operations of another downstream affiliate

Figure 3.1 Mapping the Jointly Determined Nature of Organisation Structure and Control Components

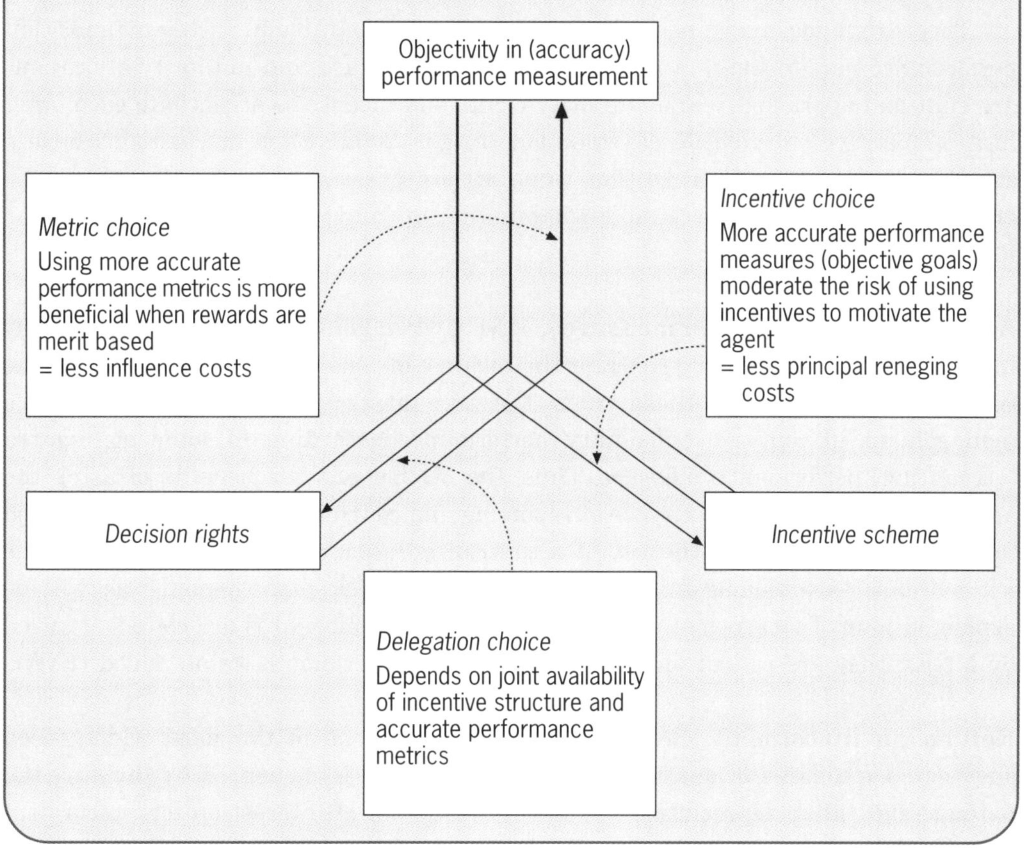

within an organisation's hierarchy are lower when decision-making rights are moved to individuals who operate at the organisational edges (e.g., purchasing and sales departments) (Christie, Joye and Watts, 2003). Jensen (1998) defines knowledge transfer costs along a knowledge continuum from specific to general that measures transfer costs from high to low.

Firms also need to objectively measure the behaviour and efficiency of functional managers, and to reward them on that basis (Jensen and Meckling, 1995). The increased weighting placed on objective measures in the objective/subjective performance measurement mix means that the measurement is increasingly "free from personal bias" (Merchant, 1989, p. 26). This is important to performance monitoring as greater objectivity reduces the superior's discretion in the evaluation process, which in turn reduces the potential gains from influencing activities as perceived by the agent (Prendergast, 1999). Finally, agency theory prescribes the use of incentive compensation that is based on the performance of agents, because the resultant information asymmetries make their behaviour costly or difficult to observe (Gerhart and Milkovich, 1990).

These three mechanisms are interrelated and inseparable in such a manner that performance monitoring is a foundation on which reward and authority allocations are built and appraised, while authority rights and incentives accentuate each other in a competitive yet volatile environment (Nagar, 2002). Such mechanisms have a complementary association, so that when all are present, the incentive alignment effect is stronger than the simple combination of individual effects (Milgrom and Roberts, 1995).

Aggregated performance measures. MNEs, when going internationally, typically impose universal accounting rules for the purpose of consolidation. As a result of the consistent application of these rules, the accounting system allows head office management to compare subsidiary performance according to some aggregated (accounting) performance measure. Thus, the MNE gains the benefits of using the accounting system for the purpose of reporting and control. However, due to the need for comparable reporting, the use of a centralised accounting system for control is not without its problems (e.g., controllability and risk management), as will be explained later. Two types of aggregated performance measures are commonly used by MNEs; they are return on investment (ROI) and economic value added (EVA).

Return on investment. Return on investment is one of the most widely used aggregated measures of subsidiary performance. ROI is measured by dividing the net earnings (after depreciation but before deduction of interest on long-term debt and taxes) by net assets (total assets minus goodwill and other intangibles, current liabilities and reserves for depreciation) and can be broken down into return-on-sales and sales-to-assets ratios.

In the early studies on US MNE subsidiaries, researchers found that ROI was the most used measure of performance. In Europe, Appleyard, Strong and Walton (1990) studied the performance evaluation practices of seven British MNEs and found that they, unlike their American counterparts, preferred to use budget/actual comparisons. However, some form of ROI was also widely used for measuring foreign subsidiaries' performance. In contrast to the US MNEs, Japanese MNEs tend to rely on sales volume as their most important criterion – ROI is rarely used (Bailes and Assada, 1991).

There are, however, several shortcomings in the ROI measure. First, managers may take steps to maximise the ROI but decrease the long-run value of their business units. Second, an increase in divisional ROI may not mean an increase in the economic wealth of the whole corporation because managers tend to reject new viable projects that may decrease their division's ROI but are well above the division's cost of capital. Third, ROI measures may motivate divisional managers to dispose of an asset even though it is earning above the division's cost of capital. Moreover, where inter-corporate transfers are significant and not at arm's-length prices, the ROI measure is highly arbitrary. In addition, subsidiaries that operate in different countries may have different objectives and operating environments. It is also wrong to treat all subsidiaries as independent autonomous operations (Radebaugh and Gray, 2002).

Economic value added. Economic value added is a residual income type of aggregated performance measure. It has several advantages over the ROI that relate to the shortcomings noted in the preceding section. First, the EVA measure will always increase when a division adds investments, which can provide a rate of return above the cost of capital or can eliminate investments that have a rate of return below the cost of capital. Thus, at least two shortcomings of ROI can be overcome. Second, the EVA measure is also more flexible than ROI because a different percentage of cost of equity and/or cost of debt derived from the capital asset pricing model can be applied to investments of different risks. For example, the cost of capital for divisions in different countries may differ.

EVA is calculated as follows:

EVA = (EBIT − Taxes − Capital charges (i.e., Invested capital × Cost of capital)

Where:

EBIT = earnings before interest and tax
Invested capital = Equity + Long-term and Short-term debts
Cost of capital = Weighted average cost of capital (WACC)
(i.e., Net cost of equity × % of equity used
+ Net cost of debt × % debt used).

In the 1990s, more and more US companies adopted EVA (Ehrbar and Stewart III, 1999). According to Stern and Shiely (2001), more than 300 [large] companies worldwide have adopted EVA. However, the exact nature of the value added is unclear. For example, Chen and Dodd (1997) found that "the association of EVA with stock return is not as strong as suggested in anecdotal EVA stories". Biddle, Bowen and Wallace (1997) found that EVA does not significantly outperform earnings before extraordinary items in tests of relative information content.

Informal and Subtle Mechanisms

Informal controls are those that focus on a particular behaviour as their object of control. Informal or subtle mechanisms are employed to manage the communication and learning routines in an organisation. These routines become more critical in the international context as the complexity of information flows that are necessary for competition increases. Examples of such controls include communication routines (meetings), socialisation, training and the employment of expatriates. These mechanisms vary according to the cost of implementation, maintenance and effectiveness.

Informal communication. This is a relatively low-cost option that involves the network of personal contacts that one develops over time in an organisation. At a more formal level, such communication routines are organised through specific task forces and meetings which are held to accomplish the corporate objectives. Frequent communication enhances transparency and the information sharing that is necessary for strategic integration (e.g., taking advantage of collaborative opportunities) and control of the subsidiary (Lane and Lubatkin, 1998).

Socialisation routines. These are an important control mechanism through which managers learn to share attitudes and knowledge of the organisation. Socialisation routines include personal relationships, customs and rituals, training programmes, information sharing, meetings, visits to and from parent headquarters and recruitment criteria (Van Maanen and Schein, 1979). The aim is to develop task knowledge and personal relationships, and to internalise organisational goals, customs and rituals. Corporate norms foster desired behaviour and help to bridge parent–subsidiary differences in strategic orientation and culture. As a result, socialisation has been proposed as a key tool in the management of foreign subsidiaries and joint ventures to improve mutual information sharing and commitment between partners with different competencies and knowledge (Ostroff and Kozlowski, 1993).

Expatriates. This is an expensive option that allows for specific training and control over specific functions in the subsidiary. For this reason, expatriates are typically employed in critical areas such as administration and finance or in high-tech production operations which require particular expertise that is difficult to transfer to local managers. Ultimately, expatriate management leads to a greater transmission of values and goals from the parent to the subsidiary (Isobe, Makino and Montgomery, 2000).

THE MNE SUBSIDIARY CONTROL FRAMEWORK

Often the management control system is designed to fit with firm strategy, the size of the firm or the management culture. However, in the international setting, the MNE depends to a greater extent on the environment in which it operates. Therefore, management's desire for particular controls should be made within the range of choice afforded by each subsidiary environment. The international environment creates several complications for maintaining the basic tenets of a good management control system. To begin with, the information asymmetry problem may be exacerbated due to both the physical and cultural distance between the head office and the subsidiary. Other problems such as how much responsibility should be built into various performance benchmarks and how to tailor various controls to the local environment need to be considered. Figure 3.2 maps several linkages between independent and management control system variables that are associated with three important choices made by MNE and subsidiary managers: decentralisation, the focus of head office control and the extent to which controls need to be adapted to the national culture of a subsidiary's domain.

First, as part of the MNE strategy, there are several factors that shape the manner in which the head office is likely to decentralise control over the subsidiary – that is, the extent to which decision rights are assigned (and the scope of their assignment) to the subsidiary manager: 1) whether the subsidiary is part of a global or multidomestic strategy, 2) the rationale for country location of the subsidiary (e.g., resource efficiency or market expansion), and 3) the nature of the role of the subsidiary in this strategy. Is the subsidiary an integrated part of the global supply chain? Or is the subsidiary using specialised (e.g., patented) production technology? In addition, the environment (political and economic uncertainty) is likely to shape the scope and extent of the decentralisation of control (see top part of Figure 3.2).

Second, after the head office has decided on the extent and the scope of subsidiary decision authority, one of the next important choices is the focus of head office control over the subsidiary. The focus of head office control can range from the subsidiary as a unit (e.g., investment centre) to the subsidiary manager (e.g., cost centre) or both (e.g., profit centre) (see middle part of Figure 3.2). Several issues need to be addressed here: 1) the extent to which the subsidiary manager should be held accountable for factors outside of their control (e.g., foreign exchange), 2) the extent to which we can compare the performance or contribution of different subsidiaries to the MNE (e.g., How do you compare the contribution of a sales subsidiary with a production subsidiary while at the same time encouraging their cooperation in the global supply chain?),

Figure 3.2 Integrative Framework of MNE Subsidiary Control

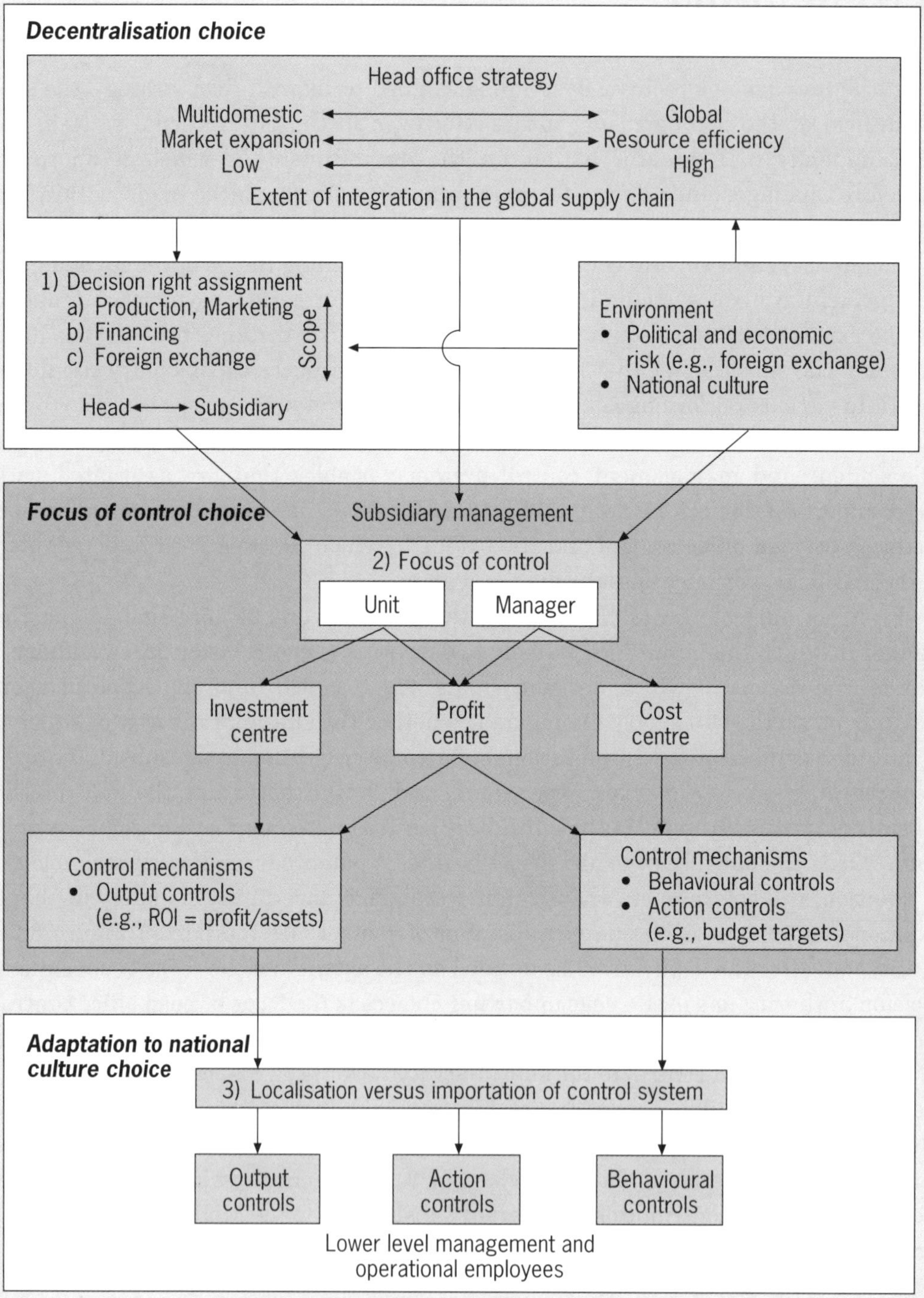

3) verifiability issues concerning the use of output measures to measure the performance of the subsidiary (e.g., ROI is arbitrary in that subsidiary managers can borrow heavily to lower the denominator), 4) how to effectively communicate the scope and focus of the performance measures used to evaluate the subsidiary, so that it is understood and used by the subsidiary, and 5) where budgets are used for the purposes of planning and control – how to obtain a reasonable budget level? Due to the distances mentioned earlier, subsidiary managers are frequently able to negotiate more slack in the budget than domestic managers.

Finally, once the formal control and reporting mechanisms are determined between the head office and the subsidiary, a decision has to be made about whether the same controls are to be used in the lower levels of the subsidiary operations. This is the issue of how the controls in the subsidiary engage with the host nation's national culture (see bottom part of Figure 3.2). National culture is an important consideration for control to the extent that is likely to affect information sharing and the nature of the incentives that are required to motivate staff in the subsidiary. Some of the key issues relating to the three choices are expanded upon in the next section.

KEY ISSUES IN MNE SUBSIDIARY CONTROL

Within the MNE subsidiary control framework there are three key issues that have occupied much of the international management literature: centralisation/decentralisation, controllability of subsidiary manager responsibility and the ability to adapt to the subsidiary country's national culture.

Centralisation/Decentralisation Dilemma

The MNE has three means of coordination available to achieve control that relate to the formal and informal control groups presented at the beginning of this chapter: formalisation, centralisation and socialisation. These can often be associated with using different resource flows: goods and products can be coordinated using formalisation; resources and skills may need to be coordinated using centralisation; and information may require a socialisation process to accomplish control. The critical challenge is to develop a control system that is consistent with the overall decision-making approach of the MNE. As the coordination network in the head office is vertical, the decision-making process is in accordance with centralisation. Table 3.3 shows the nature of the costs that are associated with centralisation and decentralisation. The centralisation costs reflect the level of control and coordination that is necessary to implement a global strategy. The decentralisation costs reflect the need to adapt to the host country environment; for example, different products to suit the market preferences.

Table 3.3 The Centralisation/Decentralisation Dilemma

Strategy towards world markets	Factors	Control mechanism
Multidomestic strategy • Products differ greatly across country markets	• High transportation costs • High government barriers to trade • Industry lacks sufficient scale economies • Research and development may be tied to a specific market • Distribution systems are fragmented and too hard to penetrate	Greater decentralisation
Global strategy • Where significant benefits can be gained from worldwide volume	• Significant benefits gained from worldwide volume – reduced unit costs or superior reputation or service > costs of serving worldwide • Large production runs, more efficient logistics networks, higher-volume distribution networks, multi-country benefit of research and development	Greater centralisation

Controllability of Subsidiary Manager Responsibility

The second key issue facing international subsidiary management is the extent to which subsidiary managers can be made responsible for the environment in which the subsidiary operates (see Figure 3.3). In other words, should subsidiary manager performance be separated from subsidiary performance? In the international environment, several factors outside the control of the subsidiary manager are likely to affect subsidiary's performance (e.g., foreign exchange gains and losses, royalties, interest and taxes). The extent to which these factors are brought into the measures used to evaluate the subsidiary manager is likely to depend on head office strategy and the role of the subsidiary in the multinational enterprise.

If the subsidiary is part of a global strategy and is centrally managed (e.g., the subsidiary is part of the global supply chain within the multinational) and the finances and foreign exchange are centrally managed, then it makes sense for the subsidiary manager's responsibility to be limited to the operations of the subsidiary and conditions that affect the performance of the subsidiary in the supply chain. For example, the manager will have more knowledge of conditions that affect the logistics environment in the country in which the subsidiary operates. By contrast, if the head office has decentralised the foreign exchange management to each of its country subsidiaries, then it would make sense to bring such factors (currency fluctuations) into the subsidiary manager's responsibility. This is especially the case

Highlights

Understanding the Different Levels of Independent Variables – The Centralisation and Decentralisation of Decision Authority

Example 1: A firm that has an aggressive product development strategy (build strategy, or prospector strategy) may decentralise decision authority pertaining to sales, thus allowing sales managers to sell to anyone, offer bulk discounts and so on. However, if the firm is in a medical device industry, which is under strict regulatory control (in the US), then certain sales procedures may need to be centralised (policies formulated for who it can sell to, etc.). Here, the environment dictates the extent to which authority can be decentralised with respect to the strategy adopted by the firm.

Example 2: A firm that manufactures chemicals. In an industry with global economies of scale, it may be unable to decentralise decision authority for product development across many of its factories, as efficiencies dictate that the operations be coordinated in a centralised manner to reach the economies of scale necessary to compete in the industry. Here the industry dictates the extent of decentralisation of product development strategy.

Example 3: McDonald's has franchised its product across the globe. In the past, its marketing strategy was global. However, recent events in the form of protests by groups in certain countries have shown this strategy to be inappropriate. For example, in India, McDonald's had to modify its product line by providing hamburgers that fit in with Hindu diet dictates. Here is an example of the location (country, or dominant religion) dictating the extent to which a global-centralised product market strategy is feasible.

in developing countries that have very volatile currencies (e.g., Argentina), which would prove to be very difficult to manage centrally on a daily basis. Even so, with this extra responsibility, other factors such as political events, wars and strikes are out of the subsidiary manager's control. It is important that such factors are taken into consideration when evaluating the subsidiary manager's performance.

The issue of foreign exchange and the use of budgeting for international operations presents a major controllability problem for the subsidiary. The basic

Figure 3.3 Controllability and Responsibility

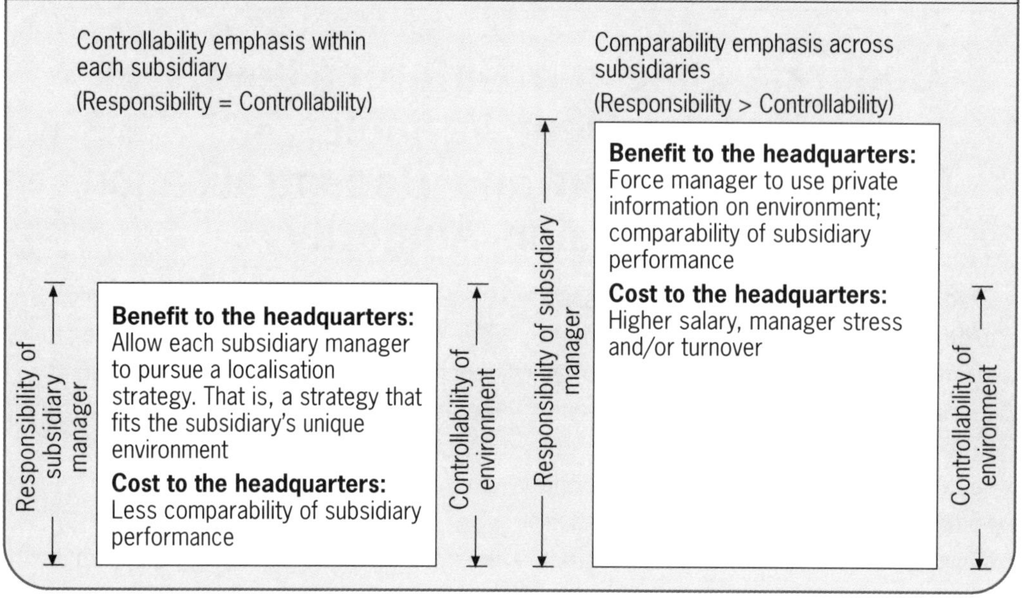

question is, to what extent does the headquarters include fluctuations in foreign exchange in the budget line item under the responsibility of the subsidiary manager? Several options are available to management ranging from zero responsibility to full responsibility. Following the Lessard and Lorange (1977) framework of budgeting and foreign exchange responsibility, a brief explanation can be given for some of the likely scenarios in MNEs today (see Table 3.4).

At the budget-setting stage the head office can require the subsidiary to set the budget and have it adjusted into the head office currency on the basis of the foreign exchange rate that 1) exists on the budget-setting day, 2) is projected to be at the end of the budget period, and 3) will be back adjusted at the end of the budgeting period. There are two practical approaches to dealing with the exchange rate at the budget-setting stage: 1) using the exchange rate at the time of budget setting and 2) using the projected exchange rate at the time of budget setting. Although head office may use the actual exchange rate at the end of the performance period to back adjust the budget when evaluating the effectiveness of the subsidiary manager in projecting the forward exchange rate, the same result can be obtained by comparing the budget calculated according to the projected rate with performance calculated according to the actual rate. Thus, the third option is really a variation of the first option with an adjustment at the end of the budgeting period. In short, six basic scenarios reflect the practical options that are available to MNE management. The scenarios are discussed in terms of purpose: that is, the nature of the responsibility given to the subsidiary manager.

Table 3.4 (see A1) shows that at the zero level of responsibility, the subsidiary budget is set according to the exchange rate on the day of budget setting. Subsidiary performance is also evaluated against actual performance, which is adjusted for changes in foreign exchange currency during the performance period. The same outcome can be achieved by using the same projected exchange rate to adjust the budget at the beginning of the performance period and to adjust actual performance at the end of the performance period (see P2). This leaves the head office with responsibility for fluctuations in the exchange rate.

Table 3.4 In What Ways can Foreign Exchange be Brought into the Budgeting Process

Rate for budget	**Rate for evaluating performance to budget**		
	Actual at budget	***Projected***	***Actual at end of period***
Actual at time of budget	A1 Zero level of responsibility for managing foreign exchange	A2 Moderate level of responsibility for managing foreign exchange	A3 High level of responsibility for managing foreign exchange
Projected at time of budget	P1 Moderate level of responsibility	P2 Zero level of responsibility – encourages management to forecast the future exchange rate as accurately as possible	P3 High level of responsibility – exchange rate variance should be minimal with accurate forecast
Actual at end of period	E1[1]	E2[1]	E3[1]

[1] Although the head office can use the actual exchange rate at the end of the performance period to back adjust the budget and evaluate the effectiveness of the subsidiary manager in projecting the forward exchange rate, the same result can be obtained by comparing the budget calculated according to the projected rate with performance calculated according to the actual rate.

Source: Lessard D. and Lorange P., Currency changes and management control: Resolving centralization/decentralization dilemma. Copyright 1977 by *Accounting Review*. Reprinted by permission of American Accounting Association.

At a higher level of responsibility (see P1 and A2), the head office seeks the private information of the subsidiary manager to help accurately forecast the level of projected exchange rate. The more accurate the forecast, the less uncertainty there will be in the evaluation of the subsidiary manager's performance. Hence, the subsidiary manager has an incentive to provide the head office with forecasts that are as accurate as possible. This is likely when the subsidiary is in a geographically distant country with higher uncertainty about the fluctuations of the foreign currency. Having the subsidiary manager project the exchange rate at the time of the budget helps the head office in consolidating it into the group's forward budget projections for its public reporting responsibilities and worldwide strategic plan.

At the highest level of responsibility (see A3 and P3), the head office uses the actual exchange rate at the end of the budget to evaluate the performance of the subsidiary. From the head office's point of view, the difference between these scenarios is that P3 serves two purposes: 1) to aid in head office strategic planning and reporting by using a projected foreign currency exchange rate, and 2) to motivate subsidiary management to use its private expertise and information to manage the influence of foreign exchange fluctuations on subsidiary profits. A3 serves only the second purpose and does not force the subsidiary manager to forecast a projected exchange rate. A3 however is likely to impose a level of responsibility on the subsidiary manager that is greater than his controllability. This in turn requires compensation for the greater risk likely to be faced by the subsidiary manager.

In summary, bringing foreign exchange differences into the budgeting process serves two main purposes: strategic planning and motivating the subsidiary manager to manage and use their private information and expertise. The drawback with attempting to achieve the second purpose is that of managing the lack of subsidiary manager control over the foreign exchange environment.

National Culture and the Transfer of Management Controls

The decision by the parent company to adapt or transfer its management control system remains problematic given the demands for internal consistency and local isomorphism that exert differing pulls on various organisational functions. Table 3.5 illustrates the various trade-offs that are involved for a subsidiary which operates in a culture that is different from the MNE head office home country. At the simplest level, the decision involves a choice between transferring home nation controls, adopting host nation preferred controls or a hybrid of the two. There are different costs and benefits associated with each strategy. The benefits from transferring the home office control system is in being able to compare the performance of two or more subsidiaries and savings in the costs to design a new accounting and control system. The cost

Table 3.5 Trade-offs in the Transfer of Controls

Control strategy	Transfer home nation controls	Hybrid	Adopt host nation controls
Formal controls	Yes	No	No
Informal controls	Yes	Yes	No
Processes of adopting the control strategy	Significantly alter forgoing employee's preferences • selection • socialisation	Accept foreign employee's preferences • de-emphasise formal controls • emphasise informal controls through socialisation	Set up a new control system that fits foreign employee preferences
Benefits of the strategy	Home/host nation comparability in planning and control	Reduced home/host nation comparability	No home/host nation comparability
Costs of the process	Selection and socialisation	Reduced selection socialisation costs	Minimal selection and socialisation costs
Externalities	High dependence on labour market	Reduced dependence on labour market	Host government support Minimal dependence on labour market

associated with this strategy is in the misfit with the local way of doing things which can result in lower productivity, and higher staff turnover than average.

Hofstede's (1980) framework. Support for the influence of national culture on control system design is found in Hofstede's (1980) definition of culture as the collective programming of the mind that distinguishes one group of people from another in terms of norms and values. Culture is this part of our conditioning that we share with other members of our nation, region or group (Hofstede, 1983a). Working with the view that the norms within a group or category of people refer to standards for particular values, Hofstede (1980) identified a set of four norm values, termed *dimensions* of culture. These dimensions are power distance, individualism, uncertainty avoidance and masculinity. He developed the dimensions from an attitude survey of individuals employed by a large MNE across 50 nations and three regions, which was administered in 1968 and 1973. In an initial analysis of 40 nations (Hofstede, 1980) and a subsequent analysis of 10 nations and three regions

(Hofstede 1983b), he found that half of the variation in a nation's mean scores could be explained by the four dimensions below.

Power distance – a measure of the extent to which a society accepts that power in institutions and organisations is distributed unequally. The level of power distance is related to the degree of centralisation of authority and the degree to which cultures prefer a more autocratic leadership style.

Individualism – a measure of the relative importance of the individual's self-interest and immediate family compared to the wider group interest and that of the extended family. Within organisations, goals and independence in the form of more autonomy are stressed in high-individualism societies, whereas less autonomy and more dependence on particular workgroups in the organisation are favoured in low-individualism societies.

Uncertainty avoidance – the level of uncertainty avoidance indicates the extent to which a society feels threatened by uncertain and ambiguous situations and tries to avoid them by providing greater career stability, establishing more formal rules, not tolerating deviant ideas and behaviour and believing in absolute truths and the attainment of expertise. Organisations in a high-uncertainty avoidance environment favour rigid rules to decrease uncertainty.

Masculinity – a measure of the extent to which the dominant values in society are masculine; that is, assertiveness and the acquisition of money and material things compared to the importance of work relations, cooperation and security.

The more recent study by the Chinese Cultural Connection (1987) is the most significant piece of work from an East Asian perspective. On the basis that Hofstede's dimensions may be culturally bound, being Western in origin, the Chinese Cultural Connection developed a survey based on 40 Chinese values. From a survey of 100 students (50 men, 50 women) from various disciplines in 23 different nations, they empirically derived four dimensions known as integration, morale discipline, human heartiness and Confucian work dynamism. Hofstede and Bond (1988) undertook an analysis of this study in comparison to Hofstede's (1980) results. Using a sample of 20 nations that overlapped with those reported by Hofstede (1983b), the scores on these dimensions were found to correlate highly with the scores obtained by Hofstede for power distance, individualism and masculinity. The *integration* and *moral discipline* dimensions were highly correlated with power distance and individualism, while *human heartiness* was highly correlated with masculinity.

They discovered a fifth dimension that was not highly correlated with the original four dimensions and termed this dimension *Confucian dynamism*. *Confucian dynamism* relates to the teachings of Confucius and can be explained in terms of society's search for virtue, or the degree of long-term versus short-term orientation.

A sample of countries representing different scores on the five dimensions is shown in Table 3.6. Note that the first four dimensions were taken from Hofstede (1983b) and the fifth (Confucian dynamism) taken from Hofstede and Bond (1988). The scores for the first four dimensions were based on formulas designed by Hofstede (1980) in his original study of 40 nations, which ranged between 0 and 100. Thus, when the same formulas were applied to other countries some scores occured outside of the original range (e.g., Malaysia: power distance = 104).

Table 3.6 Power Distance, Individualism, Uncertainty Avoidance, Masculinity and Confucian Dynamism Scores for a Select Group of Nations

Nation	Power distance	Individualism	Uncertainty avoidance	Masculinity	Confucian dynamism[a]
Australia	36	90	51	61	31
United States	40	91	46	62	29
United Kingdom	35	89	35	66	25
Germany (F.R.)	35	67	65	66	31
Mexico	81	30	82	69	–
Indonesia	78	14	48	46	–
Singapore	74	20	8	48	48
Malaysia	104	26	36	50	–
Philippines	94	32	44	64	19
Hong Kong	68	25	29	57	96
Thailand	64	10	64	34	56
Taiwan	58	17	69	45	87
South Korea	60	10	85	39	75
Japan	54	46	92	95	80

Source: Hofstede G. and Bond M.H., The Confucius connection: From cultural roots to economic growth. Copyright 1988 by *Organisational Dynamics*. Reprinted by permission of Elsevier.

Empirical research on the influence of national culture on management control. The use of budgets in the performance evaluation of managers in subsidiaries has been widely researched in the cross-cultural domain. For example, power distance, individualism (Bailes and Assada, 1991) and Confucian dynamism (Harrison, McKinnon, Panchapakesan and Leung, 1994) have been identified as potentially relevant to the preference for the use of budgets in performance evaluation in the Anglo-American versus Asian comparative context. Although the findings of Daley, Jiambalvo, Sundem and Kondo (1985) and Harrison (1993) indicate that budget criteria are perceived as culturally appropriate in Asian societies, the results of Bailes and Assada (1991), Harrison, McKinnon, Panchapakesan and Leung (1994), Chow, Shields and Wu (1999) and O'Connor and Ekanayake (1998) indicate otherwise (see Table 3.7 for a summary of expectations and findings associated with these studies). The findings for a preference of budgets in the West are consistent with Hofstede's (1968) argument that budgets are a Western game.

HUMAN RESOURCE SELECTION AND CONTROL IN CHINA

To enable foreign offices to employ locals, the Chinese government has designated specialised service companies, known as foreign enterprise service corporations (FESCO), to provide related services for employees of foreign offices. For the representative office, the payment of a service fee typically covers retirement benefits, social insurance, various taxes, unemployment insurance and funds for recreational activities. The benefit of using an FESCO is that foreign firms do not need to advertise for any replacement of staff. The local Labour Bureau needs to approve a draft of the position requirements before placing the advertisement for staff recruitment. For selection by agency, a cash deposit is required for most agency offices in China, whether they are successful or not.

Two recent studies have shed light on the enormous difficulties that accompany the use of cheap labour in China. In the first, Chan (1999) interviewed the managers of two Hong Kong-based joint ventures in China and found that workplace regionalism and inactive information sharing were critical issues facing management. Workplace regionalism resulted in disputes between workers of different provinces, unfair treatment of workers from a different province and appeals by some workers not to report misconduct. In terms of information sharing, workers were found to be inactive in reporting production errors and in giving

Table 3.7 Summary of Eastern versus Western Nation Comparative Studies of Budget Emphasis in Performance Evaluation – Methods Used and Results Obtained

	Instrument used to measure budget emphasis	Results expected – differences in means and or slopes	Results obtained
Daley, Jiambalvo, Sundem and Kondo (1985)	• Comparison of means. Summated scale-six-item, five-point Likert scale	United States > Japan	Japan > United States
Harrison (1993)	• Comparison of slopes (associations) between budget emphasis and affective outcome variables • Comparative measure, ten-item, five-point Likert scale	Slope between RAPM and JRT (JS) more positive for Singapore than Australia	Slope between RAPM and JRT (JS) more positive for Singapore than Australia
	• Two budget items, summated, multiplied by four and divided by summation of eight non-budget items		Mean level of RAPM Australia = Singapore
Harrison, McKinnon, Panchapakesan and Leung (1994)	• Comparison of means Three items, five-point Likert scale	Eastern cluster (Hong Kong and Singapore) > Western cluster (Australia and United States) of three items	Western cluster (Australia and United States) > Eastern cluster (Hong Kong and Singapore) for two out
Bailes and Assada (1991)	• Comparison of means Four items, seven-point Likert scale	No theoretical priors	United States > Japan
O'Connor and Ekanayake (1998)	• Comparison of associations – a relative measure of superior emphasis on objective (four items) versus subjective (four items) criteria in performance evaluation (seven-point Likert scale)	Western cluster (Australia and Singapore) > Eastern cluster (Hong Kong and Sri Lanka)	Western cluster (Australia and Singapore) > Eastern cluster (Hong Kong and Sri Lanka)
Chow, Shields and Wu (1999)	• Comparison of means along with comparison of fit between preferred level and actual level of budget emphasis Six items, five-point Likert scale	Japan > Taiwan > United States	United States > Japan

suggestions. Chan (1999) recommended that companies should separate production workers from different provinces, have surprise workplace inspections and take a tough stance on region-based disputes. In dealing with information sharing, companies should provide detailed instructions, attend and lead workgroup meetings and encourage suggestions and participation in decision making

In the second study, Bruton (2000) interviewed managers, consultants and venture capitalists in ten private firms with significant operations in China. Four main problems were identified. First, selection problems occurred, with foreign firms being forced to hire as many employees as possible. There was a lack of knowledge of which employees had *guanxi* with government officials and the practice of hiring relatives and friends was encouraged by local officials. Bruton recommended that MNEs select their Chinese staff themselves, and ask prospective employees to provide a list of connections. Second was the extensive training and development required to help employees overcome their fear of doing anything outside their job description and to make employees productive for the enterprise. Bruton recommended detailed production steps and tight schedules to overcome this problem. Third was finding an appropriate structuring of the appraisal and reward system – it was difficult to measure *guanxi* and retain good employees. Bruton recommended structuring the reward system by what it prevented (e.g., penalties from the government), providing bonuses for minimising entertainment expenses and offering housing loans, career tracks and education benefits to overcome this issue. Finally, there were issues of controlling company assets and socialising employees into adopting a Western approach to work. Bruton suggested the employment of Hong Kong managers as expatriates, hiring fresh graduates to maintain and develop corporate culture and the use of mentoring, company slogans, songs, outings and short holidays to deal with such difficulties.

SUMMARY

This chapter introduced the control issues that are associated with the management of a wholly owned subsidiary. The first part of this chapter presented a basic framework of control that focuses on the degree of formality (formal and informal) and the object of control (action, output and behaviour). Various control mechanisms that have different objects of control were identified. The second part introduced a framework of MNE subsidiary control that brings together the issues and factors surrounding three important choices that MNEs and subsidiary managers face: decentralisation, the focus of head office control and the extent to which controls need to be adapted to the national culture of a subsidiary's domain. The role of the subsidiary as part of a global strategy, the nature of production technology and the environment were highlighted as potential drivers of decentralisation. The degree of controllability over the subsidiary versus comparability of subsidiary performance was highlighted as a key issue associated with the focus of head office control. The national culture context of the subsidiary highlighted the extent to which controls should be adapted to the subsidiary's host nation environment. Within each of these issues various trade-offs existed that could be characterised in terms of the degree of globalisation versus the localisation of the subsidiary. Finally, some of the human resource selection and control issues in China were briefly introduced, which emphasised the importance of coaching and monitoring workers to ensure that they become productive members of the firm.

QUESTIONS

1) What important independent variables does agency theory identify for understanding the compensation structure of functional managers? List two.
2) Why is understanding of the cost/benefit trade-off between external and internal contracting important to the management accounting system design?
3) Refer to the following model of independent and dependent variables.

Centralisation/Decentralisation

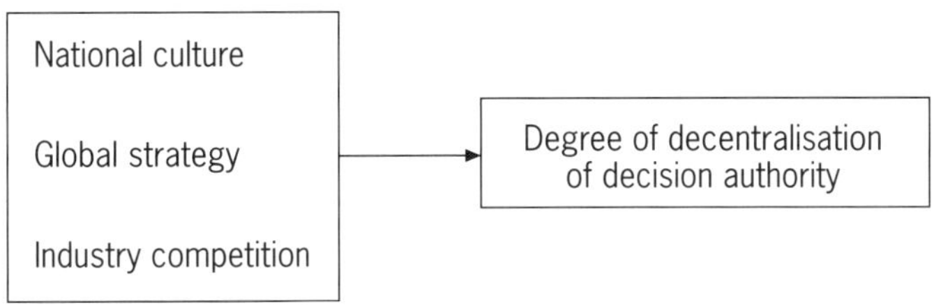

   a) What are some of the costs of the centralisation of decision authority in an MNE?
   b) What are some of the benefits of the centralisation of decision authority in an MNE?
4) Using examples of costs and benefits, explain how national culture can influence the effectiveness of delegating decision authority?
5) In what ways can Hofstede's dimensions of national culture be related to the effectiveness of various control mechanisms? Select four control mechanisms and explain the possible relationships of each with one or more cultural dimensions.

6) What is the theoretical rationale for giving responsibility for exchange rate risk to subsidiary managers?
7) In evaluating the performance of subsidiaries operating in nations of different currencies, there are various options available to management for setting the budget and evaluating performance against the budget. What are the main factors that explain the different options pursued by MNEs? List at least three factors.
8) The measurement and comparison of performance in the international environment is a difficult issue for management. Why? List three factors with one line explanations for each.
9) The separation of managerial and subsidiary performance is an important consideration in international performance measurement. What factors can cause managerial and subsidiary performance to be different?
10) The following are three key questions about international performance evaluation.
    a) What are the key choices/decisions to be made about performance evaluation, in
        - domestic operations?
        - international operations?
    b) What factors influence these decisions?
    c) What theories help you to understand the linkages between these factors and the decisions made?

EXERCISES

1) **Management control of global operations**
   Learning objective
   The aim of this exercise is to examine the following dimensions of control systems that are found in your own organisation.
   Exercise and discussion plan
   a) Provide details about organisational structure according to the list in i) and ii) below.
      i) **Organisational structure**
         Indicate the location of the following key areas of authority:
         - product
         - investment
         - human resources

ii) **Centralised/decentralised control**

For each key area of authority above, indicate the nature of controls used:

- formal controls
- informal controls

b) Discuss, with reference to the level of decentralisation of control, the extent of formalised controls and the degree to which controls reflect local or home office conditions.

c) Reflect on how the types of control dimensions discussed in theory compare with the controls that you see in practice.

CASE STUDY 8

ABC Ltd – Managing a Service Department in China

BACKGROUND INFORMATION AND MANAGEMENT PROBLEM

ABC Ltd is a Hong Kong-based garment manufacturing and trading company. It undertakes yarn trading and sweater manufacturing in Hong Kong, China, the Mauritius and India, and sells sweaters to the US, Europe and Southeast Asia. The company is an efficiency seeker. About five years ago, it decided to shift its service department from Hong Kong to mainland China to take advantage of the lower manpower and rental costs.

After years of preparation, the company's accounts department shifted to Shenzhen. Instead of laying off all Hong Kong staff, the company encouraged them to work across the border by the provision of a hardship allowance. As about 20% of the original staff resigned, their jobs were either shared by existing staff members or taken up by newly employed mainland staff members. However, the job schedules that were delayed during the transition period were never rectified. More errors were found and increasing effort was exerted to find other errors, which necessitated more overtime work. The effectiveness, efficiency and quality of work were worse than before.

Using payment processing and report preparation as an example, more time was required to prepared individual cheques and monthly ended bulk cheques. As compared to two years before, there were more errors such as wrong company names, currencies or amounts on the cheques. The report finish dates were delayed by about eight to nine days, and the number of entry errors increased (see Table 1).

I wish to acknowledge the assistance of Mandy Lee Sui Man in the preparation of this case study. This case was developed as a basis for class discussion rather than to illustrate either effective or ineffective handling of an administrative situation.

Table 1 The Efficiency and Effectiveness of Payment and Report Preparation

	Efficiency (Completed dates)		Effectiveness (Number of errors)	
Cheque	2000	2002	2000	2002
Individual cheque payment processing time	3 days	5 days	< 1	3–4 cheques
Monthly cheque payment processing time	Before month end	5th of the next month	< 1	2 cheques
Report				
Monthly financial report	22nd of the next month	30th of the next month	1–2 items	> 5 items
Monthly financial analysis	26th of the next month	5th of the next month	1–2 items	> 5 items

Moreover, problems of regionalism arose between the Hong Kong and mainland staff members. Most of the mainland staff were unwilling to work overtime or do assigned work that was not in their job descriptions, whereas the Hong Kong workers usually sought greater responsibility and were more eager to work overtime. Retaining good employees is crucial to a firm's success as turnover costs can be a significant part of salary expenses. In this case, the high turnover cost also increased the cost of recruiting and the risk of recruiting unsuitable staff.

ANALYSIS

The following factors are the independent variables that influenced the effectiveness and efficiency of the company's operation.

Recruitment Process, Staff Quality and Turnover

The recruitment process only considered department head requirements and ignored the opinions of lower-level supervisors. Many problems can be avoided if the recruitment process identifies staff who meet the requirements of their immediate supervisors. The labour market in China is more active than that of Hong Kong's. Hence, the turnover rate for mainland staff members was much higher than it was for their Hong Kong counterparts. Many staff resigned during the transition period, particularly those in middle management who had better bargaining power in the labour market. Junior staff usually took the vacant jobs, and their old jobs were in turn transferred to newly employed mainland staff members.

Communication Barriers

The use of Cantonese by the Hong Kong staff and Putonghua by the mainland staff created a communication barrier. This prolonged the training period for new staff and hampered the effectiveness of communication between junior and senior staff.

Performance Appraisal and Job Duty Expectations

Some of the mainland staff were unaware that performance appraisals were being carried out, and they complained that they were not told the results. They worried that they would not know their strengths and weaknesses, which would reduce their chances of promotion. The mainland staff preferred a clear list of detailed job duties. They were unwilling to do anything that was outside their job descriptions. The Hong Kong staff, in contrast, were more flexible, and in particular were more willing to work unpaid overtime.

CONSULTANT'S RECOMMENDATIONS

The following recommendations are made to improve the company's efficiency and effectiveness.

Staff Selection

Staff selection is an important process. In particular, the company should employ staff members who are familiar with the Hong Kong management style. It should also allow inter-company transfers, set recruitment priorities and have minimum qualification and experience standards. The first is important because staff recruitment is a long process but some jobs may require immediate staffing. Allowing for inter-company staff transfers may reduce the risk of employing the wrong candidates. The minimum criteria, on the other hand, may prevent departments that require immediate staffing from accepting applicants with lower qualifications and less experience. Some seniors prefer better communication (e.g., the ability to speak Cantonese) to higher qualifications and more experience. Secondly, staff members with sufficient qualifications and experience should perform the difficult jobs. If the company's policy is to employ mainland staff, then it should employ those with suitable qualifications and experience in middle-level positions. However, to save cost, less qualified mainlanders are often employed, in the hope that the firm can train them to be as good as more highly skilled staff. The employment of such mainland staff reduces the company's staff quality as a whole.

Staff Training

Senior management should offer language seminars to all staff members. To encourage staff members to attend these seminars, language proficiency should be included in performance appraisals. This would enhance inter-team communication and inter-company communication. Furthermore, to match the expectations of the mainland staff members, written job descriptions should be provided to clearly identify the duties and deadlines for each job. This would reduce the number of disputes about working hours and overtime.

Reward and Appraisal

As staff recruitment is a time-consuming and cost-intensive process, management should consider more effective ways of retaining the company's existing staff, especially those from the mainland. Frequent appraisals would motivate staff members by offering evaluation and therefore a higher chance of promotion. To ensure that staff members are aware of company requirements, quarterly performance appraisals should be conducted.

CASE STUDY QUESTIONS

1) What are the most important human resourcing factors in operating a service department in China?
2) Which human resource management activity appears to be most critical to the efficient operation of the service department in China?
3) To what extent can each of the components of the Merchant (1989) control typology be effective in this case?
4) What do you think of the consultant's recommendations?
5) What other recommendations would you make to improve the company's efficiency and effectiveness?

CASE STUDY 9

Sanyung Ltd – Can Activity-based Costing Improve Sanyung's Management Decision Making?

CASE BACKGROUND

Sanyung Electric Company Ltd, incorporated in 1950, is a public-listed Japanese company. Sanyung Electric (Hong Kong) Ltd (Sanyung), is one of the Sanyung group's affiliates, with an operational office in Hong Kong and manufacturing operations in mainland China. One of its factories located in Dongguan operates as a manufacturer of various kinds of motors and parts for CD ROM drives. Its main customers include IBM and Sony.

However, in the last two years, due to the economic recession in the US and Japan, and increased competition in motor market, both market price and gross profit of the Dongguan factory's motors have dropped significantly. In addition, the increased pace of new product offerings to the consumer market has effectively shortened the product life cycle of each motor design.

In view of these six months ago, the factory considered implementing a new cost allocation method, including an activity-based costing (ABC) system to have a clearer understanding of the factory's overhead cost structure. However, as top Japanese management was very conservative, the adoption of a new allocation method and concomitant organisation change is costly. After long and tedious discussions, the factory decided to implement the ABC system to provide a new way of evaluating product and customer profitability through a process-oriented perspective.

I wish to acknowledge the assistance of Tsui Chun Kau in the preparation of this case study. This case was developed as a basis for class discussion rather than to illustrate either effective or ineffective handling of an administrative situation.

IMPLEMENTATION OF THE NEW ABC SYSTEM

Before the introduction of the ABC system, the factory did not have a sophisticated costing system. The prices of steel coils, magnets and harnesses – the three basic raw materials – were closely monitored. They represent 70% of the cost of production. Thus, they were used to estimate the cost of producing motors. Freight charges were tracked as separate cost on each invoice. Price quotations were based only on the price of these materials, direct labour and overheads plus a mark-up.

During implementation of the ABC system as part of the existing enterprise resource planning (ERP) system, it was very fortunate that a good relationship had been developed with the in-house ABC team. Some documentations related to ABC could be reviewed, for example, the main processes of the factory, warehouse material sub-processes and assignment of cost pools to each activity and then how they were charged to motors and customers. Also, through the ERP system, the data-related cost structure and product cost of motor, and profitability of customers could be collected.

DEVELOPING THE ABC MODEL

The ABC model for the Dongguan factory was set up in several stages. First, the main processes were defined by the senior management group. Then key employees (factory manager and supervisors) were selected to develop the flow charts for the processes. After detailed analyses, six business processes were identified as shown in Figure 1. Within each business process, a total of 168 activities were identified. Four resource drivers were identified for allocating resources costs to the various activities: time spent, headcount, number of motors and space charge. For example, for time spent, the 568 employees were surveyed to estimate how they allocated their time to different activities. All overhead resources were then collected in 78 cost pools. For each cost pool, an activity driver was assigned. In Figure 2, sub-process warehouse materials is selected as an example of assigning activity drivers to cost pools for each activity. After the cost was assigned to activities, they were charged to motors as well as customers.

IMPACT OF THE NEW ABC SYSTEM

After the implemention of the ABC system, owing to production volume, complexity

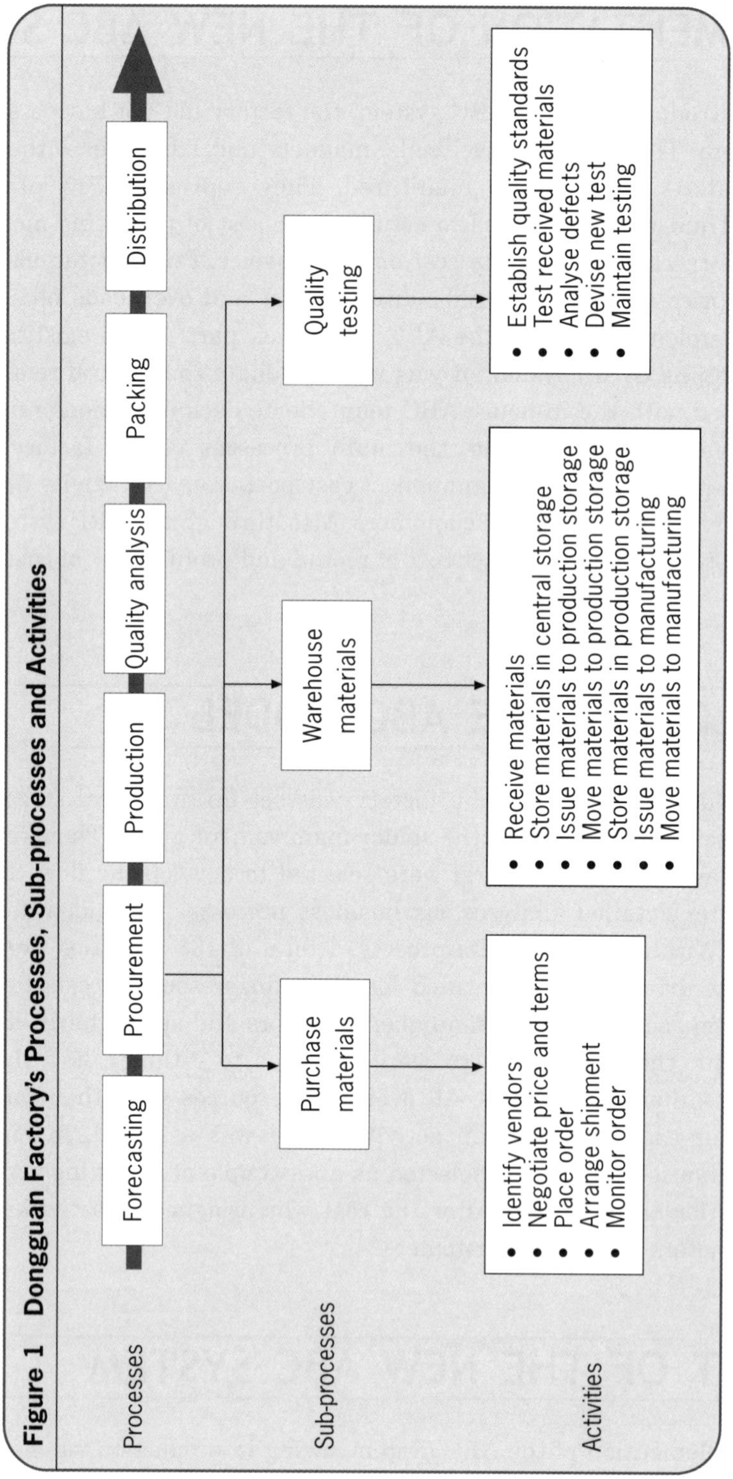

Figure 1 Dongguan Factory's Processes, Sub-processes and Activities

Figure 2 Combining Activity Costs from Activity Cost Pools for Sub-process Warehouse Materials

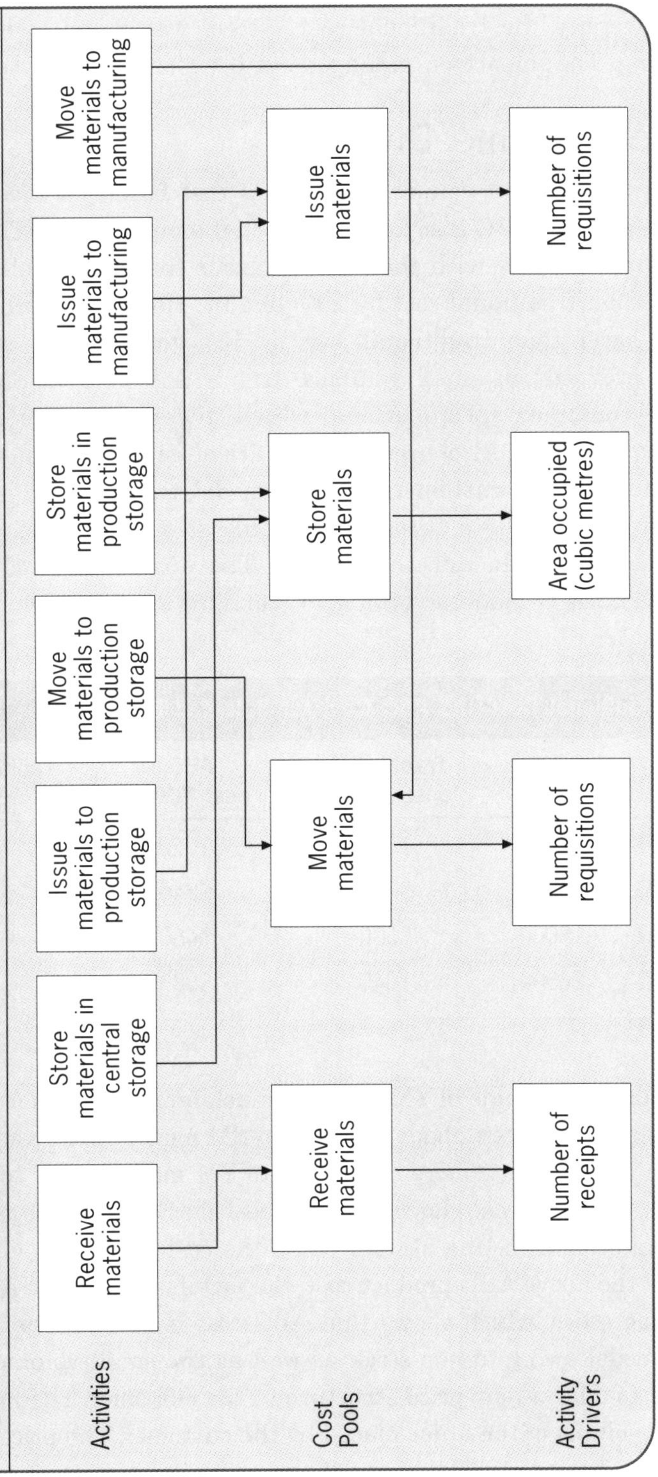

and set-up diversity, the traditional cost system was found to have distorted the product costing. The impact on management decision are analysed here.

Production Volume Diversity

Table 1 shows production volume, traditional cost based on raw materials, direct labour, overheads and ABC cost for four selected motor models. The traditional cost can be compared directly with the ABC cost. For the SM models, the ABC cost is much higher than traditional cost by 20% to 40%. However, for the YM models, the ABC cost is lower than traditional cost by 15% to 23%. SM model is normally ordered and produced in small volumes, and is not stocked. SM model is made according to customer specifications, which always changes according to the customer's requirements. Also, urgent orders are often placed. Thus, extra manpower is necessary to serve the customers. For YM model, the situation is totally different. The customer can provide a three-month forecast of the model, which allows the factory to plan for production in advance. The order and production volume is normally big and it is made according to standard specification.

Table 1 Traditional Cost and ABC Cost for Selected Models

Model	Volume (PC)	Traditional cost ('000)	ABC cost ('000)	Traditional compared with ABC cost
SM-01187901	2000	$1320	$1620	+22.70%
SM-01191700	3500	$600	$840	+40.00%
YM-01202602	18000	$600	$460	–23.33%
YM-01204900	26500	$1040	$880	–15.38%

Since production volume of YM model is much larger than that of SM model, YM model takes up more direct labour hours than SM model. As a result, the traditional cost system allocates much more overheads to YM model owing to its large volume of production. The ABC cost shows that the cost for SM model is much higher than that of the traditional costing system while the cost for YM model is much lower.

In view of the above ABC product cost, the factory shared the ABC analysis with the Hong Kong office, which shows that ABC cost is much higher than traditional cost for SM model owing to non-stock as well as the small volume of orders. Hong Kong decided to offer a new price structure to the customer. The main purpose is to stimulate the volume of the order placed by the customer. The price structure allows the customer to have a 10% discount if the order volume is up to a certain level, while the price would increase by 30% for a small volume order to reflect the actual cost. Because of the new price structure, the sales volume placed by the customer is increasing gradually. This demonstrates that Sanyung is becoming a major source of customer's supply.

Set-up Diversity

The profitability distribution (see Figure 3) shows how profitable 20 of Sanyung's customers were to the company. Few customers were profitable to the factory. Many of them brought limited profit or even loss to the factory. The profitability of the models to the customers are shown in Table 2. About 25% of customers contributed over 220% of total profit, 65% of customers broke even and the remaining 10% customers contributed a loss that was equivalent to 120% of the total profit.

Figure 3 Customer Profitability for Selected Customers

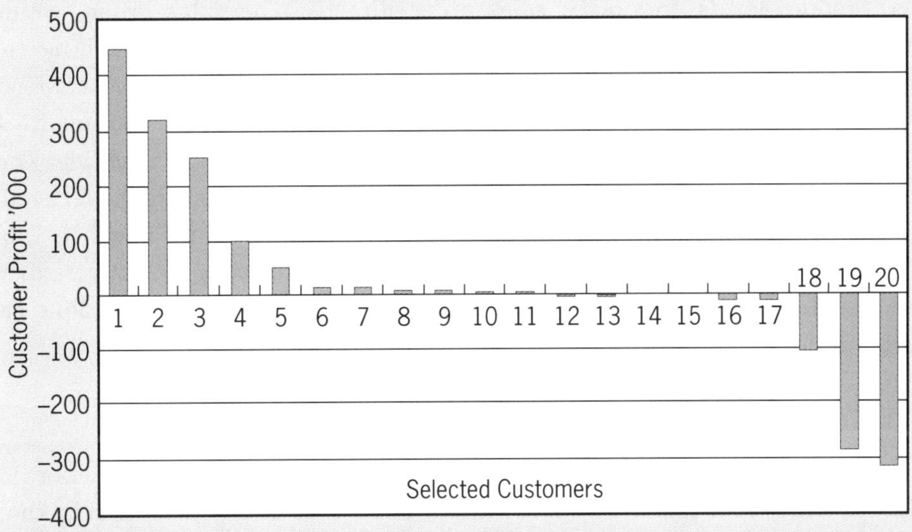

Note: Customer names have been replaced by numbers to preserve confidentiality.

One of the most unprofitable customers was selected by the company to study the reasons for the lack of profitability. It was found that the customer placed a large number of small and unique specification orders. The customer was using just in time (JIT) and tailor-made its products for its own customers. As a result, the factory incurred extra set-up costs for scheduling production and administration of expenses to handle its large number of small orders.

Table 2 ABC Costing Changes for New/Old System

Model	Volume (PC)	Manufacturing overhead		Percentage change
		Old system ('000)	New system ('000)	
XM-03290831	2,500	$1250	$870	–30.40%
XM-02287600	3,500	$1640	$1216	–25.85%
XM-02376901	3,800	$1600	$1140	–31.25%
XM-01237680	2,100	$1320	$1020	–22.70%

Instead of imposing extra charges on the customers, Hong Kong office introduced a creative solution to reduce set-up costs and administration expenses. It developed a computer application for the customer. The program allowed the customers to review product levels and place sales order directly. The sales orders would be transferred to the computer system in the Donggang factory. According to the requirement date of sales order, the computer system would group small orders together and schedule production accordingly. The customer could monitor its sales order according to the factory's stock level as well as production schedule. Though the development cost of the system was quite high, the manufacturing overheads for four selected models declined sharply from 22.70% to 31.25% as shown in Table 2. Therefore, the factory could decrease its set-up costs and administrative expenses, which meant that the profit margin for customers with smaller and unique orders could be improved.

Complexity Diversity

Before implementation of the ABC system, engineers designed motors according to the functionality and customer specification. They did not pay attention to the cost of the components and production process complexity. In addition, the traditional cost system focused on direct materials and labour, which gave a message to engineers that they should reduce the cost of purchased materials. This caused the engineers to increase the number of the components and search for vendors who could provide the cheapest materials.

Further analysis of certain motors revealed that expensive components and complicated production process did not aid functionality or performance of motors. As a result, management directed the engineers to redesign several motors by eliminating certain components without significantly affecting motors' functions and performance. As part of the ABC system, the number of different parts was selected as a new cost driver so as to deliver a clear signal to engineers about the cost of increasing the number of components as well as vendors. Engineers were also encouraged by the new system to use less expensive common components that were purchased in high volume. As shown in Table 3, after the redesign of some motors and increasing the use of common components, the ABC costs for four selected motors were found to have declined sharply, from 18% to 31%.

Table 3 Cost Comparison Before/After Redesign of Selected Motors

Model	ABC cost before redesign ('000)	ABC cost after redesign ('000)	Cost comparison before/after redesign
EM-01188912	$1,020	$770	–24.50%
EM-01192802	$640	$440	–31.25%
DM-01217023	$720	$588	–18.30%
DM-01348119	$950	$738	–22.32%

CONCLUSION

Table 4 summarises the impact of the three diversities on management decision. It is obvious that production volume diversity significantly affects pricing decisions. For setup diversity, management should review the process and therefore, improve process efficiency. Finally, complexity diversity affects both process and product management depending on the source of origin of complexity.

Table 4 Impact of Diversity on Management Decision

Diversity	Management decision	Level of significance
Production volume diversity	Product management	Low
	Pricing	High
	Process improvement	Low
Set-up diversity	Product management	Low
	Pricing	Medium
	Process improvement	High
Complexity diversity	Product management	High
	Pricing	Low
	Process improvement	Medium

CASE STUDY QUESTIONS

1) How is diversity in production volume, setup and complexity a significant factor in determining the value of information that is generated by the ABC system?
2) What decisions are influenced by the ABC system in this case?
3) What are the weaknesses in surveying the employees about the time they spend on each activity? How can this potential weakness be overcome?

CASE STUDY 10

TSL Jewellery Ltd – Activity-based Costing

INTRODUCTION

Tse Sui Luen Jewellery Co Ltd (TSLJ) carries out manufacturing and retailing of jewellery products in Hong Kong and the Asia-Pacific region. The company is currently employing over 1,300 employees and has established its own absorption costing system over the past ten years. The existing pricing system is based on a percentage mark-up on the product cost. The overhead absorption basis is based on the value of direct materials used in each product. The management has considered that this absorption base may unrealistically reflect the characteristics of the given cost centre and not truly show the costs of the products. Management hopes to improve its competitive power by allocating its scarce resources more effectively and efficiently to those higher profit margin products. Figure 1 illustrates the organisation chart of TSLJ.

Due to the drastic economic downturn in 1997, both the jewellery industry and the retail market experienced dramatic adverse changes, which had not been seen before. As jewellery products are luxury goods, a decrease in sales was unavoidable. In the fall of 1998, a cut-throat price war was sparked and many competitors joined the price war. Keen competition in the jewellery industry and weak market sentiment both affected the business of TSLJ. However, as a market follower, TSLJ cannot set the prices of their products higher than its competitors. Currently, the company faces a problem that the existing costing system does not reflect the true cost of its products and is confused as to which costing system is the best for them.

I wish to acknowledge the assistance of William Yau in the preparation of this case study. This case was developed as a basis for class discussion rather than to illustrate either effective or ineffective handling of an administrative situation.

Figure 1 Organisation Structure of Tse Suai Luen Jewellery Ltd

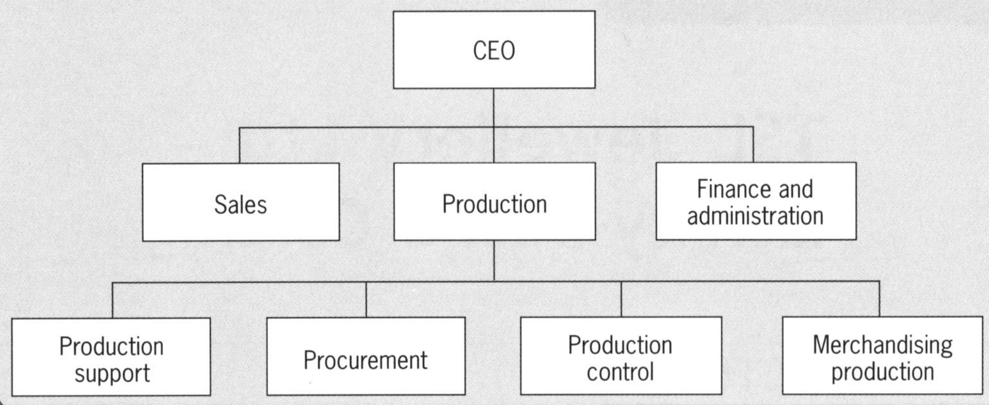

In order to compete successfully and positively in the industry, the company should try to set up a more reliable and accurate costing system. This can help management develop a better product strategy. Moreover, a costing system that expands the bases on which costs are allocated can improve the efficiency and effectiveness of operations by providing guidance in resource allocation. An expanded cost system would go beyond standard production variables to include the extensive allocation of fixed costs. Therefore, it is to the company's benefit to investigate whether it is cost effective to adopt activity-based costing (ABC). We examine how, by using ABC, the company can analyse the profit contribution and impact of interrelationship of products to develop a more appropriate product strategy. In this case study we identify the costs and benefits of adopting the ABC system to TSLJ as compared with the traditional overhead absorption costing system. The analysis is based on data of the company from a site visit and interviews.

CASE STUDY ANALYSIS

Traditional Costing System

The costing system used by the company is *absorption costing*. This is a product costing system in which all costs, such as direct materials, direct labour and manufacturing overhead considered necessary to manufacture the products, are included in the product cost. Direct material includes those materials that become a significant component of the finished product and can be specifically traced to the product. For example, gems, diamond, precious metal and jades used in jewellery products are typically classified as direct materials. We can trace other items such as packing boxes and pricing labels to the finished products, but only at a significant expense. Such items would likely be regarded as indirect materials and classified as part of manufacturing overhead.

Likewise, only those labour costs directly identified with manufacturing the product are considered as direct labour. The labour costs of goldsmith workers and assembly workers would be direct labour costs. Indirect labour would typically include supervisory costs, maintenance and quality control. The efforts of indirect personnel are essential to the manufacturing process, but they cannot be traced directly to the product. Such costs become part of manufacturing overhead. Manufacturing overhead includes all costs other than direct material and direct labour that can be identified with the manufacturing process.

Activity Analysis

The objective of activity analysis is to reduce the detailed task inventory in order to produce a listing of the major activities within the plant. Table 1 represents the major activities in each interviewed department. As certain activities represent an accumulation of work undertaken in several of the existing departments a cross-department boundary grouping is necessary in order to pool the total information on each activity.

Table 1 Major Activities in Departments

Department	Major activities
Production support services	Production control
Procurement	Material procurement Material selection Material handling
Product control and inspection	Inspection
Merchandising	Customer order process Material planning

Cost Driver Analysis

The existing TSLJ costing system consists of one main cost centre: the entire manufacturing facility. Table 2 represents the possible cost drivers for each activity.

Figure 2 shows that this costing basis allocates overheads to the products by means of the material costs.

Table 2 Main Cost Drivers in Major Activities

Major activities	Main cost drivers
Production control	Numbers to be supervised Number of defective stock Demand movement Production volume Batches size Product quality
Material procurement	Number of batches of material purchased Number of orders Volume of material receipts Stock discrepancies Materials available Number of suppliers
Material assembly	Volume of orders Stock differentiation
Material handling	Material storage Number of material transactions Stock discrepancies
Inspection	Production volume Batches of despatch
Order process	Order volume
Material planning	Complexity of ordering product Product style (new/old style)

Figure 2 The Cost System at Tse Suai Luen Jewellery Ltd

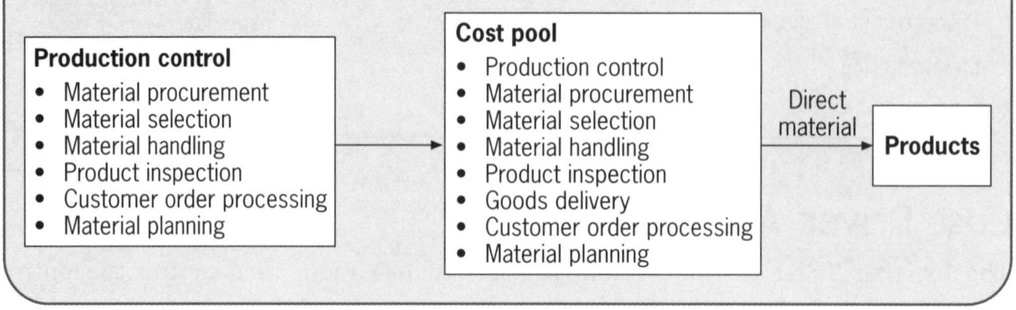

In the proposed ABC system, a unit-level activity driver is used to attribute unit-level expenses. For possible batch-level activity drivers, the time handled is the possible and appropriate cost driver to attribute those expenses accurately to the products. For the product-level cost pool, the cost driver of the number of components is appropriate (see Figure 3).

Figure 3 The Proposed ABC System at Tse Suai Luen Jewellery Ltd

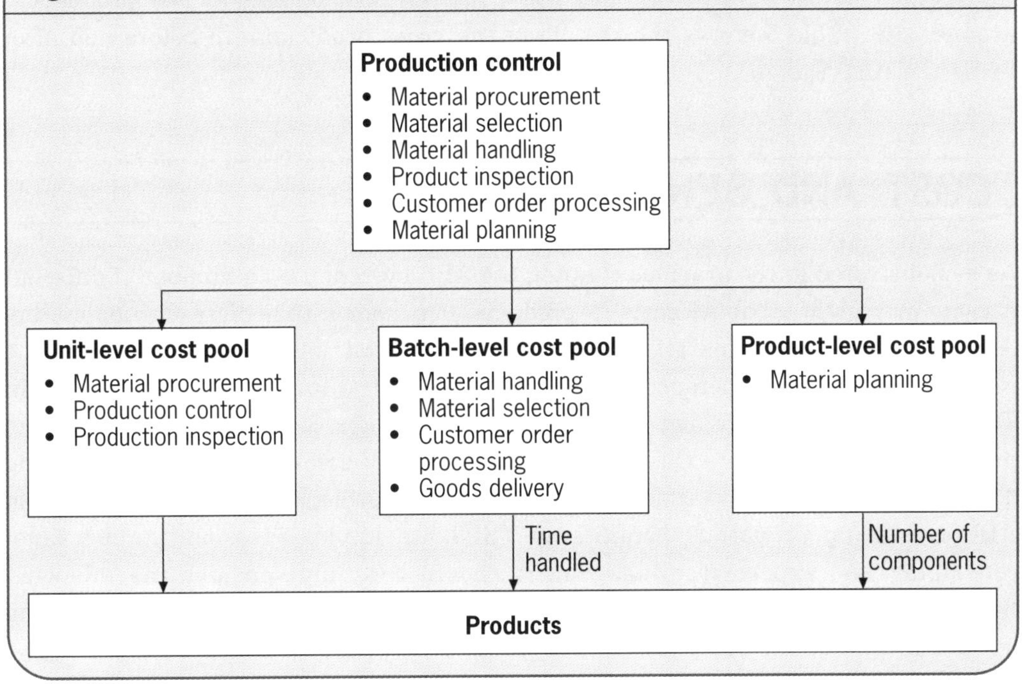

Basically, TSLJ manufactures thousands of kinds of products. They can be categorised according to their different attributes, such as difference in products' style, difference of gems stone assembled on the products and variety of order volume. In order to facilitate the consultation study in this preliminary stage, we chose our subject products according to their different categories. Generally, the product line of TSLJ can be classified into four main categories according to the characteristic of material assembled. They are diamond, ruby, sapphire and jade. Diamond is the hardest and most valuable material in the world; from past experience, the defective rate during handling and assembly is around 0.3% (around HK$30,000 per month) of the material costs assembled, which is the least among the products. Ruby and sapphire are less solid materials, however, their value is also much less than diamond and the defective rate is comparatively higher. It is around

0.33% (around HK$10,000 per month). Jade is the most fragile and highly-priced material. The value lies between diamond and ruby and sapphire but the hardness of this material is much less than the others. The defective rate is around 0.5% (around HK$10,000 per month) which is also the highest as compared to the other materials. Tables 3 and 4 show the cost data of these four categories of products under the existing costing system and the ABC system.

Under the current market situation, TSLJ is a market follower in determining the company's pricing strategy. The gross margin of each category of products is around 35%. Table 5 shows the results of the gross profit margin before and after using the ABC system.

COST AND BENEFIT ANALYSIS

As demonstrated in the previous chapter, the ABC system uses a number of different activity drivers to attribute costs to products. It is shown that after the adoption of ABC, the gross profit margin of products P2 and P4 have dropped 5% and 6% respectively. From the perspective of management, the implementation of ABC in TSLJ can help them reflect the accurate production costs of each category of products and thus restate their own product strategy according to the new costing data in order to maximise their profit and returns. Although the implementation of ABC can bring numerous benefits to TSLJ, its implementation can be time-consuming and expensive. Management should carefully consider the following factors before the full implementation of an ABC system since this will bring additional cost to the company.

We think that the main benefits will come from activity elimination and better resource allocation to more profitable products. Regarding the marginal cost, we expect that the curve will have two effects depending on the stage of implementation of ABC. At the early stage of implementation, staff training is required to provide them the knowledge of ABC. Moreover, resistance to change is expected because the current costing system has run for ten years. These two effects will cause cost increases. However, when ABC is developed at a later stage, these marginal costs will decrease due to the learning curve effect and the production of more useful management accounting information with the help of computer facilities.

Table 3 Product Costing Data of Existing Costing System

	Cost related to: Unit-level activities		Batch-level activities		Product-sustaining activities		
Product Category (HK$)	*Material*	*Direct labour hours*	*No. of selections*	*No. of orders*	*Time handled*	*No. of components*	*Total overhead costs*
Diamond (P1)	15,000	11	4	5	4	4	–
Sapphire (P2)	2,000	2	2	1	2	2	–
Ruby (P3)	2,500	2	2	2	2	2	–
Jade (P4)	2,500	3	1	1	3	1	–
Amount consumed	22,000	18	9	9	11	9	–
Activity costs (overhead)	200	2,000	400	400	200	400	–
Aggregated activity costs		2,200			1,000	400	$3,600

Product category	**Units produced**	**Direct labour hours consumed**	**Overhead rate[1]**	**Costs allocated**	**Reported unit cost**
P1	4	15,000	$0.164	$2,455	$614
P2	2	2,000	$0.164	$327	$164
P3	2	2,500	$0.164	$409	$205
P4	1	2,500	$0.164	$409	$409
		22,000		$3,600	

[1] Overhead rate: Total overheads/Total material cost ($3,600/$22,000 = 0.164)

Table 4 Product Costing Data of Proposed ABC System

	Unit-level activities	Batch-level activities	Product-sustaining activities
Total overhead costs	$2,200	$1,000	$400
Total cost driver units	18 hours	11 selections	9 components
Consumption intensity	$122 per hour	$91 per selection	$44 per component

	Cost related to: Unit-level activities			Batch-level activities			Product-sustaining activities		
Product category	*Direct labour hours*	*C.I.*[1]	*Costs traced*	*No. of selections*	*C.I.*[1]	*Costs traced*	*No. of components*	*C.I.*[1]	*Costs traced*
P1	11	$122	$1,344	4	$91	$364	4	$44	$176
P2	2	$122	$244	2	$91	$182	2	$44	$88
P3	2	$122	$244	2	$91	$182	2	$44	$88
P4	3	$122	$366	3	$91	$273	1	$44	$44

[1] C.I.: Consumption Intensity

		Reported unit cost			
Product category	*Total costs traced (ABC system)*	*Proposed ABC system*	*Existing system*	*Difference from existing system (Unit cost)*	*Difference from existing system (%)*
P1	$1,884	$471	$614	$–143	–23%
P2	$514	$257	$164	$93	56%
P3	$514	$257	$205	$52	25%
P4	$683	$683	$409	$274	66%

Table 5 Results of Gross Profit Margin

		Existing costing system			ABC system		
Product category	*Current selling price*	*Unit cost per existing system*	*Gross profit*	*Gross profit*	*Unit cost per ABC system*	*Gross profit*	*Gross profit*
P1	$6,500	$4,364	$2,136	33%	$4,221	$2,279	35%
P2	$1,750	$1,164	$586	33%	$1,257	$493	28%
P3	$2,200	$1,455	$745	34%	$1,507	$693	32%
P4	$4,350	$2,909	$1,441	33%	$3,183	$1,167	27%

CASE STUDY QUESTIONS

1) How does absorption costing differ from ABC?
2) What are the potential benefits provided by an ABC system?
3) What additional cost was brought into the cost pool under the proposed ABC system?
4) Why were the product costs different under the proposed ABC system?
5) Which of the two main independent variables of ABC were used to analyse the adoption of ABC and why?
6) Should management adopt the ABC system? Explain your reasoning.

CASE STUDY 11

Healthcare Ltd – Multiple Performance Measures

INTRODUCTION

Healthcare Ltd is a Singapore-based retailing company in Hong Kong whose main activity is to trade health care products such as massage chairs, ear scans, intelligent thermometers, foot rollers and slimming belts. The products are imported from Japan and distributed through the retail outlets located in large shopping malls. Current marketing strategies are almost wholly devoted to the massage chairs as they are the key products of Healthcare Ltd and are expected to generate the highest revenue. At the initial stage of its operations in Hong Kong, the scale was very small and no specific internal organisational structure and comprehensive management system existed. In recent years, Healthcare Ltd was on a steadily growing trend and now it has become a major health product retailer in Hong Kong with over 30 outlets. However, the growth has slowed down recently. The management thinks it may be due to increased competition from several major competitors in Hong Kong sourcing similar products from Japan.

The corporate mission of Healthcare Ltd is to become the market leader of the health care products industry by providing high-quality health care products to the general public. For Hong Kong, the objectives are to expand the market share from the current 20% to 40% within two years and to increase retail outlets to more than 50 shops by 2002. It plans to penetrate the market by establishing more retail outlets in new shopping malls, maintaining close communication with the parent company and fellow foreign subsidiaries, exploiting any new products suitable to the Hong Kong market; and training staff to enhance the sales services.

I wish to acknowledge the assistance of Meisy Wong in the preparation of this case study. This case was developed as a basis for class discussion rather than to illustrate either effective or ineffective handling of an administrative situation.

The company's organisational structure is simple (see Figure 1). The top management comprises a managing director and a regional general manager. Both of them are Singaporeans and are assigned by the parent company in Singapore. The local functional departments include sales, marketing, administration, store, repairs and maintenance and accounts. Management control is highly centralised because decision-making rights reside with the top management in Singapore who frequently travel within the Asia-Pacific region. The managing director makes the decisions on the development of new products, the source of inputs and the selection of large investments, while the regional general manager decides on pricing policies, allocation of budget among alternate users, hiring and firing of management personnel and performance evaluation of functional managers. The local management is mainly responsible for making daily operational decisions and advising the top management on strategic decisions with regard to the local market conditions since top management is not familiar with the local market and operating environment. The local accounts department reports functionally to the financial controller of the parent company and operationally to the regional general manager. It has a certain extent of autonomy in dealing with accounting issues to fulfil local accounting requirements.

Figure 1 Organisation Structure of Healthcare Ltd

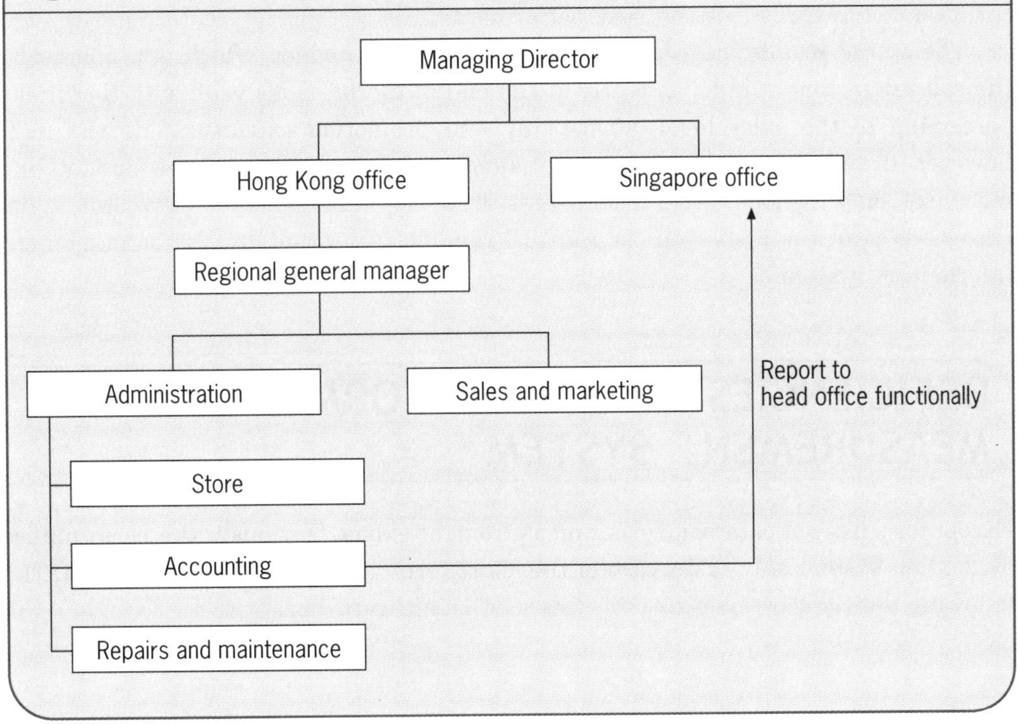

PERFORMANCE MEASUREMENT SYSTEM

To achieve the corporate objectives, the management focuses on the turnover level and the number of outlets. The performance evaluation system is naturally established in this direction. Sales figures, financial reports and budgets are generated in the existing management information system. Among the departments of local functions, the performance of the sales department draws the highest attention from the top management, while the other departments provide a supporting role. The management aknowledges that the performance of the sales teams represent the performance of the overall business because they are the vehicle to achieve the corporate objectives. The sales teams, in order to compete with their competitors, tend to suggest the opening of outlets in their vicinity to contest for the market share. Very often, free gifts are offered without pre-approval to attract high sales.

The major information for performance evaluation is the daily sales summary which gives updated information on the sales volume of each outlet. On-line sales analysis is also available after the data is uploaded and checked by the accounting staff. The salesmen are entitled to rewards on a team basis according to the turnover level. Once the team has achieved the pre-determined target, the whole team enjoys a prescribed percentage of the sales amount as commission. Another basis of judging the outlets' performance is sales turnover. The outlets which achieve high levels of turnover are regarded as the best performers.

The actual results are compared with the annual budget, which is prepared by the sales department independently at the end of the previous year, with line items pertaining to the sales level, advertising and promotion expenses. The variance, however, draws little attention from management. Among the three budget line measures, only the sales level is of interest from the management's viewpoint, while the other two are just seen as routine reports generated by the management information system.

DEFICIENCIES IN THE PERFORMANCE MEASUREMENT SYSTEM

Except for sales indicators, no other measurement exists. Obviously, the performance evaluation system only takes care of the short-term goal of sales maximisation. The following deficiencies exist in the system of Healthcare Ltd:

Team-based Measurement

The team incentive base is designed to motivate the salesmen to achieve a higher sales level both in quantity and in sales amount. However, without an assessment of the individual performance, the overall results are dragged down by incompetent staff and a fall in morale of high-performing staff is conceivable.

Incomplete Financial Indicators

From the monthly financial reports, the management sees the profitability of each outlet and the overall performance of the business. The performance of each outlet is based on the turnover and the associated direct costs. Financial information is a common and basic source of information for management that gives a picture of the business performance. Since, Healthcare Ltd is operating with 30 outlets, it is important for the management to assess the performance of each individual outlet. However, the management has a wrong perception that the outlets are profitable and are maintained within the appropriate sales network based on the information in the financial reports. Sales turnover is just a superficial indicator of the outlets' operating results. High turnover does not imply high profitability. The management only focuses on turnover and the gross profit of each outlet ignoring the huge centralised costs, like advertising expenses, marketing expenses, storage costs and repair and maintenance costs which are not allocated to the outlets. Furthermore, free gifts are often given away without prior approval. The offer of such unauthorised free gifts actually increases the cost of sales. However, the salesmen are not penalised and still receive the same commission. Therefore, the indicators cannot fully reflect the outlets' performance. The sole reliance of the management on this indicator for resource allocation to respective outlets, future expansion planning and salesman reward programme is highly critical. Further, the focal point of their workforce is on the sales level. This short-term objective may not achieve the long-term strategy – to be a market leader – if the business is persistently unprofitable and over-expanded.

Non-comprehensive Planning

Planning is an important function of management for effective business arrangements, pre-determining control measures to deal with any discrepancies and deriving contingency plans. Although, Healthcare Ltd has a prepared budget, little effort is directed towards the discrepancies. Furthermore, the budgets are made on a piece-meal basis in the sense that there are only budgets for sales levels, advertising and promotion expenses. Other operating expenses, such as delivery and storage expenses, are not projected. An incomplete budget can result in a misallocation of resources. For instance, the management expands aggressively so that the sales network can contest for market share; new outlets are opened simply due to the existence of competitors' outlets in the same location. As opening of a new shop involves huge costs and expenditure, including rental deposits, lease rental and renovation expenses, thorough planning beforehand is required. The management also places little value on the local accounts department. The value of this function can be enhanced with better communication with the management and the attainment of more information from other departments. The under-developed management information system impairs the ability to provide information to executives for corporate planning.

Ignorance of Non-financial Performance Indicators

There is no consideration of non-financial performance indicators like customer satisfaction. Customer services are important to the retailing industry, especially in this vigorously competitive environment. Healthcare Ltd aims at providing high-quality customer service, but the measurement of such quality is unclear and not well established. As there is no customer services department in the current organisational structure, the administration picks up such responsibilities on a supporting basis. As a result, there is no systematic policy to handle customer complaints relating to on-site sales services – delivery arrangement, quality of products and the frequency of repairs. No statistical records for these cases are maintained for evaluation. Although Healthcare Ltd has provided training in respect of the techniques of dealing with customers and professional product knowledge to the sales staff, the actual performance is not reflected in the management information system.

SUMMARY

The success of Healthcare Ltd is not just assessed by the sales performance and financial results. High-quality customer services can consolidate the corporate image and customer loyalty. Customer complaints spoil corporate reputation and potential customers will hesitate to buy Healthcare Ltd's products. Healthcare Ltd's competitiveness will be severely weakened if the management is not aware of the problem and fails to respond. Without performance evaluation with respect to non-financial performance, management is not alerted to the dilemmas and therefore, is unable to control strategically the deficiencies. Therefore, the recent slowdown of growth rate may have something to do with customer service problems which management is unaware of.

CASE STUDY QUESTIONS

1) What are some of the key success factors for Healthcare Ltd?
2) In what effective ways can performance evaluation assist the management of Healthcare Ltd in decision making?
3) The current performance measurement system is a product of the Chinese way of management. Comment.
4) How are the deficiencies in the current system similar to the balanced scorecard approach to measurement?
5) What recommendations would you make for improving Healthcare Ltd's performance measurement and evaluation system?
6) What are the likely system costs associated with introducing the new measurement system?

CASE STUDY 12

Yunhong Group – Delegation and Performance Measurement

INTRODUCTION

In MNEs, organisation structures can be very complex, and different dimensions of authorisation can induce conflicts of interest between parties. There is no golden rule in determining which decision-making authority is better. This case study examines a conflict of interest between the sales and purchasing functions of the Yunhong Group. Yunhong is a Hong Kong-listed company with a multinational network. As of 30 June 2003, the group's turnover was more than HK$15 billion with net assets of about HK$3.5 billion. The group has 69 offices in 40 countries and territories and is a premier global trading group managing the supply chain for high-volume, time-sensitive consumer goods. Garments make up a large part of the group's business, which also covers the sourcing of hard goods such as fashion accessories, furnishings, gifts, handicrafts, home products, promotional merchandise, toys, sporting goods and travel goods. As a supply chain manager across many industries and countries, the group provides the convenience of a total value-added package from product design and development, raw material and factory sourcing, production planning and management, quality assurance and export documentation to shipping consolidation.

In view of the complexity and wide range of product lines, the group's business is divided into several streams. An independent sales and purchasing team is assigned to each stream. The sales function is mainly located in Hong Kong and is headed by a sales manager who coordinates with overseas customers mainly in the US and Europe. The purchasing function is headed by a purchasing manager who

---

I wish to acknowledge the assistance of Thomas Kwok Yick Hung in the preparation of this case study. This case was developed as a basis for class discussion rather than to illustrate either effective or ineffective handling of an administrative situation.

is usually located somewhere in Asia. Such managers are fully responsible for the purchasing function in their countries. They mainly deal with local suppliers and vendors. Sales managers are mainly responsible for customer searching, product design and development. Purchase managers are mainly responsible for raw material and factory sourcing, production planning and management and quality assurance (see Figure 1).

GOAL CONGRUENCE PROBLEM

The sales managers mainly work with US and European customers, but in some cases they contact Asian suppliers for purchases. The purchasing managers work mainly with their local suppliers, but in some cases they deal with overseas customers directly. The customer and supplier information is shared in the group's sales and purchasing system. However, this structure means that the decision rights of sales managers and purchasing managers are often in conflict with each other. There may be lack of goal congruence between two functions – one manager may focus on higher sales turnover but ignore the purchase cost, whereas another manager may focus on a lower purchase cost but ignore the sales volume.

Because sales managers and purchasing managers both have full control over their functions, bonus rewards are based on the financial outcomes of their performances. The existing performance measurement for sales managers is based mainly on sales turnover in comparison to budgets and quarterly forecasts. Bonuses are granted based on the level of excess turnover. Therefore, the sales managers have an incentive to boost sales turnover. However, a higher turnover volume does not mean higher profits, for example, a higher-quality product may increase the turnover but may not increase profit due to higher costs.

The performance measurement for purchasing managers is based mainly on purchases (cost of goods sold) in comparison to the budget and quarterly forecasts. Bonuses are granted based on the purchasing costs saved. Hence, purchasing managers have an incentive to lower the purchasing costs. However, lower purchasing costs may not mean higher profits if they come at the expense of quality. The existing performance measurement system does not take into account the interdependency between the sales and purchasing managers. Hence, each manager is concerned about how to maximise his own interest (see Figure 2).

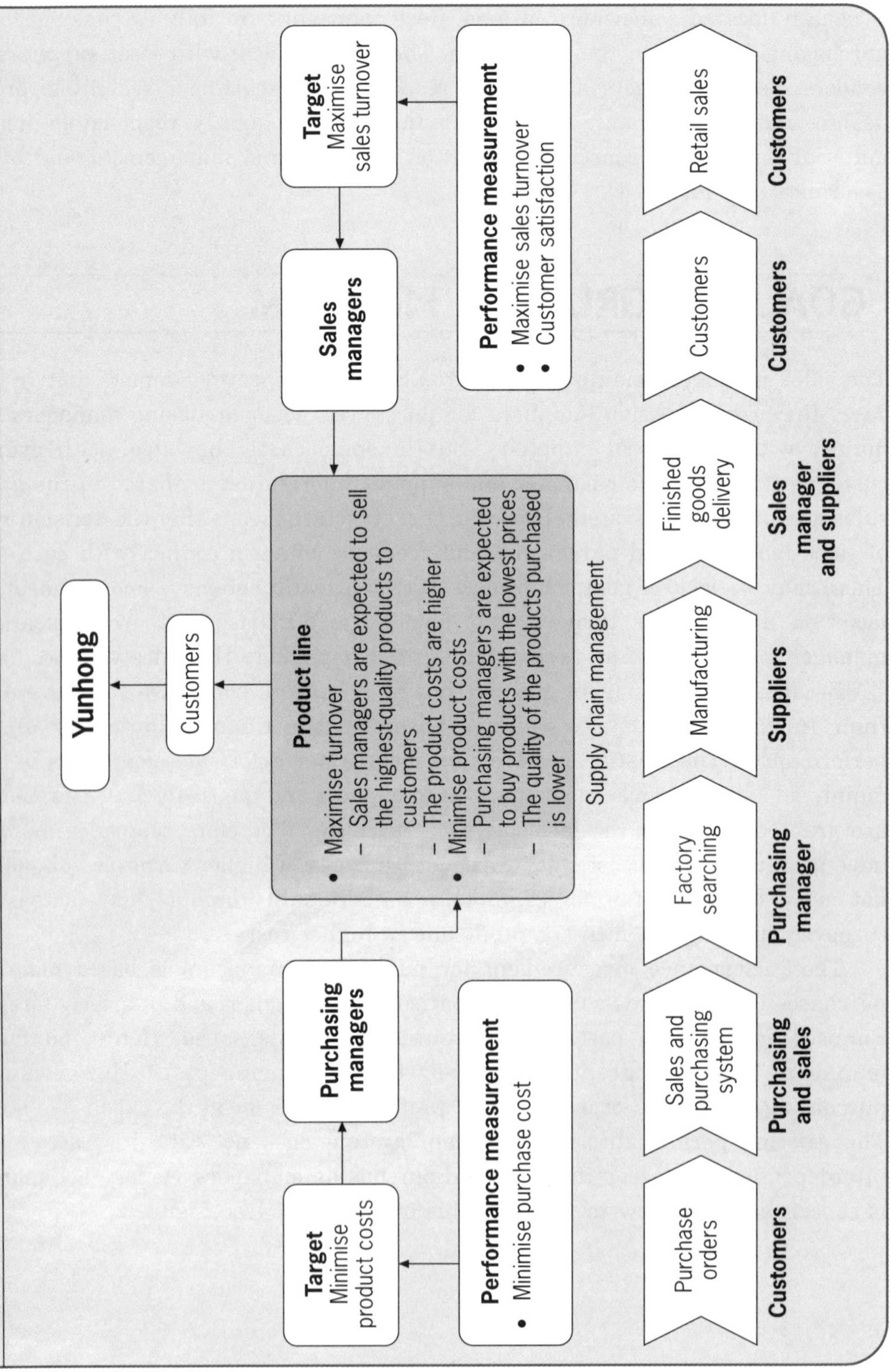

Figure 1 Organisation Structure of the Yunhong Group

Figure 2 Goal Congruence Problem

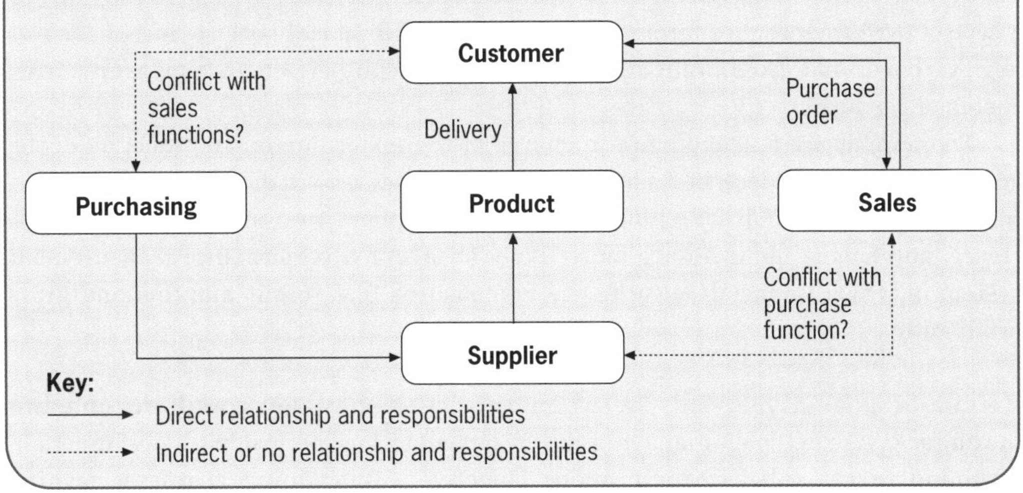

DRIVERS OF GOAL INCONGRUENCE

Because sales managers work more globally and purchasing managers work more locally, to rationalise the structure of the established resource-based and/or market-seeking investment in a way that it can gain from the common governance of geographically dispersed activities, the group has to achieve operational efficiency by means of an efficient resource allocation. As both sales managers and purchasing managers are experts in their areas, the new performance measurement system must best reflect the efficient use of the resources that are allocated to these two groups of managers. Apart from resource allocation, three other factors drive the lack of goal congruence.

Level of dependence on host country's operation. The sales managers sell goods to customers around the world upon the placement of orders, and the sales operations are dependent on the operations of the host country (Hong Kong). The purchasing managers purchase goods from different suppliers in Asia, and they operate quite independently of the host country. Hence, the new performance measurement system must reflect the different mode of operations of each functional group of managers.

Sales and purchasing managers' attitudes. The sales managers play the role of the major sales force of the group in Hong Kong, and are responsible for coordinating with overseas customers, mainly in the US and Europe. They are more customer oriented in looking for new customers, ensuring customer satisfaction and product quality and maintaining target sales. In this regard, the sales managers may favour a type of performance measurement that is a mix of financial performance measures (e.g., turnover and gross profit ratio) and non-financial performance measures (e.g., customer feedback).

The purchasing managers are in charge of the major purchasing function of the group, which takes place in Asia. They are more cost oriented, and profit margins, cost minimisation and searching for quality suppliers are their main concerns. Hence, purchasing mangers are more likely to favour a performance measurement system in which financial performance is measured (e.g., profit margins and gross profit ratio).

Extent of goal divergence between the sales managers and purchasing managers. As the sales managers are responsible for the group's sales function, attaining target sales is their major objective. Maintaining customer loyalty, boosting sales figures, increasing market share and ascertaining product quality is their focus. In contrast, the purchasing managers are fully responsible for the group's product sourcing. Bidding for the most favourable product purchase price, maintaining product profit margins and researching into quality suppliers are their main concerns.

COMPARISON OF INCENTIVES AND PERFORMANCE MEASURES WITH CONTEXTUAL VARIABLES

In accordance with the group's strategy of providing a total value-added package to customers, it is important to maintain good-quality products to maximise customer satisfaction. Moreover, due to keen competition the group cannot ignore the need for minimising its product costs to maintain its selling price. However, good-quality products will bring higher costs. To ensure the continued success of its business, the group must bear in mind how to measure quality and how to determine its costs for good quality (see Table 1). Such measures should be built into the performance measurement system to ensure that sales and purchasing managers are encouraged to perform in line with the group strategy.

To enhance goal congruence, the group's performance measurement system should be redesigned. In consideration of the above measures of costs and quality, a detailed comparison of various incentive and performance measures is given in

Table 1 Measures of Cost and Quality

	Measurement
Quality	• Number of customer complaints • Number of customer re-orders • Number/amount of sales return • Expenditure on research into new suppliers for high-quality products
Costs for achieving good quality	• Increase in product costs in exchange for high-quality product features/styles • Expense of market research for understanding customer preferences • Costs of increasing the quality guarantee for customers, such as revising an 80% guarantee of good quality to a 100% guarantee • Increase in quality assurance costs to ensure product quality before shipping to customers • Time cost incurred for tracing customer needs and requirements rather than waiting for feedback

Table 2. A mark is given for each incidence where a particular incentive or performance measure attribute is related to either of two types of performance goals (financial and non-financial) and four contextual variables: *basis of resource allocation (O-1)*; *level of dependence on host country's operation (O-2)*; *sales and purchasing manager attitudes (I-1)* and *extent of goal divergence between sales managers and purchasing managers (I-2)*. The design of a new scheme to solve the group's problem consists of having an appropriate mix of performance measures and the right type of incentive. The selection of components is based on the score in Table 2. The two incentive components along with the performance measurement components with a score of five will be discussed below.

Profit sharing scheme. This has the highest score of all components and can be the most appropriate tool with which to align the interests of the sales managers and purchasing managers. It also encourages different functional managers to work closely with each other because the maximisation of profit is the ideal outcome of both sales and purchasing. A notional profit can be assigned to sales function (50%) and purchasing function (50%) so that a profit-sharing scheme can be applied to both sales managers and purchasing managers.

Bonuses for extra sales or purchasing costs saved in comparison to budgeted figures. A special bonus for managers with outstanding performance in

Table 2 Comparison of Various Incentive and Performance Measures in Terms of Their Relevance to Contextual Variables[1]

	Achievement		Relevance to contextual variables				
	Financial	*Non-financial*	*O-1*[2]	*O-2*[3]	*I-1*[4]	*I-2*[5]	*Score*
Incentives							
• Profit-sharing scheme	✓		✓	✓	✓	✓	5
• Bonus on extra sales, purchase costs saved in comparison to the budget	✓		✓	✓	✓		4
Performance measures							
• Level of customer satisfaction		✓	✓	✓	✓	✓	5
• Number/amount of sales returns	✓		✓		✓	✓	4
• Acquisition of new suppliers for high-quality products		✓	✓	✓	✓	✓	5
• Acquisition of information on market/customer preferences		✓	✓		✓	✓	4
• Sales turnover in comparison to the budget	✓		✓	✓	✓		4
• Purchase cost in comparison to the budget	✓		✓		✓		3
Number of measures achieved/relevant	5	3	8	5	8	5	

[1] The basis of resource allocation and sales and purchasing manager attitudes are the most important contextual variables in determining the success of the new scheme.
[2] O-1: Basis of resource allocation
[3] O-2: Level of dependence on host country's operation
[4] I-1: Sales and purchasing manager attitudes
[5] I-2: Extent of goal divergence between sales managers and purchasing managers

comparison to their budgets may encourage them to boost sales and save costs. However, it would also induce the problem that the sales and purchasing functions may work in their own interests and lack goal congruence.

Level of customer satisfaction. Customer satisfaction is the major non-financial measure, and is the most important non-financial component of the group's strategy. Periodic feedback should be obtained from customers. The feedback should be divided into concerns about the sales side (e.g., customer services and product design) and the purchasing side (e.g., product quality). The feedback should be obtained by an independent department (e.g., the finance or internal audit departments) so that it is more reliable.

Acquisition of new suppliers for high-quality products. Product sourcing is a major function of supply chain management. New and high-quality products are essential for business operations. This measurement may encourage purchasing managers to look for new and high-quality products so that sales turnover can be increased. However, to balance the performance measurement between the sales and purchasing functions and minimise implementation costs, this measurement should be paired with determination of the level of customer satisfaction.

CASE STUDY QUESTIONS

1) What is the underlying problem in this case?
2) What are the likely key performance indicators for each of the sales and purchase functions in the Yunhong Group?
3) What are the costs and benefits of using a) financial and b) non-financial performance measures?
4) What is the rationale for using objective performance measures? Why do firms persist in using subjective performance measures?
5) How would you solve the problem in this case? What are the trade-offs involved in this recommendation?

CHAPTER

4

Management Control of International Joint Ventures

LEARNING OBJECTIVES

- Understand how joint ventures are different from wholly owned subsidiaries.
- Understand the typologies of control in joint ventures.
- Understand the difference between agreement and management controls in joint ventures.
- Understand the current issues in joint venture control and performance in China.

INTRODUCTION

International joint ventures involve the establishment of a new entity with a partnership of two or more partners (typically a company) from different countries. International joint ventures have been a dominant mode of entry for FDI from developed countries into developing countries in the past 20 years. Joint ventures provide an additional challenge for management control because there is more than one owner and each typically has different strategic reasons for joining the venture. As a result very few joint ventures are successful. Empirical evidence from firms operating joint ventures in China such as Rockwell, Caterpillar, Kodak and General Motors suggest that local "environmental unpredictability, lack of bureaucratic transparency and partner unreliability" make joint venture investment difficult (Cooper and Johnson, 2000, p. 7). However, even in the absence of government regulations that stipulate joint ventures as the mode of entry, they are still considered to be the contract of choice, especially in cases where partners have different resources and capabilities that they can share for mutual benefit.

This chapter describes the various management control problems in international joint ventures with specific reference to Sino-foreign joint ventures in China. The first part explains the ways in which a joint venture is different from a wholly owned subsidiary, and outlines the influences on the use of management controls in joint ventures. The second part details the various frameworks of control that have been examined in the literature. The third part outlines the various joint venture agreements and control mechanisms that are typically employed. The fourth part summarises the empirical studies on controls in joint ventures with specific reference to the issues of control that pertain to the management of Sino-foreign joint ventures in China.

JOINT VENTURES ARE DIFFERENT FROM PARENT PARTNERS

There are several reasons behind the suggestion that the management control systems and performance evaluation criteria which are applied to joint ventures should be different from those applicable to parent partners or their wholly owned subsidiaries. The fact that two or more partners are involved renders the structure of joint ventures very much different from that of the parent company or a wholly owned division. First, the parent partners have different strategic objectives for the venture, and often these objectives are conflicting. Part of this conflict is due to the different social, cultural and political backgrounds, and the other part is due to the different contributions and dependencies that each partner has on the other. Such differences are even more apparent in the case of international joint ventures. Consequently, the control over and performance objectives for the joint venture are likely to be different between the partners.

Second, although joint ventures may be "given" independent management structures, they ultimately face a dual reporting/loyalty dilemma. This is particularly the case in international joint ventures in which one partner supplies human capital and the other partner supplies the management know-how and technology. Although systems may be put in place for congruent reporting, employee loyalties are likely to remain with the partner of their home country. Finally, the organisational politics of joint ventures are much more complicated than those of parent partners and, because of their "distance" from the parent company, joint ventures are more likely to be used as a "scapegoat" by parent company management to justify their company's/division's failures.

Given this contrast, the choice of management control systems for the joint venture and the choice of how to evaluate its performance is critical for the long-term stability of the venture. Parent companies will often want to employ systems with which they are familiar and are thus not aimed at overcoming the above differences. According to Anderson (1990), corporate headquarters often apply to joint ventures the same criteria used for the management control system and the evaluation of the performance of wholly owned subsidiaries. However, it is often the case that joint ventures are to be operated as independent entities with strategic objectives that are different or in conflict with the partners. It is then possible that in a simple joint venture with two parent partners, up to three different performance evaluation criteria sets can be used.

TYPOLOGIES OF CONTROL IN JOINT VENTURES

In an early typology of control, Geringer and Herbert (1989) argued that there are three major dimensions of control (see Figure 4.1): 1) mechanism of control, or the means by which control is exercised, such as by equity ownership, representation in management bodies, technical superiority and management skills, 2) extent of control, or the degree of the role played in decision making, and 3) focus of control, or the scope of activities over which parents exercise control. Geringer and Herbert also suggested that these control elements interacted with the strategy of the head office and/or subsidiary to influence joint venture performance. They conceptualised the extent of control as dependent upon the centralisation or the locus of the decision-making process, which is regarded as a continuous variable. For the focus dimension of control, Geringer (1986) suggested that the exercise of effective control should emphasise selective control over those dimensions that a parent perceives as critical, rather than attempt to control the entire range of the joint venture's activities.

Figure 4.1 A Strategy Control Model of Joint Venture Performance

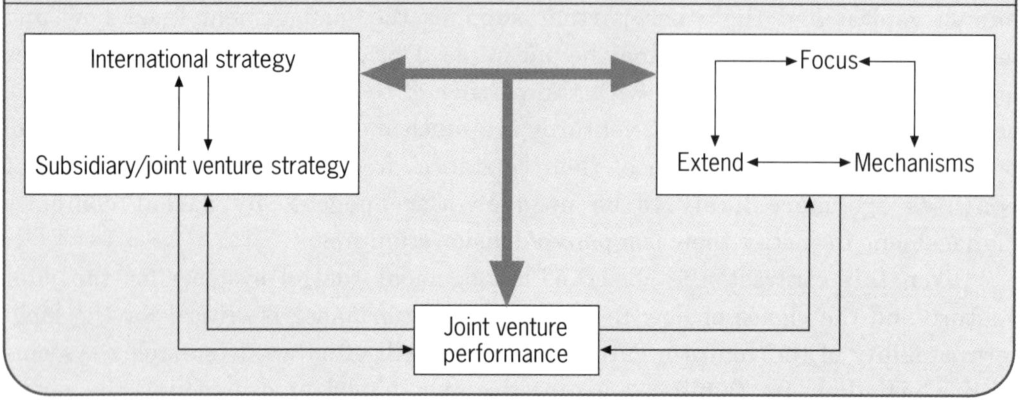

Source: Geringer J.M. and Herbert J., Control and performance of international joint ventures. Copyright 1989 by *Journal of International Business Studies*. Reprinted by permission of Palgrave Macmillan Ltd.

These issues in the management of joint ventures can be more specifically summarised in terms of a framework (see Figure 4.2) of antecedents, control mechanisms and performance. These three parts raise important questions for the way in which a joint venture is managed. For antecedents or determinants of control the question is: What is the extent to which partner strategy and contributions impact on relative partner bargaining power and partner risk? For example, foreign joint venture partners from developed countries often bring cash, technology and management skills to joint ventures with developing country partners. In contrast, the local partner will provide access to land, buildings and distribution networks. While these contributions provide bargaining power for each partner to negotiate for certain control over the joint venture, it is the nature of the contributions (e.g., patented technology) and strategy (e.g., if the joint venture is part of a global supply chain) that is most likely to impact on partner risk (Chalos and O'Connor, 2004).

The risk faced by each partner is also likely to be different. While the foreign partner may view the loss of technical know-how as a potential risk, in contrast, the local partner may view the failure to learn from the foreign partner as an overriding risk. The level of risk exposure and bargaining power can be thought simply in terms

Figure 4.2 Antecedents and Control Mechanisms Model of Joint Venture Performance

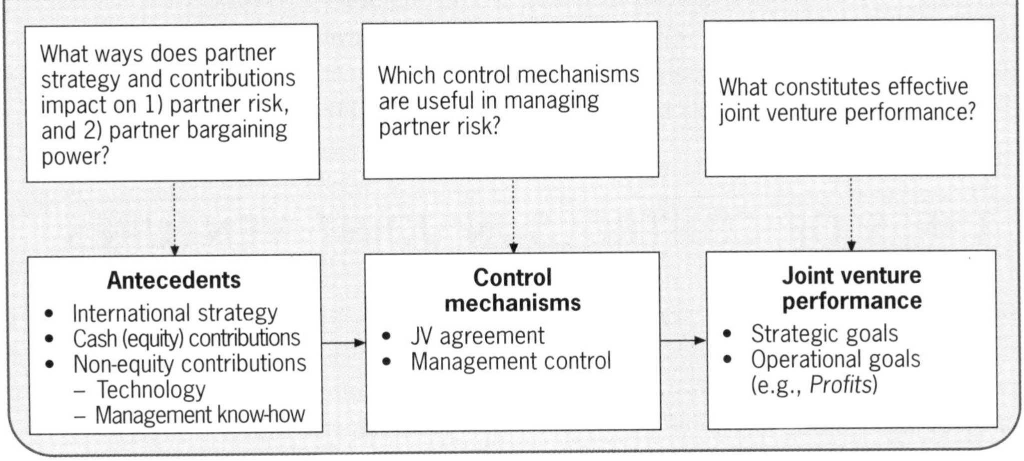

of a partner's *need* for control and a partner's *ability* to control particular operations of the venture. Often the partner with a relatively higher bargaining power has the ability to institute a range of controls but does not have the need for such controls because of a particular strategy (e.g., the venture has a high degree of autonomy) or partner contributions that are more transparent and controllable (e.g., low-tech manufacturing industries).

For control mechanisms, the question is: Which control mechanisms are useful in managing partner risk. The role of controls as perceived by each partner can range from simple prevention of asset loss to the facilitation of knowledge transfer or a combination of both. For example, specific personnel controls (e.g., expatriates) are likely to provide more assurance to the foreign partner in the management of assets, while at the same time helping the local partner learn from the foreign partner's expertise. Joint venture agreement and management controls are also determined differently and are likely to substitute for each other depending on the nature of the partner contributions and the initial bargaining set. The key here is knowing how to balance the use of management controls to fit with 1) the joint venture agreement that typically arises out of the partner's initial bargaining set, and 2) the different risks as perceived by each partner which are not fully captured by the joint venture agreement.

For performance, it is important to understand the strategic objectives of the partners in addition to the typical profit goals of the joint venture. It is the strategic performance goals which are likely to be different between partners in international joint ventures. For example, foreign partners may view the following as strategic goals, 1) overcoming government-mandated investments or regulatory barriers, 2) gaining access to less-costly labour and materials, 3) faster market entry and payback, and 4) gaining access to political and business network. In contrast, the local partner may view 1) initiating international expansion through the benefit of partner's know-how, 2) seeking alternative sources of capital investment, and 3) modernising the existing business operations as relevant strategic objectives.

TYPES OF CONTROLS IN JOINT VENTURES

As explained in Chapter 2, a joint venture agreement legally creates a joint venture through a contract, and identifies the major rights, duties and obligations of the participants. The joint venture agreement typically identifies the provisions for management and the performance of obligations, including the transfer of knowledge. However, given contractual limitations, joint venture partners typically rely on various control mechanisms. These controls serve to influence behaviour in areas that cannot be included in the joint venture agreement and to ensure the fulfilment of parts of the agreement that are difficult to enforce legally. The aim of such controls is to align partner differences and to promote a better understanding of the intangible strengths and relationships that each partner brings to the venture. Joint venture agreement controls and management controls are discussed in turn.

Joint Venture Agreement

Equity ownership and board membership. Equity ownership control is defined as the division of the equity investment or shareholding in the joint venture among the sponsoring firms (Yan and Luo, 2001). As the equity position of the partners usually determines the composition of the board of directors and the board in turn appoints upper-level management, including the appointment of expatriates, the dominant partner has the ability to exercise significant control in the management of the joint venture (Mjoen and Tallman, 1997). Yan and Gray's (1994) interview and archival data supported "the importance of the role played by the boards of directors in making strategic decisions for the joint ventures and solving critical problems regarding the partnerships in general". Child and Yan (1999) note that:

> Appointing board members is important for control, because the board approves the venture's business plan, profit distribution, major investments and other important financial decisions. In addition, board members can influence appointments to key executive positions in the joint venture and will sometimes insist on approving them.

In addition, the joint venture board has the power to determine the extent to which decision control is given to the general manager of the joint venture. According to Yan and Gray (1994), substantial power is associated with the position of the general manager in a joint venture: "The general manager made important operating decisions for the venture and represented each parent (company) in negotiations with the other partner on issues that arose unexpectedly."

Contractual safeguards. Contracting risks in China have been amply documented (Martinsons and Tsang, 1995; Yan and Gray, 1994). Despite reforms, intellectual property rights remain a serious problem for foreign firms. There are numerous cases in which local joint venture partners or local contractors have pirated aspects of product design. Even when foreign partners seek damages through the court system, foreign partners are frustrated by lack of power to enforce payment (Weldon and Vanhonacker, 1999). Nevertheless, safeguards written into agreements provide explicit means of control designed to improve joint venture performance. A clear set of safeguards at the outset can both serve as a caution to local management and make clear whether rules have been broken.

A number of explicit safeguards exist to protect partner interests in the areas of transfer pricing, quality standards, royalties, performance goals and audit procedures (Ring and Van de Ven, 1994). The greater the difference in partner expertise and asset-specific investments in machinery, land and buildings, the more joint venture partners have a mutual interest in clearly elaborating safeguards related to transfer pricing, quality standards, pricing and technology policies, royalty obligations and auditing standards. Beamish (1993) argues that Chinese culture, economic policy and politics are so far removed from the experiences of most Westerners that the design of adequate safeguards is more likely as partner experience increases. The following safeguards are typical of those found in Sino-foreign joint ventures.

Transfer price setting. Since joint ventures often transact with parties who are related to either partner, it is important to have a stipulation that transfer prices reflect arm's-length market prices. If they are at arm's length, then they are easy to negotiate because no party is better off for each transaction. It is better to include such a stipulation in the agreement to avoid misunderstanding between partners.

Benchmarking procedures. Procedures are required for comparing each partner's investment against the best market standard on quality, material price and technology. Often a partner's contributions (e.g., patented know-how and special machinery) are difficult to quantify. In such cases it is better to get independent professional valuers to value the assets. In case there is no independent valuer, this is negotiated between the partners. This safeguard is aimed at ensuring that any ex-post agreement contributions (e.g., the supply of materials from the local partner's supplier network) are of acceptable quality.

Royalties. Once the partners have agreed on the value of their respective investments, it is important to have procedures to guarantee the payment of royalties to the foreign partner. However, there is a further difficulty in repatriating the royalties outside of China. Typically, approval should be obtained from exchange control for remittance and others, such as tax authority if it is for tax deductible purposes. Another strategy that foreign partners follow is to break their cash contribution into a form of debt and equity – with arrangements for the loaning of debt from banks in China. This reduces the offshore commitment of capital to the joint venture and thus the amount of profits/royalties that are expected to be repatriated.

Performance standards. To enhance the transparency of the performance expectations of each partner, a set of minimum performance goals for each partner should be stipulated. This safeguard is a planning type of control that helps focus the partners on the minimally agreed performance terms of the joint venture. The performance goals are subject to review upon changes in the business environment.

Audit rights. Foreign firms typically insist on the right to have the business accounts independently audited by an internationally recognised accounting firm under international accounting standards or they conduct periodic internal audits. This should be agreed upon by both parties. Audits can include either a special audit or a statutory audit. If a statutory audit is used, then it should be conducted by a qualified certified practising accountant (CPA) who is recognised by the host country. If a special audit or an audit for the purpose of shareholders is used, then the extra cost should also be considered.

Management Control Mechanisms

Management control refers to control over the strategic and operational conduct of the joint venture, including the "determination of strategic priorities … making of senior appointments … control over the production processes within an organisation, in the sense of determining how the employees of an organisation perform their work" (Child, 1984, p. 138). Some of the more common management control mechanisms that are found in Sino-foreign joint ventures include the employment of expatriates and decision-making controls, performance measurement systems and socialisation and communication controls. Support for these management controls has come from the Sino-US joint venture control literature. For example, Child and Faulkner (1998) proposed similar joint venture control mechanisms that include the appointment of key alliance managers, formal contractual agreements, human resource programmes, formal planning models, standard operating procedures and competitive compensation practices. Geringer and Frayne (1990, p. 107) proposed four specific dimensions of human resource management that are often a key determinant of an effective joint venture control system: recruitment and staffing, training and development, performance appraisals, and compensation and reward strategies.

Expatriates and decision controls. Many foreign investors now insist on the right to name the chief financial officer and place their own personnel in positions that involve daily operations or that enable them to report irregularities to the corporate headquarters. The use of expatriates has been found to be an important control mechanism in Sino-US joint ventures (Firth, 1996; Schaan, 1988; Beamish and Banks, 1987). Schaan (1988) noted that key expatriate personnel appointments provide ready knowledge of joint venture decisions for foreign parent firms. Parent control that is exerted through the placement of staff can more directly affect joint venture policies and monitor performance (Cyr, 1995). Mjoen and Tallman (1997) argue that local decision control combined with expatriate expertise can be effective in protecting strategic resources and in reducing opportunism, thus resulting in better joint venture performance. However, employing expatriates is more difficult and expensive in China due to Chinese insistence on salary parity and the hardships faced by foreign expatriates.

The decision-making control that is involved in operating decisions includes the hiring and firing of personnel, the sourcing of inputs, operating procedures and pricing decisions. In China, the local partner begins with possessing relatively more knowledge about local operations. Over time, as the local partner learns more from the foreign partner, there is an increased desire to have more decision rights. However, this desire is likely to be mitigated by actions on the part of the foreign partner (such as the sharing of second generation know-how) to maintain its knowledge advantage and thus the information asymmetry between the partners (Osland and Cavusgil, 1996).

Austin (1990) observed a correlation between split control and joint venture success in market economy developing countries. In China, Shenkar (1990) found control to be effective when divided along functional lines. Having one partner make all the decisions, as would be the case in a wholly owned subsidiary or dominantly controlled joint venture, increases the probability of poor performance (Teagarden and Von Glinow, 1990). As noted by Beamish (1993), "the local economy, politics and culture in the PRC are so far removed from the experience of most Western firms and managers as to make dominant foreign control extremely risky. Similarly, the lack of technology and managerial skills by the Chinese makes dominant control by them equally risky. As a result, shared or split control is the principal means by which success may be achieved".

Performance measurement and incentive systems. Despite the egalitarian tradition in China during the communist era, employees in many joint ventures are increasingly compensated based on individual performance. Chen (1995) found that Chinese managers were very economically oriented and, contrary to communist philosophy, preferred the unequal distribution of awards and merit pay to a greater degree than did their US counterparts. The wages of the strongest performers are four to five times those of new recruits (Martinsons and Tsang, 1995). To overcome the shortage of skilled labour, many joint ventures have set up in-house training programmes and have increased the scope and extent of performance-based incentives (Wagner, 1990). Performance evaluation systems are often complex, stemming from differences in evaluation systems among partners (Zahra and Elhagrasey, 1994). Frequently, greater cash and specific asset commitment provides justification for the foreign partner to implement a unified evaluation system, which is consistent with a Western approach to management. Such variable performance-based incentives have been shown to be effective (Hagerty, 1997) and are increasingly commonplace in Sino-foreign joint ventures. Osland and Cavusgil (1996) observed that although Chinese partners attempt to manage personnel decisions, US managers have learned that they must take greater control of compensation and motivation issues to retain the best Chinese managers.

Socialisation and communication practices. Socialisation has been proposed as a key element in the management of Sino-US joint ventures to improve mutual information sharing and commitment between partners with different competencies and knowledge (Ostroff and Kozlowski, 1993). Zahra and Elhagrasey (1994) note that socialisation practices should emphasise technical skills, operational and personnel policies, the importance of the joint venture to employees' parent companies and the development of a common organisational culture when the environment is amenable to such practices. As the asset commitment to a joint venture increases, socialisation becomes more important. For example, key employees are usually sent overseas to experience successful operations first-hand. A review article emphasising the importance of organisational socialisation in cross-cultural joint ventures reported consistently positive relationships between socialisation and managerial performance (Bauer, Morrison and Callister, 1998).

Joint ventures often fail due to conflicts over decision making, managerial and corporate values, perceptions of unequal costs and benefits and the significantly different goals of managers from two parent firms (Cyr and Schneider, 1996). Communication problems between individuals with different cultural and linguistic backgrounds are inevitable, especially in relation to the interpretation of the joint venture agreement. Partner dedication to the success of the joint venture is most apparent through the use of informal and frequent communication. Such communication minimises ambiguity and improves decision making. In contrast, poor communication results in poor joint venture relationships (Zahra and Elhagrasey, 1994).

STUDIES ON JOINT VENTURE CONTROL AND PERFORMANCE

The joint venture control and performance relationship has engaged researchers for several decades. The early studies examined the relationship between equity (ownership) control and performance, whereby equity ownership was viewed as the main proxy for control. More recent studies examined the influence of non-equity (ownership) factors (e.g., intangible asset contributions by the partners) on management controls and joint venture performance. These two groups of studies are discussed in turn.

Equity Ownership, Management Control and Performance

Early studies of the control-performance relationship for international joint ventures have produced inconsistent results (Geringer and Herbert, 1991). For example, some studies have found that dominant parent ventures perform better, whereas others have shown more satisfactory performance with shared control ventures. Tomlinson (1970) found that a more relaxed attitude towards control over joint ventures by parent companies would lead to a higher level of profitability. Later, Franko (1971) used a "strategy-structure" conceptual framework to examine the joint venture control-performance relationship. This framework presumed that the degree of parental control and the joint venture's performance was contingent on the strategy and structure of MNEs. Franko found that joint ventures were more stable when their parents demanded less control.

Killing (1983) proposed and found that ventures with one dominant parent were more likely to be successful than those with shared management because management is easier when the joint venture's activities are dominated by a single parent. Consistent with Killing (1983), Lecraw (1984) found that joint ventures in five developing Asian countries, had positive, roughly linear associations between control and performance. However, Beamish (1985) reported that dominant control by foreign firms was negatively related to performance. He found no such relationship when local partners dominated ventures. Hence, he suggested that the type of economy in which a joint venture operates may moderate the control-performance relationship.

Non-equity Resource Contributions, Management Control and Performance

Given the equivocal findings about the influence of equity ownership and control, more recent empirical studies have argued that non-equity partner contributions may provide a basis of management control that is separate from that provided by equity ownership (Chalos and O'Connor, 2004). The reasoning behind this argument is that the difference in the nature of the contributions that are typically provided by each partner creates a resource dependency between the partners. That is, one partner is dependent on the other partner's intangible knowledge, while the other is dependent on the other partner's tangible assets. Using China as an example, it is common for the foreign partner to provide technical and managerial know-how, capital and access to international markets, whereas the Chinese partner contributes land and buildings, access to employees and local market knowledge. Yan and Gray (1994) found that local knowledge in areas such as local sourcing, domestic distribution and personnel management was the main resource contributed by the local partners. Similarly, Inkpen and Beamish (1997) found that the critical knowledge contribution of the local partner revolves around "an understanding of local market, cultural, and environmental conditions". This resource dependency in turn creates a basis for the partners to negotiate for control over particular areas of the joint venture operation. For example, the contribution of technical knowledge by the foreign partner may create goodwill with the local Chinese partner that enables the foreign partner to negotiate for the employment of more expatriates than what could be negotiated with the contribution of cash alone.

Several researchers have noted that the combination of partner contributions in managerial skills and knowledge can affect the venture's structure with respect to parental control (Chalos and O'Connor, 2004; Child and Yan, 1999; Yan and Gray 1994). Yan and Gray (1994) examined the relationship between partner bargaining power, control and joint venture performance in an in-depth study of four Sino-US joint ventures. They found that the contribution of non-equity resources, such as proprietary technology and know-how, management expertise, international marketing networks and information systems, gained the foreign partner a significant competitive edge in exercising control over the joint venture's decisions.

In a series of three case studies of international joint ventures operating in Europe, Groot and Merchant (2000) explored the types of control that are likely to be found in such joint ventures. They also explored the likely influences on the types

Figure 4.3 Tentative Theory as to the Factors Explaining International Joint Venture Control System Differences

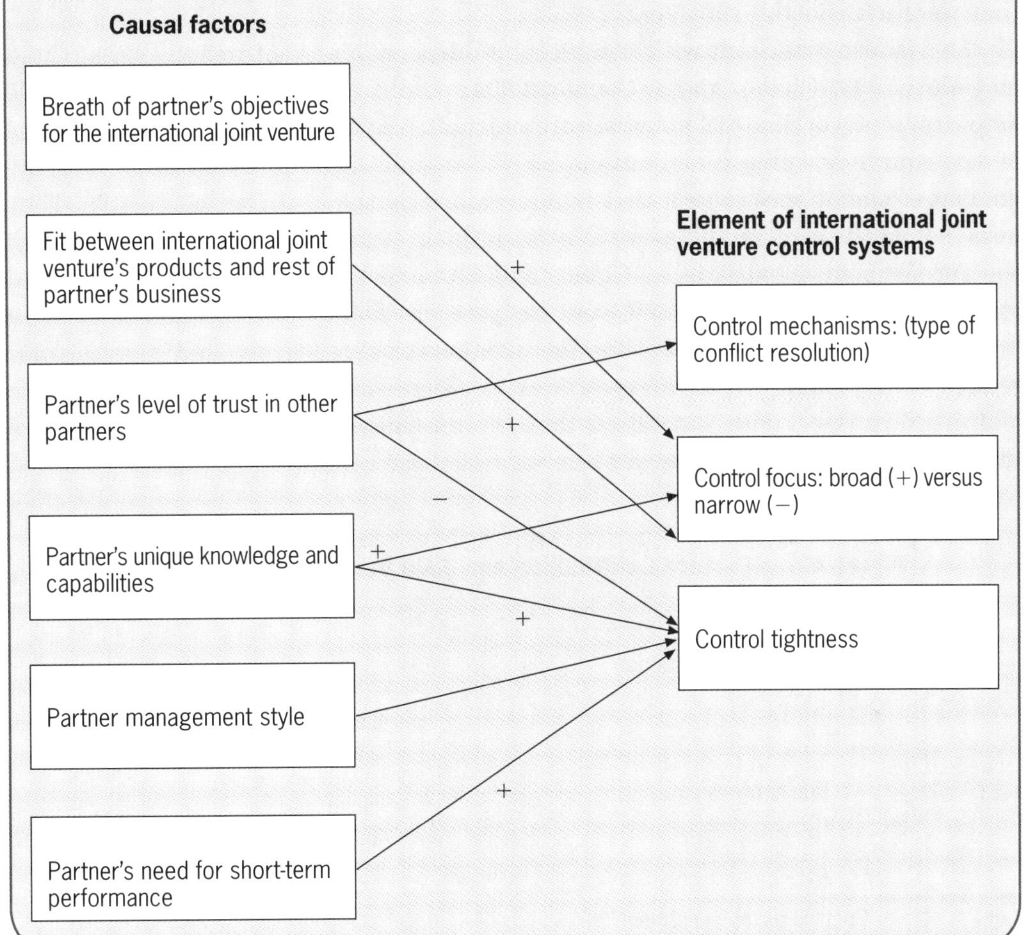

Source: Groot T.L.C.M. and Merchant K.A., Control of international joint ventures. *Accounting Organisations and Society*, 25. Copyright 2000 by *Accounting Organisations and Society*. Reprinted by permission of Elsevier.

of control. They found that several factors not related to equity ownership influenced the control focus, control tightness and the control mechanisms used in the joint venture (see Figure 4.3). These factors were the breath of the partner's objectives (positively related to a broad control focus), whether the joint venture's products were part of the core business of the parent (positively related to control tightness), partner trust (use of control mechanisms – related to control tightness), partner unique knowledge and capabilities (positively related to broad control focus and control tightness), management style (related to control tightness) and the need for short-term performance (positively related to control tightness). One of the conclusions drawn was that non-equity factors drove the types and nature of controls that were used in the joint ventures.

This is also consistent with two recent studies on joint ventures in China (Child and Yan, 1999; Chalos and O'Connor, 2004). Child and Yan's (1999) large-scale empirical study of Sino-US joint venture partners provided evidence of the influence of non-equity resource contributions on the appointment of expatriates and the amount of operational control that is maintained by the contributing partner. They note that equity ownership has an indirect influence on operational controls through the appointment of expatriates. Chalos and O'Connor's (2004) large-scale empirical study of over 200 Sino-US joint venture partners found that the higher relative knowledge contribution of the foreign partner was positively and significantly related to the employment of expatriates, decision control and socialisation in the joint venture (see Figure 4.4). Both the US and Chinese partners' responses were consistent for the significance and the sign of these relationships.

Figure 4.4 Partner Contribution and Joint Venture Control Model

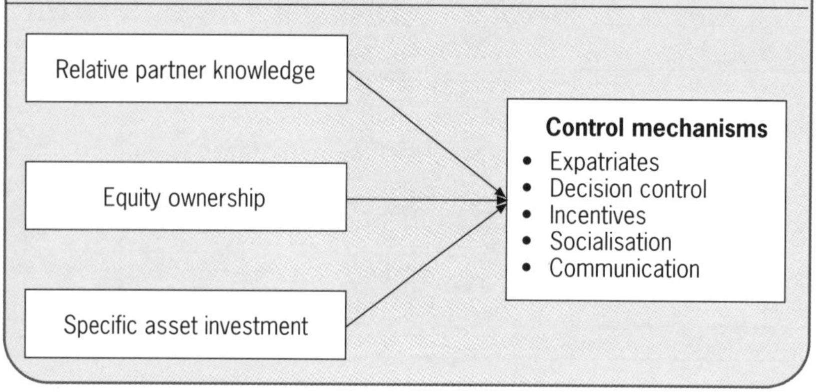

Source: Chalos, P. and O'Connor, N.G. (2004). Determinants of various controls in US-Sino joint ventures. *Accounting Organisations and Society*, 7.

SUMMARY

This chapter introduced the control issues that are associated with the management of international joint ventures with particular reference to China. The first part contrasted joint ventures with subsidiaries and presented a general framework of control that was useful in exploring the types and nature of control of joint ventures. Here it was explained how the joint venture is a special entity that is typically characterised by multiple owners, strategies, contributions and outcome expectations. While these features are often the exact reason for the formation of a joint venture, the same features make the control of the entity difficult and ultimate success elusive. The second part outlined the control typologies of joint ventures which include the special link between contributions, strategy, the location and types of control mechanisms. Several examples of control mechanisms commonly employed in the joint venture agreement and as management controls were given in the third part. Several types of controls were identified as being commonly used in joint ventures, including the use of safeguards, expatriates, decision controls, performance measurement and reward systems, and socialisation and communication routines. The final part reviewed the recent literature on the influences on the use of various controls in joint ventures, with particular reference to Sino-foreign joint ventures. It was noted that the need for and the scope of management control is particularly related to the level of non-cash contributions by the foreign partner.

QUESTIONS

1) What are the benefits of entering into a joint venture compared to setting up a wholly owned subsidiary?
2) In what ways does a joint venture add to the complexity of controlling multinational operations?
3) A joint venture can be described as two partners sleeping on the same bed but having different dreams. Explain.
4) What is the sequence of setting up agreement and management controls in a joint venture?
5) What important independent variables does transactions costs theory suggest for understanding the types of controls that should be used in joint ventures?
6) What non-equity ownership factors are likely to be important determinants of controls in joint ventures?
7) What does "obsolescing bargaining power" mean for how control over a joint venture may change over time?
8) What are the different strategic objectives that are typically associated with setting up a joint venture? Give examples of these objectives in the China context?

CASE STUDY 13

Fortune Ltd – The Balanced Scorecard in a Sino-US Joint Venture in China

CASE BACKGROUND

Fortune Ltd is a Sino-US joint venture located in Guangdong that was founded in 1994 with a 90% equity injection by a US pharmaceutical manufacturer and 10% equity held by a Chinese government department. Fortune Ltd was a state-owned enterprise before being acquired by the foreign investor. The US parent company is a large pharmaceutical company that is ranked among the top ten of generic sales in the world in 2001. Its core products include global human generics, active pharmaceutical ingredients and animal health goods. The group strategy of the US parent is: "Making medicine accessible, clear vision, dedicated leadership and quality people".

The aim of Fortune Ltd is "to be the leader in China-branded generic business in five years". In 2003, Fortune Ltd achieved a break-even position and is making profits in 2004. The main product of the joint venture constitutes 35% of total sales of the factory and a market share of 70% in southern China, all of which is from domestic sales. Although Fortune Ltd contributes around 1% of the sales turnover for the US parent, which is comparatively small, it serves as the market seeker in China for the group. In addition to the regional office in Guangdong, Fortune Ltd is projecting to set up a branch in Shanghai. It hires 460 staff, 200 of whom have technical backgrounds, and 300 are secondary graduates.

After the formation of Fortune Ltd, the US parent soon realised that the joint venture had many operational problems and concluded that:

I wish to acknowledge the assistance of Elaine Feng in the preparation of this case study. This case was developed as a basis for class discussion rather than to illustrate either effective or ineffective handling of an administrative situation.

- production staff still had an iron-bowl mindset,
- sales staff were not professionally trained,
- they had an old product range (mainly list A products, whose selling prices are determined by the government, resulting in low profit margin), and
- the cost of production and operation activities was high.

To achieve the group corporate strategies, the US parent had to implement a strategic management system to control this newly acquired joint venture to achieve the desired organisational outcomes. The main objectives were to motivate employees' performance, increase productivity and operation efficiency, enhance customer satisfaction and improve profitability.

STRATEGIC COMPETITIVE ADVANTAGE

In order to sustain a winning position in the market, Fortune Ltd identified its strategic competitive advantage (SCA) based on the key success factors analysis (see Figure 1). This analysis involves the ranking of several potential key success factors on two dimensions, value to the customer and ability to beat competitors. For Fortune Ltd's case 20 key success factors were identified by management and ranked on these two dimensions. From Figure 1, we can see that the top five key success factors are the strategic competitive advantage. The SCA statement of Fortune Ltd is: "We will win by having high quality, good customer service, long-term customer relationships, GMP products (full range) and high company awareness in Guangdong."

Amid ongoing evolution of competitors and the external environment, it was important for the Fortune Ltd senior management team to clarify their answer to a fundamental question: "Why should customers buy from our company?" In order to find the answer to this question, the senior management team analysed the value proposition of the company: "What variables are most important to our target markets, such as pricing, quality, time, selection, service, customer relationship and company image (Beiman and Sun, 2003)?"

Value proposition can be broken down into business leadership in one of the five major areas: 1) low cost, 2) product leadership, 3) customer solutions, 4) system lock-in, and 5) a unique combination of product and service.

From the above SCA analysis, the senior management found that Fortune Ltd's SCA is on customer service and relationships. So the value proposition should stress the provision of complete customer solutions. For this value proposition, customers should feel that the company understands them and is capable of providing them with customised products and services tailored to their needs. The value proposition of Fortune Ltd is outlined in Figure 2.

Figure 1 Strategic Competitive Advantage Matrix

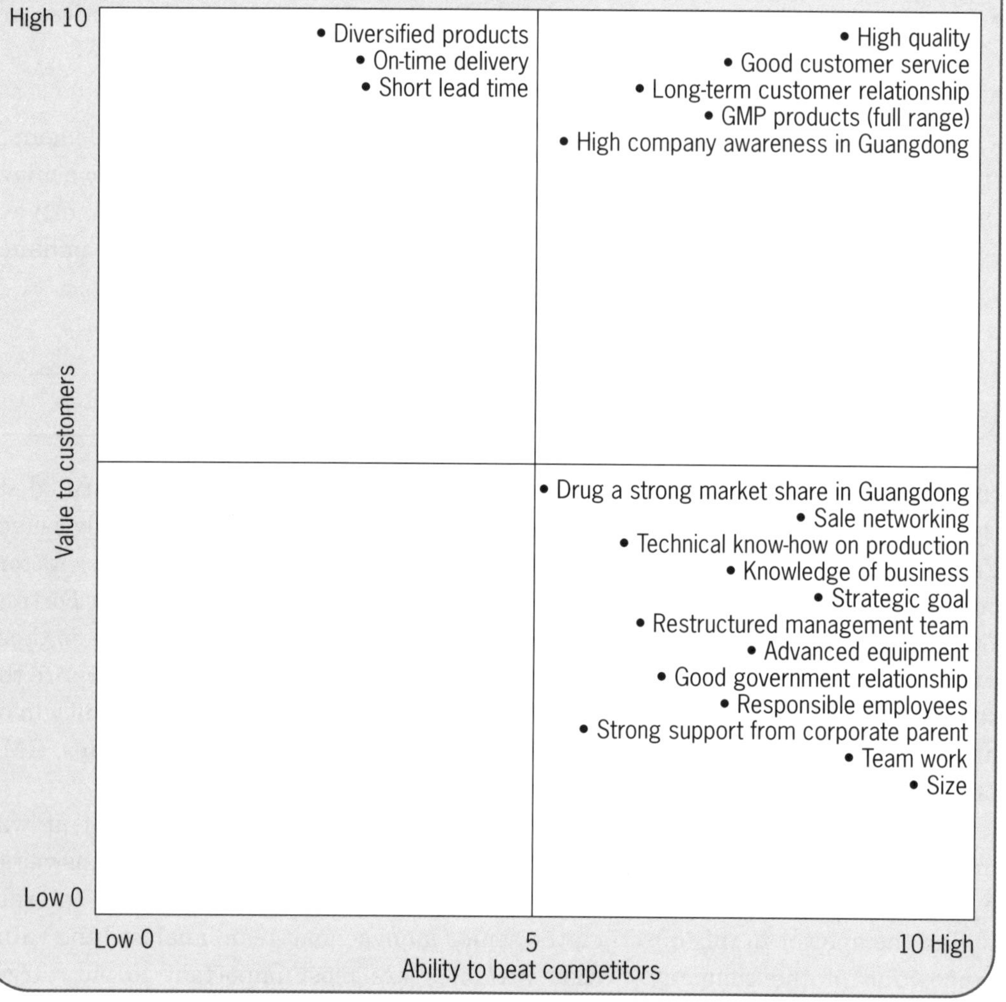

Figure 2 Customer Value Proposition (Customer Retention Strategy)

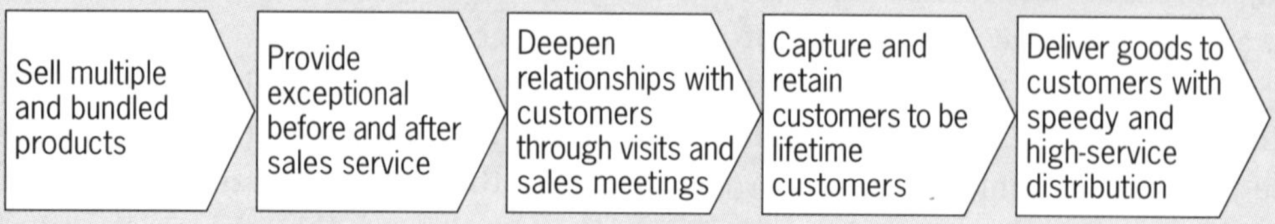

BALANCED SCORECARD IMPLEMENTATION

To tackle these main problems, the US parent must communicate its vision, mission, value and strategy to Fortune joint venture staff, and align the behaviours of managers and low-level personnel in order to achieve the group's goal. Therefore, US parent management decided to implement the balanced scorecard (BSC) approach in Fortune in early 2002. The BSC project was expected to be rolled out across managerial level and above over the first year (2002), then down to all lower functions and levels from the second year (2003). The timeline schedule for the implementation in the first year is shown in Figure 3.

The implementation of the BSC process within Fortune Ltd was supported by a head office consultant who has helped several of the US parent's regional offices to implement BSC and has many experiences in solving the management problems similar to those in Fortune Ltd. In the first of a three-month stay (January to March 2002), the consultant conducted training sessions for all directorial and managerial levels. In the second month, he helped the management team set up BSC in Fortune Ltd, including objectives and critical success factors. In the third month, he helped each department to set up their departmental key performance indicators (KPIs). The KPIs were arranged accordingly to the four perspectives of the BSC: 1) financial, 2) customer, 3) internal business and 4) learning and growth (see Table 1).

With the implementation of BSC, Fortune Ltd could achieve the following objectives, which correspond with each of the four perspectives. First, Fortune Ltd provided training courses to re-orientate production staff away from the state-owned enterprise (SOE) mindset and to enhance the professionalism of the sales staff (learning and growth perspective). Second, the production and sales staff were made accountable to meet key indicators associated with the cost of production and customer service (internal business perspective). Third, sales staff were made aware of the importance of the linkage between having good customer relationships, image and reputation such as trust (i.e., how the customer feels about the experience of purchasing from the company) and the ability of Fortune Ltd to capture market share in China (financial perspective).

RESULTS OF USING THE BALANCED SCORECARD

BSC has been implemented in Fortune Ltd since January 2002. During the BSC implementation, the US parent has achieved the expected results in Fortune Ltd.

Figure 3 The Timeline Schedule for Implementation in the First Year

Schedule	Jan 02	Feb 02	Mar 02	Apr 02	May 02	Jun 02	Jul 02	Aug–Dec 02	Jan 03	Feb 03
1) Training from consultant	■									
2) Set up balanced scorecard – objectives and CSFs		■								
3) Develop departmental KPIs and cmplete KPI form – directors			■							
4) Review all the directors' KPIs – CEO				■						
5) Develop individual KPIs and complete KPI form – managers					■					
6) The directors and managers discuss and agree upon the KPIs						■				
7) HR completes all the BSC and KPI database							■			
8) Mid-year review on results of KPI – director and manager levels							■			
9) Adopt "Plan Do Check Act" sessions								■		
10) Year-end review on results of KPI – director and manager levels									■	
11) KPI measurement – all levels									■	
12) Submit the total company KPI review to the corporate parent										■

Code:

CSFs Critical success factors
KPIs Key performance indicators

Table 1 Fortune Ltd's Balanced Scorecard Performance Objectives

Strategic theme: Internal product development

Panel A: Financial

Strategic perspective	*Objective*	*Measure (CSF)*	*Target (KPI)*	*Initiative*
Revenue growth What we want/need to achieve in the marketplace in order to reach our financial goals?	• Operating margin research	–	10%	–
	• Revenue increase annually	–	15%	–
	• Return on capital employed	–	8%	–
–	• Grow revenue from new products	–		–

Panel B: Customer

Strategic perspective	*Objective*	*Measure (CSF)*	*Target (KPI)*	*Initiative*
Innovative What we have to do for customers in order to achieve the above marketplace goals?	• Build strong brand image	• Create brand awareness via introduction to distributors • Key products and star products awareness	No. of public relations events: • Participate in national commercial meetings • Advertisement in trade magazine or journal • Survey of company awareness	• Relationship management programme • Gain-sharing programme
	• Competitive prices	• Best price to quality ratio • Benchmark with leading products – quality issue • Lower COGS (optimise purchasing of raw materials, higher production volume)	• Protect key products' prices • Achieve gross margin price level	
	• High service level	• Information regarding product status • Speedy and accurate information to customers • Product quality, logistic management	• Reduce customers' complaints • Deliver on time to customers	

Table 1 Fortune Ltd's Balanced Scorecard Performance Objectives (Cont'd)

Panel C: Internal processes

Strategic perspective	*Objective*	*Measure (CSF)*	*Target (KPI)*	*Initiative*
World class internal product What we have to do well internally to ensure the achievement of market goals?	• Improve cost of goods	• Establish database. • Material cost control • Productivity improvement • Production cycle time reduction • Facility utilisation increase	• 4% GM improvement in 2002 • Production line productivity • Inventory turn increase between 4.5–5 times in 2002 • Production cycle time reduction • Facility utilisation increased by 50% to 70%	• Supplier liaison/ technology transfer
	• Reengineering, research and development capability	• Enhance product development – pipeline management • New technology – introduction	• Identify number of new or potential products • Number of new technology and material introduction	• Development cycle time reengineering
	• Improve customer relationship	• Establish customer service function • Set up customer survey system. • Order fulfilment	• Customer satisfaction survey	
	• Improve internal operating system	• Establish database of operation and improve report system • Improve planning and inventory control system	Set up: • Database of operation and report system • Planning and inventory control system • Distribution system management	

Table 1 Fortune Ltd's Balanced Scorecard Performance Objectives (Cont'd)

Panel D: Learning and growth

Strategic perspective	*Objective*	*Measure (CSF)*	*Target (KPI)*	*Initiative*
Stable high talent workforce How do we enable competencies, systems and culture to achieve the internal and market goals?	• Upgrade skill of employee	• Professional training • Responsible and committed employee • Competency development	• Master training plan • Training courses and hours • Performance evaluation	• Competency model • New hiring programme
	• Improve internal and external communications	• Internal newsletter • Team building • Willingness to share information and knowledge • Further efforts to promote communication among divisions and business partners	• Publish internal newsletter. • Number of employee communication meetings • Number of customer communication meetings • Number of users for BSC	• Supervisory training • Benefits programme
	• Commitment- and result-oriented culture	• Implement job description for all levels • Performance management • Open-minded approach and trustworthy • Willingness to change behaviour • Positive-thinking culture	• Number of implementing job description for all levels • Number of improving projects • Number of SOPs reviews • Number of new ideas implemented	

Figure 4 Balanced Scorecard Outcomes

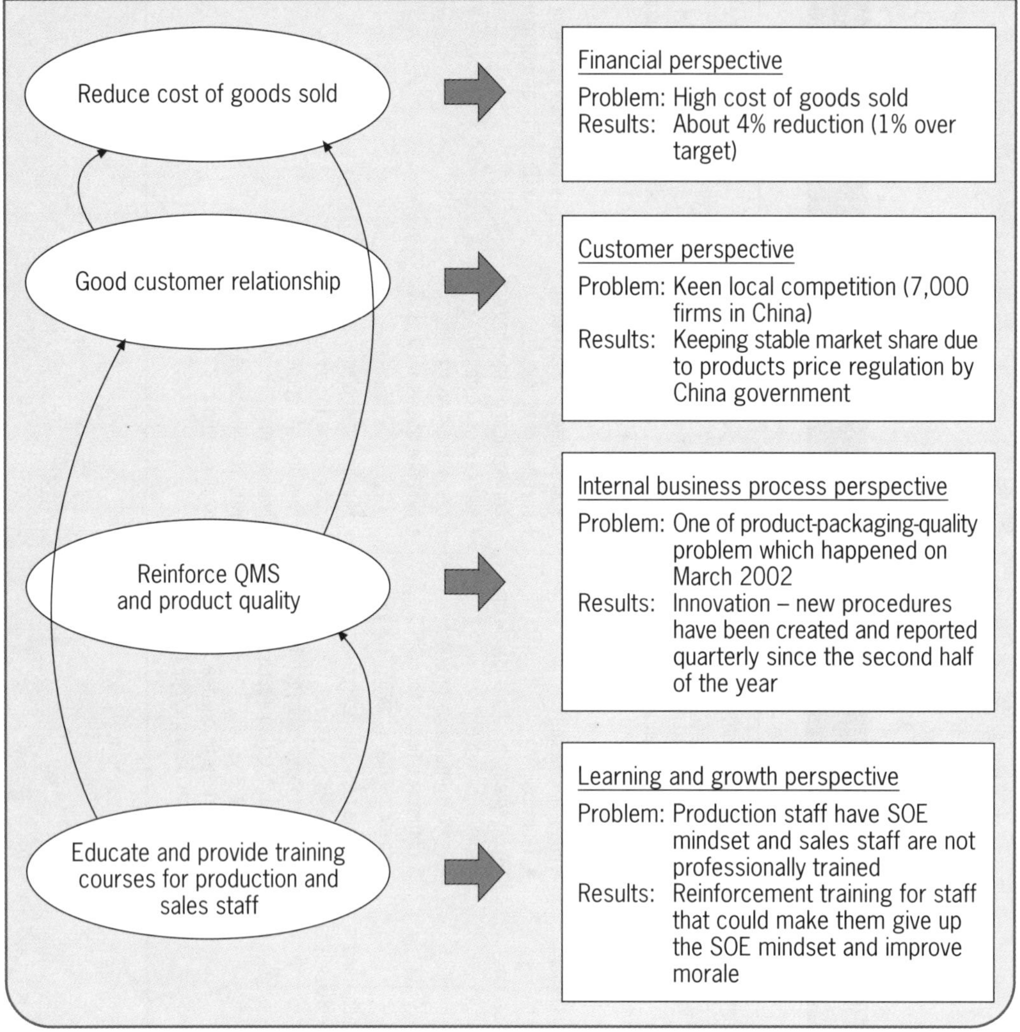

For example: the reduction cost of goods sold from 70% to 64% was 1% over target (65%). BSC helped Fortune Ltd to respond to unexpected events. For example, it traced the root cause of a product-packaging-quality problem to the operator's lack of familiarity and skill in operating the new packaging machine. This was improved after operator training, machine adjustment and reinforcement of site management (see Figure 4). The training and contingency plans present an opportunity for improving the BSC in the future.

CASE STUDY QUESTIONS

1) What are the theoretical underpinnings of the BSC?
2) What are the costs of the BSC in Fortune Ltd's case?
3) What were the main reasons for the US parent to adopt the BSC in its joint venture in China? Did the adoption of the BSC achieve its purpose?
4) In what ways may culture impact on the successful adoption of the BSC in China? What steps did Fortune Ltd take to minimise this risk?
5) Draw a strategy map that reflects the connections between the objectives under each of the four BSC perspectives (see Table 1).

CASE STUDY 14

AB Holdings Limited – A New Incentive Scheme

COMPANY BACKGROUND

AB Holdings Limited (referred to as the Group) was established in the early 1990s and successfully listed on the Main Board of the Stock Exchange of Hong Kong in the mid-1990s. The principal activities of the Group are the trading of electronic components and assisting some famous brand names in television to enter the China market. In the early part of 2000, the Group diversified its businesses into wireless applications protocol (WAP) business and telecommunication services.

In early 2001, the Group entered into a joint venture with a Hong Kong company to form a new company called CD Ltd for the purposes of promoting telecommunication services in China. The vision of CD Ltd is to become a leading provider of telecommunication services in southern China. The detailed structure is shown in Figure 1. In August 2001, CD Ltd formed an equity joint venture (EJV) called ThreeG Inc with two China partners (see Figure 1). As a result of this, the Group owns 18.33% (55% × 33.33%) of effective holdings of the EJV because the shareholding distribution is strictly bound by the telecommunication regulation of the People's Republic of China (PRC).

The core businesses of the EJV are broadly divided into three categories.

1) Selling of telephone calling cards (telephone cards) in several regions of the mainland China (i.e., Beijing, Shanghai, Guangdong and Fu Jin).
2) Selling of Internet service traffic through the establishment of the data centres in Beijing and Shanghai.
3) Operating as an Internet service provider (ISP) and Web server hosting business.

I wish to acknowledge the assistance of Ray Siaw in the preparation of this case study. This case was developed as a basis for class discussion rather than to illustrate either effective or ineffective handling of an administrative situation.

Figure 1 Organisation Structure of AB Holdings Ltd

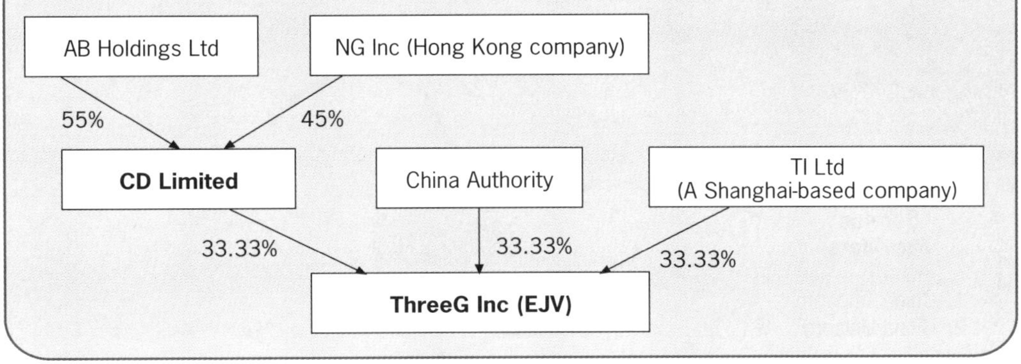

Due to the strong ties between CD Ltd and China Telecom, the rate of subscription to the Internet bandwidth service was good. However, the profit was very slim due to strong competition. Although the turnover of the EJV increased from HK$4.5 million for 12 months for the year ended June 2002 (2001/2002) to HK$17.55 million for the year ended June 2003 (2002/2003), the loss from operations increased from HK$10.05 million in 2001/2002 to HK$19.2 million in 2002/2003; there were significant differences in the two fiscal years. For the accounting purposes of associated companies, a share of the loss of the EJV was incorporated into the consolidated financial statements of CD Ltd, which ultimately affected CD Ltd's financial results. The turnover of the EJV was around RMB19.5 million in the year ended June 2004 and the net loss was about RMB2 million for the same period.

As detailed in the turnover model in Figure 2, the cash generated from Internet service provider (ISP) traffic volume and telephone card sales is passed directly from the distributors to the local agents of China Telecom and China Unicom – two of the largest Chinese telecom operators. The proceeds from the EJV are booked as accounts receivable and the amount is derived from the traffic volume reports and calling cards sales reports which are prepared by the agent.

Figure 2 Telecom Services Distribution Model

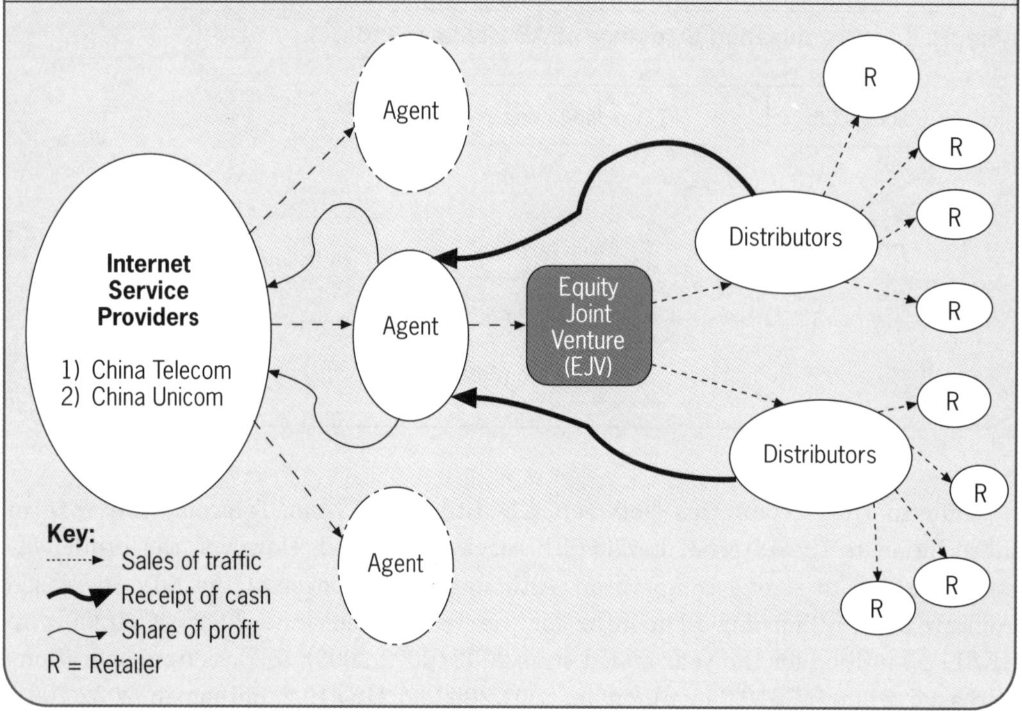

ACCOUNTS RECEIVABLE COLLECTION AND INCENTIVE PROBLEMS FACING THE EJV

Collection of Accounts Receivable

In the turnover model in Figure 3, the agent obtains the telephone card sales from the distributors and the traffic volume from the service providers for the production of the relevant reports for onward transmission to the EJV together with cash from the sales. Even though the cash collection cycle as explained in Figure 3 requires four months in total, the EJV accepts it as the business potential is large when the market of the mainland China opens as a result of China's accession to the WTO. More businessmen entering the China market will use telephone cards to make international calls.

The main problem facing the EJV is in the collection of account receivables. The cause is twofold: the lengthy receivables practice in China and the fact that the submission of turnover reports to the EJV are generally late by up to four months. First, it is a common practice in China to use invoice accounting. The duration of the

Figure 3 Cash Collection Cycle

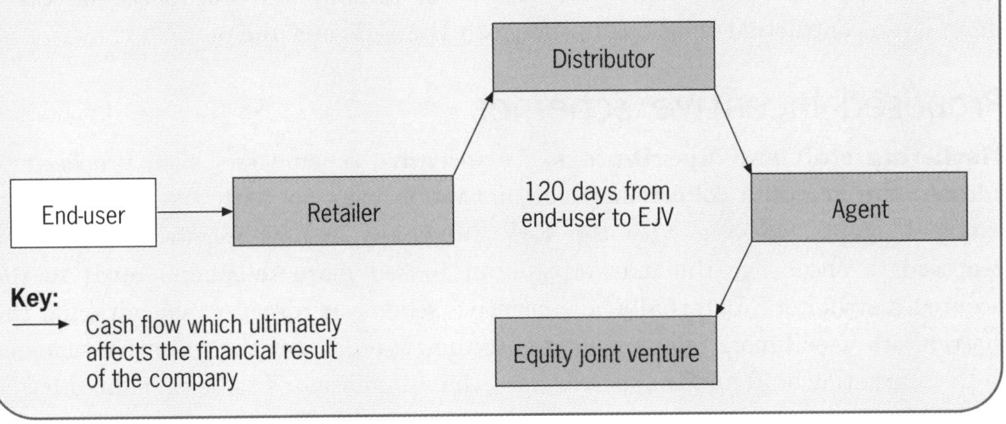

receivables is very long. This poses problems to the EJV because the risk of the debt becoming bad is extremely high. From past records, the EJV has set 10% of bad debts provision for the receivables. The management of the EJV has estimated that the receivables outstanding for four months are typically written off completely.

Second, the delayed submission of turnover reports stems from the nature of the telecom contracting arrangements in China. The EJV has a contractual relationship with the service providers but not with the agent. The agents can only be appointed by one of the two major traffic suppliers. The EJV can do business with either one of them. The monopolistic environment is very clear as the local companies that are supported by the government always dominate the market. The agents are designated by the service providers, China Telecom and China Unicom. The service provider pays the commissions to agent, one agent serves many telecommunication services companies at the same time, thus they may not be willing to boost the turnover of the company without additional benefits. As there is no contractual relationship between the agent and the EJV, the former has no fiduciary duty to submit the financial reports earlier. Though the distributors are nominated by the EJV, they will never report the sales of cards to it directly. Consequently, the agent is the only one simultaneously acting as the information collector and conveyor. He collects the traffic usage report from service providers and the analysis of sales of calling cards from distributors and conveys the information to the EJV.

Current Incentive Scheme

The EJV has an incentive scheme for the marketing staff which comprises a small percentage of commission with a maximum of RMB5,000 per staff per month. After an evaluation, however it was found that the current scheme is not attractive and does not motivate the marketing staff to sell more. As for the distributors and agents, there is no formal incentive scheme or commission reward scheme since there is no contractual relationship between the EJV and them.

Proposed Incentive Schemes

Marketing staff and distributors. An incentive scheme has been proposed to address the accounts collection problem that focuses on both the internal and external agents working with the EJV. Internally, a new incentive scheme is proposed to encourage the marketing staff to sell more telephone cards to the licenced distributors. Externally, an incentive scheme is aimed at encouraging the distributors to sell more telephone cards to the retailers. For the incentive schemes to the marketing staff and the distributors, the commission is to be calculated based on the increased number of sales of the telephone cards to end-users (see Table 1). It is assumed that the more the telephone cards of the EJV are available in the markets, the higher the chance of the cards being sold to the end-users. Commission is based on the increased number of telephone cards sold to the end-users.

Agents. The proposed incentive scheme for the agent comprises a commission that is based on the shortened number of days of submitting the reports and remitting the cash to the EJV (see Table 2). Since the agent is assigned by the service provider with no contractual relationship with the EJV, an additional clause will be added to the contract entered between the EJV and the service providers which will be subject to approval by the latter.

The bad debts of the EJV per last financial year was approximately 10% of the trade debts which was RMB2 million. From Figure 4, the curves representing the estimated amount of debts which can be collected back went up from RMB300,000 to RMB1,900,000 and the proposed amount of commission to be paid to the agent went up from RMB100,000 to RMB1,267,000 if the number of days of reporting and remitting can be shortened from 10 to 90 days respectively. The gap difference between the two lines is the expected net benefit to the EJV upon implementation of the proposed incentive scheme.

Total incidental cost (the commission) to the increased revenue is 12%. It seems justifiable. However, other additional costs such as implementation and restructuring costs also need to be taken into consideration. The normal delay in submitting the reports and the cash remittance is three months. From the financial reports, the annual bad debts written off is RMB2 million. The more the days shortened, the more commission to be paid but the more the bad debts can be reduced.

Table 1 Proposed Incentive Scheme for Marketing Staff and Distributors

• Average annual sale of telephone cards	600,000 pcs
• Total value of telephone cards sold per year	RMB65,000,000
• Share of revenue by the EJV	30%
• Average annual revenue from sale of telephone cards for the EJV	RMB19,500,000
• Average sale of telephone cards per month	50,000 pcs
• Number of licenced distributors *(approximately)*	10
• Average sale of telephone cards per month per licenced distributor	5,000 pcs
• Number of marketing staff	5
• Targeted increased revenue *(approximately double the existing)*	RMB18,000,000
• Total commission paid to marketing staff	RMB360,000
• Total commission paid to the licenced distributors	RMB1,800,000

Panel A: Marketing staff

Number of telephone cards sold by each marketing staff	Commission paid on the next 1,000 cards sold beyond each level *(RMB)*	Accumulated commission *(RMB)*
5,000	–	5,000
5,000	1,000 (1)	6,000
6,000	1,100 (1.1)	7,200
7,000	1,200 (1.2)	8,300
8,000	1,300 (1.3)	9,600
9,000	1,400 (1.4)	11,000
10,000 (Max)		

Panel B: Distributors

Number of telephone cards sold by each licenced distributor	Commission paid on the next 1,000 cards sold beyond each level *(RMB)*	Accumulated commission *(RMB)*
5,000	1,000 (1)	1,000
6,000	2,000 (2)	3,000
7,000	3,000 (3)	6,000
8,000	4,000 (4)	10,000
9,000	5,000 (5)	15,000
10,000 (Max)		

Table 2 Proposed Incentive Scheme for the Agent

No. of days shortened	Annual commission to be paid *(RMB)*	Bad debts which can be received	Total bad debt reduction
1–10	100,000	15%	300,000
11–20	167,000	25%	500,000
21–30	233,000	35%	700,000
31–40	450,000	45%	900,000
41–50	550,000	55%	1,100,000
51–60	650,000	65%	1,300,000
61–70	1,000,000	75%	1,500,000
71–80	1,133,000	85%	1,700,000
81–90	1,267,000	95%	1,900,000

Figure 4 Cost and Benefit Analysis of the Agent Incentive Scheme

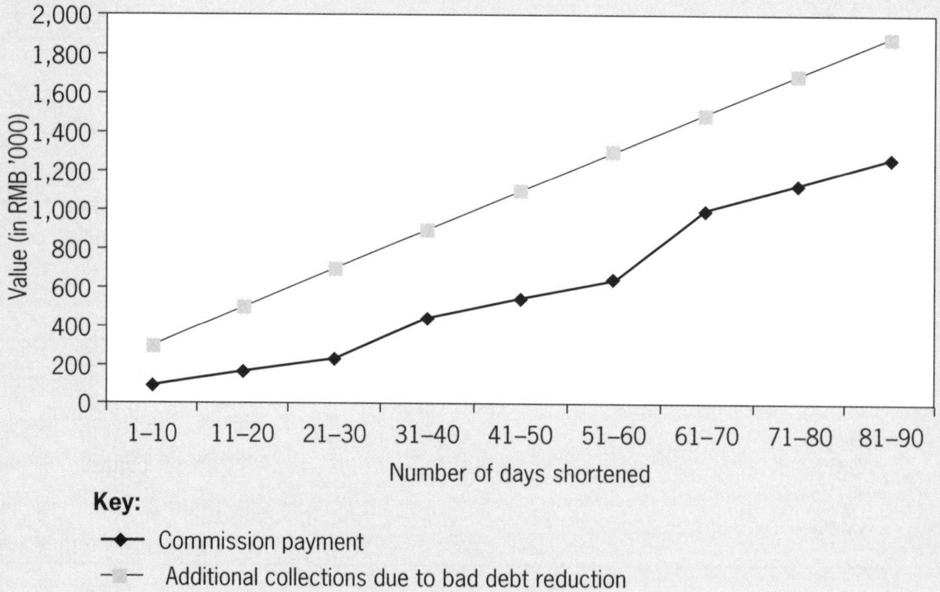

CASE STUDY QUESTIONS

1) What were the regulatory and contractual challenges faced by CD Ltd in China?
2) To what extent were these challenges imposed on CD Ltd? What were the payoffs for CD Ltd in entering China?
3) What are the advantages of the proposed incentive scheme?
4) What are the assumptions of the different incentive schemes? Are these assumptions valid?
5) What are the alternative control mechanisms that the EJV can use to motivate its marketing staff and other staff in the venture?

CASE STUDY 15

ECG Group – Fraud and the Liquidation of a Joint Venture in China

INTRODUCTION

ECG Group is a multinational enterprise that is involved in supplying building control systems to construction industry projects throughout the world. ECG Group has two main subsidiaries in the US (ECG US) and Singapore (ECG Sing Ltd). With a burgeoning construction industry, China provided an opportunity for ECG Group to expand its overseas operations. ECG Sing Ltd first developed its presence in 1990 when a representative office in Shanghai was established for coordinating selling and engineering activities. Contracts were signed between ECG Group and the client. The purpose of the representative office was to act as a liaison office between client and the head office. Periodically, the head office sent engineers to provide local engineers with product updates.

However, it was soon apparent that the representative office model was restrictive and not suitable for the potential demand and growth for the systems that were built by ECG Group. Consequently, ECG Group decided to expand its operations through a joint venture. This enabled the expansion of both its manufacturing and selling activities. In 1994, the US subsidiary formed an alliance in Shanghai with a local manufacturer in building instruments. The joint venture, known as the Realton JV, was set up to manufacture building systems equipment. The joint venture encountered problems in the years that followed and ended up in liquidation (see Figure 1).

I am grateful for the assistance of Cliff Tse in the preparation of this case study. The names, data and dates of this case have been slightly changed in order to preserve the anonymity of the firms involved. This case was developed as a basis for class discussion rather than to illustrate either effective or ineffective handling of an administrative situation.

Figure 1 Timeline for Development of Realton (Shanghai) JV Ltd

June 1994	1994–1998	1999	2000	2001
Establishment of joint venture	Manufacturing of control valves	Conversion to engineering company to install control valves	Management fraud	Liquidation

Legal and Strategic Framework

The joint venture was formed between ECG US and CIG Ltd (a Shanghai-listed company), with shareholdings of 60% and 40% respectively. Part of the joint venture agreement was that ECG US would supply the technology and train local engineers, while the China partner would undertake to market ECG Group's products. The joint venture was formed to explore the production of building system equipment such as air-conditioning valves and fire-safety equipment that is used in building construction projects (see Table 1). ECG US appointed the general manager while the local joint venture partner appointed two assistant general managers (see Figure 2.1).

Table 1 Partners in the Joint Venture

Partners	ECG US (60%)	CIG China Ltd (40%)
Core business	Building automation Proven sales track record in the US	Temperature control instrument A Shanghai-listed company with strong sales in building automation products in China
Origin	United States	China
Contribution	Contribute 60% of capital and supply technology and train local engineers	Contribute 40% of capital and market ECG Group's products
Partner strategic aim	To secure a profitable return on investment	To share a stable return to complement its main business

Figure 2 Organisation Structure of Realton (Shanghai) JV Ltd

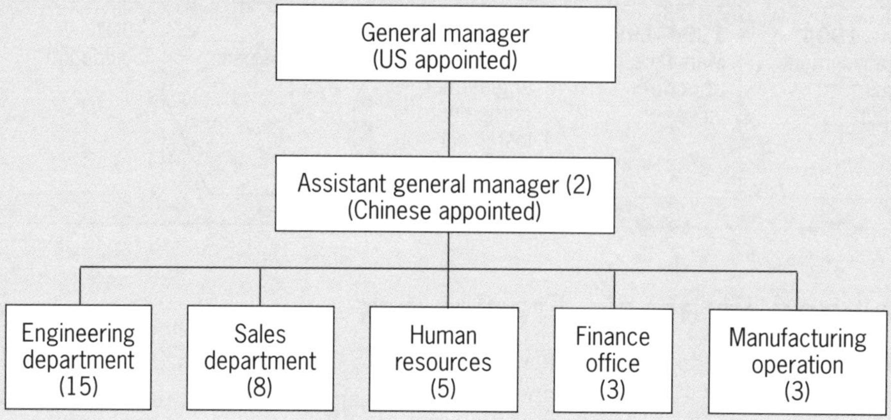

LOSS OF CONTROL AND MANAGEMENT FRAUD

The joint venture began to manufacture goods in 1994, and customers immediately complained about products not meeting their specifications. Product sales were weak and the US partner requested remedies. In mid-1997, the US partner adopted the general manager's advice to stop manufacturing products due to the lack of sales. The general manager also hired his own team of sales managers. In 1998 and 1999 sales grew, but the general manager died of heart attack in April 1999. From that time no new general manager was appointed. Operations continued without leadership and the accounting numbers were not reported. Sales managers took up contracts on their own authority. The acting general manager divided the company into separate groups that worked for his own benefit.

In January 2000, the finance director for the Asia-Pacific region discovered an unrecorded liability of US$560,000. Losses accumulated to US$690,000, and prospects for continuing the operations were not good. The finance department, which had previously been under the control of the general manager, had generated fictitious transactions involving goods or services. The order book was falsified to show good sales prospects, but 90% of the contracts secured were making losses and the finance manager did not report the irregularities. In China, each company has two common seals that are used in place of authorised signatures: a contract common seal and a company common seal. Individuals who hold either of these common seals can represent the company in banking transactions and contracts. In this case, hidden contractual obligations were endorsed with the contract seal without the need for a valid signature.

Independent auditors were subsequently brought in and they discovered that the holding company for local joint venture partners had set up parallel companies to compete directly with the joint venture, using the foreign investor's own technology and market information and diverting the most profitable contracts to their own operations. Without independent auditors to review the books and records, headquarters may never have discovered such activities.

Memo A to Vice President of ECG US from the Asia-Pacific Finance Director

I am presenting the following findings of why some contracts are signed between CIG and a trading company called YEFA, which operates under CIG.

In auditing the books and records of Realton JV, it has been discovered that Realton JV has been using a trading company controlled by CIG, Realton JV's parent company, to transact businesses. In addition to quasi-contracts signed between customers and CIG, a service contract has also been signed between CIG and Realton JV. The purpose of the transaction is that a trading company is to handle the importation of foreign equipment while arranging disbursement of US dollars to ECG US. The trading company will receive renminbi or other currency at an inflated exchange rate to cover their service fee.

Figure A: Transactions without a trading company. When Realton JV

Figure A Transactions without a Trading Company

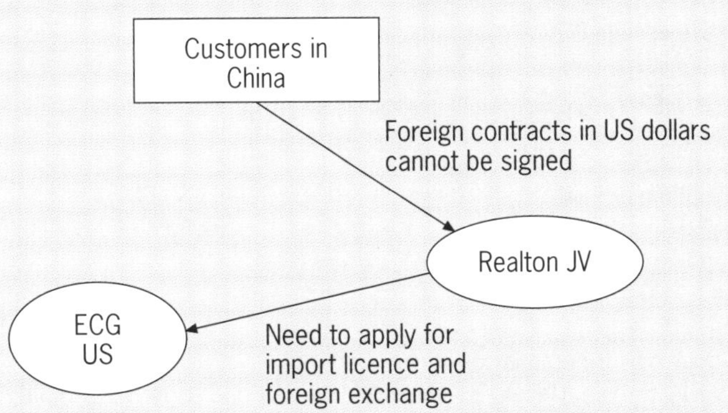

obtained the business licence, their business scope was the manufacturing of building systems equipment. At present, their business scope does not include any project installation and management. This hinders Realton JV's development into project management because the Chinese government does not allow any foreign importation of equipment or customs clearance of equipment.

Figure B: Transactions with a trading company. Realton JV has turned to CIG for assistance, using a trading company to contract for projects that Realton JV cannot transact because the scope of business is restricted under the present business licence. There are two types of contracts customers are allowed to enter into: US-dollar and renminbi-denominated contracts. For the US dollar contracts customers are able to sign contract with CIG/YEFA. In return CIG is signing service agreements with Realton JV that will entail the placement of orders with ECG US. Once CIG collects money from customers (in renminbi) it arranges a reimbursement to ECG US for the order amount that Realton JV is due to pay ECG US. Under this transaction, Realton JV receives renminbi for the difference between the contract amount and the purchase cost (after setting off the service fee that is received by CIG/YEFA). For renminbi contracts, the customers remit money to Realton JV, which is then passed on to CIG. CIG assists in the remittance of the

Figure B Contracts Handled through a Trading Company

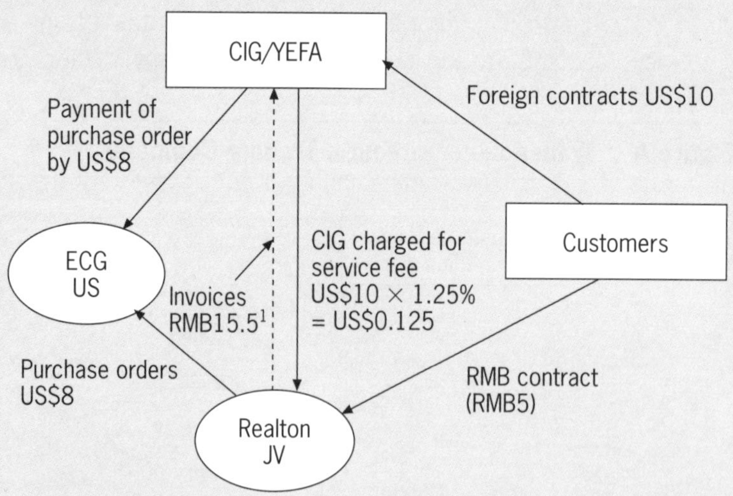

[1] Invoicing for commission
US$(10 – 8) – US$0.125 service fee = US$1.875 × 8.3 = RMB15.56

equivalent in US dollars to ECG US when it receives the renminbi from Realton JV.

The inter-company reconciliation between Realton JV and ECG US shows a balance of US$1.863 million due by Realton JV. Out of that amount, US$109,000 is owed by CIG/YEFA in that customers have not paid CIG/YEFA. There is no contractual liability between ECG US and CIG/YEFA because Realton JV has placed orders directly and CIG will settle the amount when monies are directly received from customers.

I hope that the above report will help us to gain an insight into the background of the problem, because it appears that the trading company has been taking away Realton JV's profit. Whether someone has "cooked the books" will be left to the auditors to determine.

Memo B to the Vice President of ECG US from the Asia-Pacific Finance Director

When the joint venture changed its business nature from manufacturing activities with more than RMB1.4 million of imported equipment, obsolete spare parts amounting to RMB1.98 million were not written off in accordance with the accounting standards ruling at the time. Also account receivables amounting to RMB568,000 were unaccounted for. It is uncommon to issue invoices to collect dues for which a tax invoice is raised. Controlling these activities mainly calls for action from the sales managers.

Table A shows a summarised balance sheet for the best estimate of the carrying value based on the balance value as at 31 July 2001. In determining the estimate, a prudent view is taken notwithstanding the disposable value in the fixed or current assets. No adjustment has been made for payable items because any error will end in a gain and that is not on par with the prudent view.

Internal audit views are taken into consideration on the assets value. The analysis reveals the following.

- The depicted capital value of RMB11 million should be reduced to RMB2.9 million (which represents 23.3% of the original share capital).
- The depicted net assets RMB6.7 million should be net liabilities of RMB1.5 million.

Table A Reconciliation from China GAAP to US GAAP Realton JV, 31 July 2001

	Mgt accounts	Statutory *YTD Accounts (RMB)*	Adjustments *(Estimated) (RMB)*	Estimated *Value (RMB)*	(Dec) *Inc. % (RMB)*
Tangible assets	3,603,581	3,546,917	–1,982,372	1,564,545	–81%
Fixed assets	**3,603,581**	**3,546,917**	**–1,982,372**	**1,564,545**	**–81%**
Inventory	5,194,114	10,160,632	–4,369,072	5,791,560	–43%
Construction in progress		191,587	–191,587	–	
Organisational expenses		611,827	–611,827	–	
Other deferred expenses		257,177	–257,177	–	
Debtors-net trade	5,245,987	5,676,409	–567,641	5,108,768	–10%
Debtors – inter-company	430,423	–	–	–	
Advances to suppliers		225,367	–225,367	–	
Debtors – other	4,385,216	788,089	–39,405	748,685	–5%
Creditors – net trade	–1,721,147	–1,721,147	–	–1,721,147	
Creditors – inter-company	–11,103,472	–12,665,924	–	–12,665,924	
Creditors – other	–2,601,835	–222,029	–	–222,029	
Taxation	–134,433	–134,433	–	–134,433	
Net current assets	**–305,148**	**3,167,557**	**–6,262,076**	**–3,094,520**	**–198%**
Assets employed	**3,298,433**	**6,714,474**	**–8,244,448**	**–1,529,975**	**–123%**
Share capital					
Capital reserve	18,481,095	18,481,095	–	18,481,095	
Exchange variance	–165,837	–165,837	–	–165,837	
Reserves – revenue b/fwd	–10,839,298	–6,707,410	–	–6,707,410	
YTD transfers to revenue reserve	–850,939	–1,549,220	–	–1,549,220	
Asset written-down losses			–8,244,448	–8,244,448	
Total equity	**7,742,131**	**11,158,172**		**2,913,723**	**–74%**
Cash in hand and at bank	4,443,698	4,443,698	–	4,443,698	
Total debt	4,443,698	4,443,698	–	4,443,698	
Capital employed	**3,298,433**	**6,714,474**		**–1,529,975**	**–123%**

PROCESSES AND FRUSTRATIONS IN NEGOTIATING THE LIQUIDATION

By end of February 2001, after the presentation of the irregularities in the financial statements, the US party resolved to liquidate Realton JV on the understanding that 60% of the shareholding in the company was sufficient to pass the resolution in accordance with US liquidation law. However, the Chinese partner refused to agree to the cessation because the Chinese bankruptcy law stipulates that all joint venture partners must agree to the cessation of business. In addition, the Chinese partner maintained that the accounting records were proper according to the Chinese Generally Accepted Accounting Principle (GAAP). Consequently, the Chinese partner requested US$200,000 for mismanagement by the US partner.

Many parts of the review noted differences in accounting estimates for asset valuation, which meant that historical costs were recorded for the non-use of manufacturing facilities, thus resulting in the write-off of US$1.38 million. Eventually, the Chinese joint venture partner agreed to a payment of US$100,000 in compensation. An employee meeting was held to announce the closure of the joint venture and a meeting was held on the next day to start the year-long liquidation process. Liquidation commenced with an employee meeting that explained that the company was to be wound up. In the following weeks, a liquidation committee was formed by one Chinese general manager appointed by the board of directors, one finance manager and one legal adviser.

There were several difficulties in negotiating the liquidation of the joint venture. These were related to the Chinese culture, inadequate preparation of the foreign partner and other tactics used by the Chinese partner. First, in every meeting, the Chinese partner claimed that it could manage to revive the company. In a few discussions, the Chinese participants indicated they would never close the joint venture because they would lose "face" in their immediate social contacts with friends and relatives. Second, when the US acting chief representative paid visits to the Chinese partner in Shanghai he returned empty-handed because either no meeting had been scheduled by the Chinese partner or no agenda for negotiations had been tabled. Adding to the complexity was that the parties did not speak the same language and no documents were properly prepared until at a later stage when the Chinese general manager assisted in interpretation and translation during meetings.

Third, the US acting chief representative had replaced the acting general manager who was removed from office in December 2001. No formal re-registration approval was sought from the Ministry of Foreign Trade and Economic Cooperation (MOFTEC). Legally, no agreements could be reached, and the time for getting to know each other was limited to the meeting table. In each meeting, the Chinese partner reminded the chief representative that he knew nothing of the Chinese and the company's business. Often, the Chinese participants demanded proof of the chief representative's legitimacy in conducting business meetings. Finally, in China it was typical at the time for correspondence to be sent by fax and for messages to be relayed by telephone conversations. These mediums of communication were more common than the use of email. Consequently, the confidentiality of the US partner's intentions was breached when fax messages were read by the Chinese partner's representatives.

CASE STUDY QUESTIONS

1) What were the various weaknesses in the internal control system in this case?
2) In what ways could the situation have been avoided?
3) In what ways did Chinese accounting practice interfere in the transition of the joint venture from a manufacturing entity to an engineering service company?
4) How can the process of liquidation be more effectively managed?

CHAPTER

5

International Transfer Pricing

LEARNING OBJECTIVES

- Understand the conditions that influence subsidiary transfer pricing.
- Understand the various trade-offs that have to be considered when setting transfer prices for the subsidiary.
- Understand the current trends in transfer pricing with specific reference to transfer pricing issues in China.
- Understand the current regulations in China that govern transfer pricing.

INTRODUCTION

The setting of international transfer prices involves the pricing of intermediate goods and services between various entities within a multinational enterprise (MNE). As part of the establishment of an overseas subsidiary or joint venture, head office management must decide on transfer prices that will be used for accounting for any intra-company transfers. Transfer prices provide management with the opportunity to manage the subsidiary financial reporting, to improve the subsidiary's competitiveness with regard to beating the competition and gaining access to finance, and to control decisions made by the subsidiary. As part of the later role transfer prices are viewed as a formal control mechanism that can substitute or complement the various control mechanisms discussed in Chapters 3 and 4.

The role of transfer pricing, however, extends beyond that of control and it is this multi-role complexity that makes it one of the critical challenges for the MNE. Indeed, the criticality of transfer pricing for the MNE is highlighted by the fact that up to 40% of international trade involves the transfer of goods between affiliates within the same MNE and that transfer pricing can have different tax implications for MNE affiliates in foreign countries, thus it is one area of MNE practice that is directly impacted by the government regulations of another country. Accordingly, international transfer prices are generally set due to a range of factors: tax minimisation strategies, market conditions in the foreign countries, custom duties, exchange controls, import restrictions and the desire to help the foreign affiliate earn a reasonable profit (Radebaugh and Gray, 2002).

An overview of the frameworks for setting international transfer prices is provided in the first part of this chapter. This part includes a discussion of the various transfer pricing trade-offs facing the MNE. The second part provides an overview of the empirical literature along with details of the current Organisation for Economic Cooperation and Development (OECD) guidelines. Emphasis is given to the transfer pricing issues facing MNEs and their affiliates in China.

TYPES OF TRANSFER PRICES

There are three broad types of transfer prices: 1) market price, 2) cost-based or cost-plus methods, and 3) negotiated price. The market price is an arm's-length price that is used as though a subsidiary were charging an external customer. Of these, the market price is the ideal transfer price to use in the international setting because it satisfies the different demands of various stakeholders that range from tax authorities, foreign exchange regulators, to internal parties such as head office and subsidiary office management. In the case where market price information is available (i.e., there exists a competitive market) market prices are useful in managing subsidiaries where subsidiary managers have their own autonomy or at least a minimal degree of interdependence among profit centres (Abdallah, 1989). However, it is often the case that a market price is difficult to determine because of the lack of a competitive market or the absence of a known price that can be quoted anytime. It is also common for MNEs to not use market price because of the MNE strategy and structure of decision making and control. For example, the MNE has a centralised structure in which case subsidiary managers may be restricted from buying or selling in the open market without prior approval from top management. In these cases, MNEs revert to a cost-based or negotiated transfer price.

Cost-based methods relate to full cost or variable cost, with standard or budgeting costs being preferred over actual costs. There are two reasons for this. First, timing – actual costs may not be known at the time of setting transfer prices. Second, setting standard costs helps to encourage the subsidiary to control cost efficiency. Cost-based methods motivate efficient resource allocation in the MNE. For example, variable cost-based transfer prices are likely to encourage the buying subsidiary to make optimal decisions in the best interest of the MNE. The drawback is that use of variable cost transfer prices forces the selling subsidiary to report less profits than would be the case under full-cost or market-based transfer pricing. Such practice is also likely to draw attention from tax authorities in developing countries. For instance, there is mounting evidence of increasing vigilance by the Chinese tax authorities (Chan and Chow, 1997a). Ideally, transfer prices should have a mark-up to allow the selling subsidiary to realise a profit that is comparable to the normal return on investment in the industry.

The negotiated transfer pricing method is used when the selling and buying subsidiaries freely negotiate the transfer price. Although this approach can be time consuming and inefficient, it does force managers to be more accountable for their subsidiary's costs and their contribution to the MNE.

CONDITIONS THAT INFLUENCE INTERNATIONAL TRANSFER PRICING

Transfer pricing for transactions with a subsidiary are subject to three main areas of influence: Organisation efficiency and strategy, regulatory environment and competitive environment forces. These areas of influence are presented in the form of an international transfer pricing framework. Satisfying the various demands of these influences inevitably results in a trade-off. The international transfer pricing framework is presented followed by common trade-offs faced by the MNE.

International Transfer Pricing Framework

International transfer pricing acts as a management tool, whereby a charge for goods or services between related parties is set at controlled or uncontrolled rates. Leitch and Barrett (1992) list a number of transfer pricing objectives, including profit objectives, cash flow objectives, marketing objectives, operating effectiveness and the minimisation of taxes. As several objectives can be achieved via transfer pricing, the achievement of one objective may contradict the achievements of another. For example, the minimisation of taxes may be contradictory to operational efficiency, as the later objective may involve the transfer of cheap production factors for profit maximisation. According to Anthony and Dearden (1980), a sound transfer pricing system should accomplish the following objectives:

- Motivate the divisional manager to make sound decisions and communicate information that provides a reliable basis for such decisions.
- Result in a report of divisional profits that is a reasonable measure of the managerial performance of the division.
- Ensure that divisional autonomy is not undermined.

Transfer pricing also enables MNEs to compete more effectively through the cross-subsidisation of costs. However, these purposes must be achieved within the regulatory context. There are three areas in which the role of transfer pricing can be considered – the strategic role of the subsidiary, regulatory influences (legal, taxation and government systems) and environmental influences (level of country development) (see Figure 5.1). These three factors increase the complexity of transfer pricing in the international realm.

Organisation efficiency and strategy issues. There are several roles that transfer pricing can play in enhancing organisation efficiency and strategic alignment. These are performance evaluation, resource coordination and the shielding of subsidiary profits from other stakeholders such as local partners and employees. These roles are, however, likely to be dictated by organisation strategy. Hence, the first determinant of transfer pricing policy is the strategic role of the subsidiary, which follows from the original intention of the MNE to enter a country. If the strategy is part of market expansion plans, then there is less need for transfer pricing to play a role of profit repatriation. Most developing countries prefer that profit be reinvested in the country, and a strategy of having several subsidiaries in one country for a long period will complement the host country preferences. In

Figure 5.1 Transfer Pricing Trade-offs

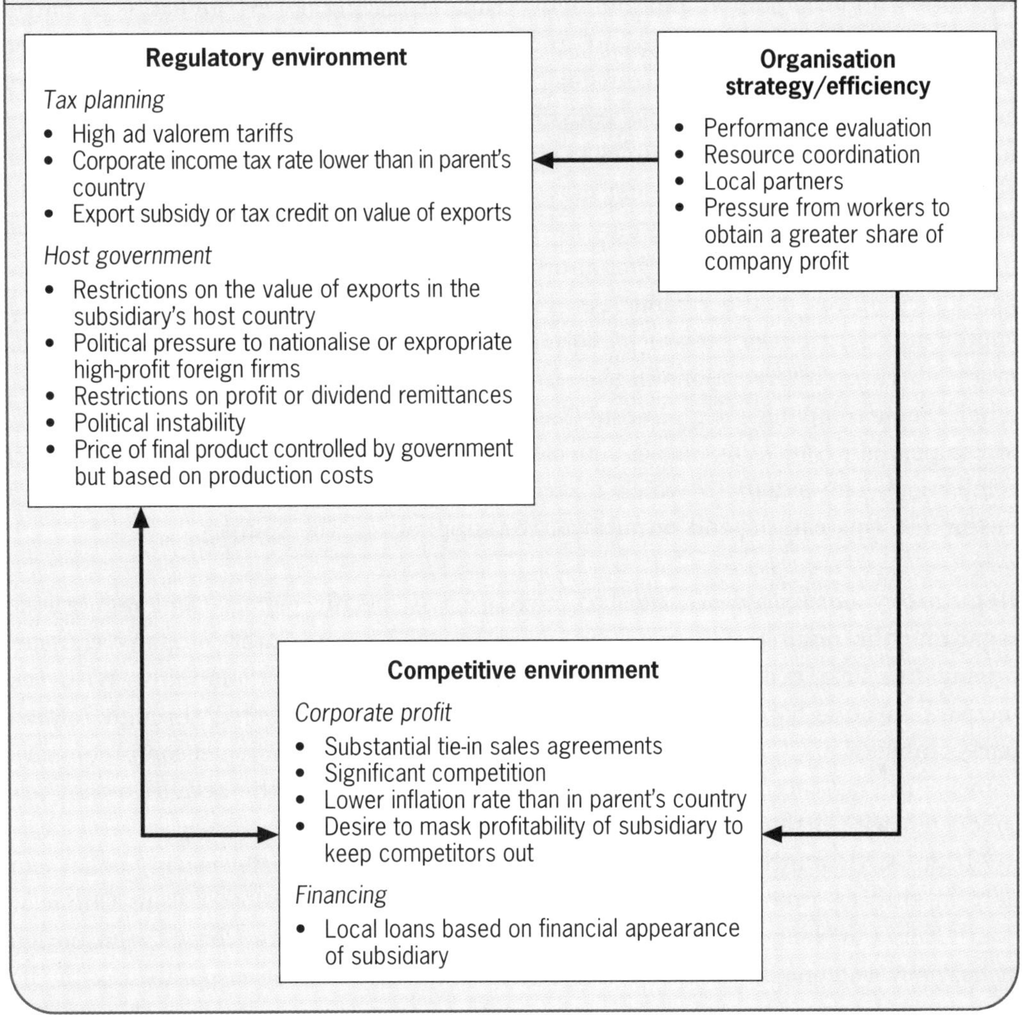

contrast if the role of the subsidiary is to exploit the assets of another country through the use of cheap labour or materials, then there may be a greater burden on transfer pricing to help the multinational derive full benefits from that cheap labour. In this case, the profits of the subsidiary are earned when the intermediate outputs are exported (creating needed foreign exchange for the host country) to the MNE's subsidiaries in another country. The multinational has less desire to retain profits in the subsidiary for growth and development compared to an MNE that is planning to expand its market. Thus, transfer pricing may play a greater role in aiding profit repatriation.

Within the constraints of organisation strategy and other influences (e.g., the regulatory and competitive environment) transfer pricing policy can act as a control (facilitate performance evaluation) and resource coordination mechanism. To be effective in this role, however, transfer prices need to be used with a complementary control mechanism. For example, transfer prices can be used to provide an incentive for management to direct resources to subsidiaries that face profitable opportunities. However, for MNEs that use a just in time (JIT) approach to inventory management, such a role for transfer pricing may need to be complemented with more centralised management (e.g., having a regional office to direct the resource flows between the subsidiary offices in the region). As developing countries are yet to fully develop supply and distribution networks, foreign sourcing can create big risks in the JIT process because interruptions in the supply line can bring the production process to a halt. Some companies (e.g., Lucent Technologies) have back up plans for the supply of components from alternative sources (even a subsidiary in the same group of companies). The extent to which a company depends on local suppliers is also a factor, and this can depend on alternative suppliers in the country.

Regulatory environment. Most countries have specific policies and regulations regarding the pricing of transferred goods by MNEs, and inter-company transfer pricing has long been a central feature of international tax planning. With the increase in cross-border trade and investment that is conducted through related party transactions, tax authorities in many countries have developed comprehensive transfer pricing compliance rules to ensure fair returns for the activities that are conducted within their borders.

If the MNE wants to minimise its corporate tax, then transfer pricing policy can help in shifting profits from high tax country to tax havens (e.g., from China or South Korea to Hong Kong). However, this shifting of profits may draw the attention of host government due to the lower contribution in terms of corporate tax to the society. This can affect the relationship with the host government and also may induce tax audit by the tax department. Ultimately, MNEs face the trade-off between the importance of host government relations and tax minimisation.

Competitive environment. Several environmental issues confront subsidiaries with respect to the setting of transfer prices such as: differences in cost structure, inflation rate and associated foreign exchange risk, masking profitability and financing opportunities. First, what problems are involved in using standard costing in a rapidly changing technological environment? How does an MNE set standards for costs in different countries that are at different stages of technology development? The cost base may be different; for example, among vehicle manufacturers who have production operations in China, it is well known that average worker productivity is less than half that of comparable workers in the US. The learning (and hence cost) curve may be different.

Second, there may be a need to shift profits of a subsidiary in a country that has significant inflation risk that threatens the associated capital investment. In another way, transfer prices can be used to mask the corporate profits of a subsidiary in certain countries in order to keep competitors out. Finally, transfer pricing policy is significant in assisting corporate financing objectives. As is normal practice in most countries, local loans are based on corporate local financial appearance. Therefore for MNEs that require financing for investment in subsidiaries through host country loan arrangement, it is necessary for subsidiaries to report "profit" figures in their financial statements by shifting income from one subsidiary to another through transfer pricing policy.

Trade-offs among the Elements of the International Transfer Pricing Framework

Given the three general areas of influence on transfer pricing policy, it is important to consider how components of these areas influence the type of transfer pricing adopted. Table 5.1 shows how different transfer prices between a parent company and its subsidiary could be set according to the conditions in the country in which the subsidiary is operating.

In most countries however, it is rare for the conditions favouring a particular transfer pricing policy to be aligned. For example, China has certain foreign exchange restrictions on the repatriation of profits which point to the use of higher transfer prices on intermediate goods inflows to the subsidiary from the parent. However, the desire to achieve a certain level of export profits to meet the conditions of entering China reduces the value of such a policy. These and other trade-offs need to be carefully considered when setting transfer pricing policy for the subsidiary. Indeed, MNEs have to make several trade-offs in using transfer pricing for various roles and in the process deploy other mechanisms such as centralised management or formal controls to complement the transfer pricing policy that is in place. The following examples provide an overview of the more common trade-offs.

Tax planning versus resource coordination. Even though the use of a transfer pricing policy can facilitate resource coordination between subsidiaries of a group, it may be at the cost of a higher tax liability for the group as a whole. For example, if the sales performance of a subsidiary in South Korea is better than the one in Singapore, by reason of profitability, the regional management may transfer more stock to Korea instead of Singapore but this will increase the corporate tax liability for the group as a whole due to higher corporate tax rate in Korea against that in Singapore.

Table 5.1 Conditions Influencing Transfer Pricing

Conditions in the subsidiary's country that induce *low transfer prices* on flows from the parent and *high transfer prices* on flows to the parent	Conditions in the subsidiary's country that induce *high transfer prices* on flows from the parent and *low transfer prices* on flows to the parent
High ad valorem tariffs	Local partners
Corporate income tax rate lower than in parent's country	Pressure from workers to obtain a greater share of company profit
Significant competition	Political pressure to nationalise or expropriate high-profit foreign firms
Local loans based on the financial appearance of the subsidiary	Restrictions on profit or dividend remittances
Export subsidy or tax credit on value of exports	Political instability
Lower inflation rate than in parent's country	Substantial tie-in sales agreements
Restrictions (ceilings) in the subsidiary's host country on the value of products that can be imported	Price of final product controlled by government but based on product cost
	Desire to mask profitability of subsidiary operations to keep out competition
	Import duty – affect on imported inputs
	Profit-cost centres

Source: Arpan, Jeffrey S., *International intracorporate pricing*. Copyright 1972 by Praeger Publishers. Reprinted by permission of Greenwood Publishing Group.

Performance evaluation versus resource coordination and corporate profit. When transfer prices are used as an incentive mechanism (i.e., as a profit performance measure) individual subsidiaries will direct effort towards maximising its reporting profits in return for higher rewards from the group. However, the profit margins of products are different between countries due to differences in brand product reputation and the living standards of people. The group may desire to mask the profitability of a subsidiary to keep competitors out of the country. As a result, such transfer pricing performance measures are likely to conflict with the optimisation of resource coordination and corporate profits among the group.

Financing versus corporate profit and tax planning. Due to various reasons such as the need to mask corporate profit, or to minimise foreign exchange risk, subsidiaries may be required to shift higher than normal profits to other subsidiaries in different countries through a transfer pricing policy. The consequent reporting of lower profits may in turn diminish the subsidiary's ability to apply for finance. Alternatively, if the subsidiary reported higher profits for the purpose of applying for local loans, then it will need to pay higher corporate tax. A trade-off is required between financing, corporate profit and tax minimisation when considering a transfer pricing policy.

Despite the complexity posed by these different trade-offs, transfer pricing policy can be effectively managed with the complementary use of various control mechanisms such as the level of decentralisation and the use of various control mechanisms (including those discussed in Chapter 3). One of the most critical of these mechanisms is the level of decentralisation between the MNE head office and the subsidiaries. Table 5.2 provides an example of a European MNE that recently centralised its Asia operations by changing the Hong Kong sales subsidiary into a regional head office. This change had several implications for how the MNE could use transfer pricing to deal with the various organisation efficiency, regulatory and competitive environment factors.

EVIDENCE OF INTERNATIONAL TRANSFER PRICING

Much of the early transfer pricing literature focused on the organisation and competitive environment rationales for setting transfer prices in the MNE. With the advances in government regulations, especially in the developing economies, the recent literature has revealed the greater influence of the regulatory environment. The influence of the regulatory environment is especially pronounced in the China foreign investment environment where the majority of the world's foreign direct investment (FDI) occurs.

Early Empirical Studies

Early transfer pricing studies were characterised by a range of factors that influenced transfer pricing. MNEs used transfer pricing as a mechanism to shift profits from less developed countries because there were restrictions on profit repatriation either through dividends or royalty payments. Taxation also figured in transfer pricing policies. According to the review of studies undertaken by Abdallah (1989), a range of factors influenced transfer pricing policies, such as relevant cost information, differential income tax rates, foreign exchange risks, restrictions on

Table 5.2 Organisation Structure and Transfer Pricing Policy for a European MNE Operating in Asia

	Decentralised strategy *(Decentralisation of controls and operations over Asian subsidiaries)*	**Centralised strategy** *(Centralisation of controls and operations in Asia through the Hong Kong regional headquarters)*
Business	Watch and jewellery distribution business throughout Asia	
Role of subsidiaries	• All Asian subsidiaries act as sale agents in each host country and report directly to the head office	• HK subsidiary acts as a sales agent and regional headquarters for the Asia-Pacific region. All other Asian subsidiaries report to the Hong Kong regional office
Organisation efficiency		
Performance evaluation	• Performance evaluation and incentive to subsidiaries is based on individual performance • At the firm level, there exists greater conflicts of interest. Thus, it is difficult to achieve goal congruence between individual subsidiaries and the group.	• Performance evaluation and incentive to subsidiaries is based on regional performance. • At the regional level, there is greater goal congruence; the group focuses on managing of business matters that affect the group
Resource coordination	• Difficulty in inventory control for the group	• Elimination of inventory control problem within the Asian region resulting in better resources coordination
Regulatory environment		
Tax planning (minimising tax)	• Difficult to control and achieve by the group due to long distance and knowledge transfer cost issues • Minimising individual tax for each subsidiary does not mean minimising the tax for the group as a whole	• Can be achieved at regional level due to centralising control and operation of the subsidiaries in Asia, for example, shifting income within the region from high corporate tax location (e.g., China – 33% or Korea – 29.7%) to a low-tax location (e.g., Hong Kong – 17.5%) • Requires individual subsidiaries' support through knowledge transfer, for example, information about tax system of each host country

Table 5.2 Organisation Structure and Transfer Pricing Policy for a European MNE Operating in Asia (Cont'd)

	Decentralised strategy *(Decentralisation of controls and operations over Asian subsidiaries)*	**Centralised strategy** *(Centralisation of controls and operations in Asia through the Hong Kong regional headquarters)*
Government regulation (issue of tax audit)	• Individual subsidiaries will have better knowledge about the government regulation in their own countries. Thus, they are better able to manage tax planning and avoid tax audit.	• Due to the short distance within the Asia region, the costs for tax knowledge transfer from other Asian subsidiaries to HK management is lower thus tax audit issues are manageable.
Relationship with local government	• Difficult to establish and manage by the head office due to long physical and cultural distance with the Asian subsidiaries.	• HK management can establish better relationships with China and Taiwan. It is easier to shift income and investment within Asia through the centralisation of transfer pricing policy.
Political risk in terms of foreign currency exchange and sensitivity to political changes	• Higher risk in foreign currency exchange due to different subsidiaries using different functional currencies	• Through centralisation of the transfer pricing policy, the risk in foreign exchange can be reduced.
Competitive environment		
Corporate profits	• Maximising individual profits may not be conforming with the group strategy; for example, masking of profit to keep competitor out.	• Corporate profits can be maximised at the regional level and greater flexibility exists for shifting profits to fit in with the group strategy.
Financing	• Only highly profitable subsidiaries can gain local financing.	• By centralising the transfer pricing policy, it is easier to arrange local finance from banks through shifting of profits between subsidiaries if and when necessary.

cash transfers, tariffs, competition and inflation rates. Organisational factors such as performance evaluation, motivation and goal congruence were not as important in the determination of transfer pricing policies. In another review of the early literature, Leitch and Barrett (1992) found that MNE decisions about transfer pricing were constrained by the numerous economic, socio-political, operational and regulatory bounds and their objectives.

In a study of 164 multinationals (88 of which were operating in less-developed countries), A1-Eryani, Alam and Akhter (1990) found that legal compliance and size were significant, and that anti-dumping and antitrust legislation and financial reporting rules were influential in transfer pricing policy. In contrast, exchange controls, price controls, import restrictions, socio-political conditions and the extent of economic development were unimportant. Among the sample companies, market-based and cost-plus transfer pricing methods were popular. Performance evaluation did not figure in the transfer pricing decisions of the sample companies.

Tang (1992) studied the transfer pricing practices of 143 out of the Fortune 500 companies in 1977 and 1990. He found that income tax considerations, good relationships with host governments, local financing and antitrust legislation became more important from 1977 to 1990. In contrast, factors such as performance evaluation, the rules and requirements of financial reporting and the rate of inflation in host countries became a less important consideration during the same period.

Recent Empirical Studies on Transfer Pricing

During the 1990s there was growing concern among developing nations about the transfer pricing manipulations undertaken by MNEs. In view of this concern, Borkowski (1997) studied the perceived extent to which transfer pricing manipulations were undertaken by resident and foreign-based MNEs. He found that the majority of the sampled nations preferred traditional methods based on the arm's-length principle. No tax haven country preferred strict transaction-based methods, and most tax haven countries considered income shifting by home-based MNEs to be an issue of concern.

Cravens (1996) studied 542 US-based MNEs and found that several factors influence transfer pricing practice: 1) those that are taxation related, such as tariffs, tax compliance and tax burdens; 2) those that are internal management oriented, such as fair performance evaluation, motivation and goal congruence promotion; and 3) international factors such as cash transfer restrictions, competitive position and the reflection of actual cost and income. Similar to previous studies, corporate performance evaluation did not figure in the transfer pricing equation.

Empirical Studies on Transfer Pricing in China

Chan and Chow (1997b) examined the extent to which foreign investors might have been shifting profits out of China by the transfer pricing mechanism. They studied 238 imported and 1,062 exported commodities from the Chinese government's statistics on imports and exports by foreign companies during 1992. The conclusion was that foreign companies paid an average of 11% higher prices for imports than domestic companies. They also charged higher prices on exports by about the same percentage. These findings are inconsistent with the allegation that foreign investors shift profits out of China by transfer pricing manipulations. The result indicates that MNE transfer pricing is constrained by internal organisational and behavioural considerations.

To determine whether fiscal authorities focus their tax audit efforts on certain industries as well as large companies and certain forms or nationalities of foreign investment, Chan and Chow (1997a) studied 81 tax audit cases in 1992 and 1993. Six of the cases were also studied in more detail. They found that both political and practical considerations accounted for the confinement of tax audits mainly to medium- and small-sized foreign companies and the transfer of tangible goods. In particular the types of business screened had lower technology, tangible goods, no local partner, were medium or small-sized, of Hong Kong nationality and had tax haven affiliates. They also found that tax audits focused on profit rather than prices. Persistent losses, low profitability and the lack of monitoring by local partners were the most likely circumstances to draw the attention of the tax authorities.

Sun (1999) examined the question of whether tariffs were a factor in determining MNE transfer pricing policies. He studied the prices of exports and imports to and from China and Hong Kong in 1994, as sourced from the commodity trade statistics published by the United Nations, and found that MNEs had under-invoiced Chinese exports by at least 10% on average and over-invoiced Chinese imports by around 9%.

Chan and Chow (2001) studied how MNE choices of international transfer pricing methods were affected by their specific corporate attributes in China. They surveyed the controllers/general managers of 63 companies selected from the directory of the top 500 industrial foreign investment enterprises in China. They found that companies in which the local partner participated in management tended to use the market-based transfer pricing method (others used the cost-based method). They also found that another corporate attribute (source of investment) was significant in interacting with the local partner condition, while activity orientation, such as domestic market or advanced technological production, was less significant.

REGULATORY GUIDELINES

The trend has been for regulatory bodies to agree to a common set of guidelines so as to control the flow of capital away from higher-taxed jurisdictions to their lower-taxed counterparts via inter-company transactions. One outcome of this push is a set of guidelines agreed to by the OECD countries. While these guidelines have a large influence since most of the world's MNEs are from OECD countries, MNEs need to be aware of the guidelines set by China.

OECD Guidelines

The use of the transfer pricing of tangible goods and intangible services as both a strategic business decision and an international tax decision has increased in step with the increasing globalisation of daily business transactions. Concurrent with the increase in cross-border taxable income is an increase in scrutiny by cross-border tax authorities which want to ensure that their country receives a fair share of tax revenues. Tax authorities justify their heightened audit activity by citing the magnitude of taxable income that is related to transfer pricing. One strategy to reduce or eliminate the risk of a transfer pricing tax audit for several years is to seek an advance pricing agreement (APA) with the tax authorities of the countries in which an MNE generates taxable income (Borkowski, 2000). The use of APAs is a means of limiting controversy about transfer pricing issues. The OECD has produced several guidelines to facilitate international transfer pricing (see Figure 5.2).

Transfer Pricing Guidelines in China

The Chinese transfer pricing regulations are primarily based on rules of foreign countries and on the OECD report, *Transfer Pricing Guidelines for Multinational Enterprises and Tax Administration*. The law states that when the payment or receipt of charges or fees in business transactions between a company with foreign investment and its associated companies is not made in the same manner as in business transactions between independent companies, and results in a reduction of taxable income, the tax authorities are authorised to make reasonable adjustments. The detailed regulations for implementation of the law provide the definition of associated companies and stipulate the pricing methodology.

China has its own law with respect to transfer pricing guidelines. This law carries with it a set of implementing rules and heavy penalties are imposed for discrepancies found in a tax audit. Aware of these developments, MNEs have begun to register for advanced pricing agreements with the China tax authorities. In 1998, the tax authority of China issued more detailed and complete rules and regulations on transfer pricing between related parties. Although the tax law stipulates that companies with foreign investment are required to pay corporate income tax at a rate of 30% and a surcharge of 3% levied by local governments, the tax incentives that are offered by central and local governments could significantly reduce the tax rate.

Figure 5.2 OECD Guidelines on Transfer Pricing

Guidelines	Current work	Cost contribution agreements (CCA)	Monitoring	Advance pricing agreements
• To determine the arm's-length price • Set out in Article 9 of the OECD model tax convention • Maintains the arm's-length principle of treating related enterprises within a multinational group and affirming traditional transaction methods as a preferred way of implementing the principles	• Provides guidelines on how to apply the general principle to complex situations • Monitors practical implementation of the guidelines and amends and updates the existing guidance given in the light of the monitoring • Improves the administrative procedures • Encourages countries outside of the OECD to associate themselves with the guidelines	• Arm's-length principles • Agreed international standard governing-related-party cross-border translations • CCA can be used by business enterprises to share the costs and risks of developing, producing or obtaining any assets, services or rights	• Covers the application of countries' transfer pricing rules and their consistency with the guidelines/ cases in which mutual agreement proceedings have not reached a satisfactory conclusion, the use of APAs and the frequency with which profit methods are used by tax administrations	• Provides guidance on conducting APAs under the mutual agreement procedure

Foreign investment and foreign enterprises (FEIT) implementing rules. Article 13 of the *Income Tax Law* of the People's Republic of China for Enterprises with Foreign Investment and Foreign Enterprises (FEIT Law) stipulates that transactions between a foreign investing enterprise or the establishment of a foreign company in China, and its associated companies, should be conducted in the same manner as that between independent parties or at arm's length. If the transactions are not carried out at arm's length, then the tax authorities can adjust the company's income. Article 13 is supplemented by Articles 52 to 58 of the detailed rules for the implementation of the FEIT Law. While these laws are generally consistent with the OECD transfer pricing guidelines, a broader definition of related parties is applied, (including companies with direct or indirect ownership of 25% or more), which makes the guidelines much more stringent.

In China, the burden of proof regarding the arm's-length price in related party transactions rests with the tax authorities, but without any requirement to prove the existence of intention to avoid Chinese tax on the part of the foreign company. When the tax authorities suspect that a foreign company's income has been reduced as a result of non-arm's-length pricing, they will notify it to provide relevant information regarding transfer pricing (Huang and Yu, 2002).

If the auditors are of the opinion that the related party transactions are not conducted in an arm's-length manner, then an adjustment is made based on the three arm's-length pricing methods that are stipulated in the regulations: the comparable uncontrolled price method, the resale price method and the cost-plus method. Other methods (e.g., the comparable profit method (CPM) and the profit split method) can be used when the above three methods are not appropriate to the circumstances or cannot be adopted. However, the three arm's-length pricing methods have not been used frequently in audit cases because it is very difficult for auditors to establish arm's-length standards in practice. Therefore, tax auditors always rely on CPM and profit split method for adjustment. As a result, Chan and Chow (1997a) argue that tax audits in China focus on profits rather than prices.

Transfer pricing audits. In the past, transfer pricing was not a major practical concern to foreign companies in general because tax authorities in southern China rarely carried out tax audits and made transfer pricing adjustments. However, foreign companies can no longer afford to take this issue lightly because pricing legislation enforcement has become increasingly stringent in China. Local tax authorities have begun to focus on tax issues arising from related party transactions within China and across its borders. To support this development, the State Administration of Taxation (SAT) has established a specialised taskforce and provided it with rigorous training. Wang, Wee and Koh (1999) reported that the transfer pricing taskforce increased from 130 members in 1997 to more than 1,000 in the year 2000. Other than the tax inspectors from the SAT, local tax bureaus also have their inspectors conduct tax audit in case of suspicion.

As of 2001, there were 390,183 foreign investment projects totalling US$744.9 billion (*People's Daily*, 2002). When compared to the total number of tax inspectors who were conducting transfer price audits, the percentage seems minimal. Nevertheless, the consequence of triggering a tax audit is that the tax bureau can make transfer price adjustments to a taxpayer's income retroactively for up to ten years, and can conduct a three-year post-audit review (Li, 2000). This can pose serious trouble to the enterprises being closely supervised by the tax bureau for a certain period of time.

The SAT has become more aggressive in challenging the transfer price policies adopted by foreign companies. It has strengthened its efforts in transfer price audits and has introduced detailed transfer price guidelines. From 1988 to 1998, the transfer price practices of approximately 5,000 enterprises were audited, and the total amount of transfer price adjustments was RMB6 billion (Li, 2000).

In the meantime, Circular 59 identifies several criteria for selecting audit targets, notably when a company, 1) has significant transactions with associated enterprises, 2) has production and operational decisions that are controlled by associated enterprises, 3) has a sudden and significant drop in profits after the expiration of a tax holiday period, 4) has incurred losses for more than two consecutive years, 5) has marginal profits or losses for an extended period, but continuously expands the scale of its operations, 6) has profits that fluctuate, 7) has transactions with associated enterprises in tax havens, 8) has lower profitability than that of other enterprises in the same industry or in the same corporate group, 9) pays unjustifiable fees to associated enterprises, and 10) is suspected of avoiding tax by other methods.

Advanced pricing agreements (APAs). Advanced pricing agreements are legal arrangements between the tax authority and the taxpayer that set out the method for determining the future transfer pricing policies for related party transactions. It is designed to resolve actual or potential transfer pricing disputes in a principled and cooperative manner, as an alternative to the traditional adversarial process like transfer pricing audit and defence (Lee, Wu and Kuo, 2004). Since its adoption in China in 1998, more than 130 APAs have been concluded in various regions and cities such as the Pearl River Delta, Shanghai, Tianjin and Xiamen (SAT, 2003). APAs are generally based on the type of agreements used in the US, but with local variations which depend on the local tax authorities' level of transfer pricing experience.

A typical APA can take up to 18 months to complete and requires a substantial input of resources. For example, an APA requires that the MNE establish proper transfer pricing documentation, including a functional analysis, a benchmarking study and inter-company agreements, which could be filed for APA application to Chinese tax authorities. MNEs should also consider their past transfer pricing behaviour which can have an impact on obtaining an APA.

Tax holidays for foreign-invested enterprises. To attract foreign investment and production technology, the central government offers a preferential tax rate of 15% to foreign companies that are located in designated zones (including Special

Economic Zones, economic and technology development zones, new and high-technology development zones and the Pudong New Development Zone), foreign companies with investments over US$30 million and foreign companies that are engaged in infrastructure development and advanced technology. It also offers preferential tax rate of 24% to foreign companies that are located in open economic zones and cities. Furthermore, local governments have the authority to waive the 3% surcharge.

Foreign industrial companies that are scheduled to operate for at least ten years can enjoy a five-year tax holiday that includes full exemption from income tax for the first two profit-making years and a 50% tax reduction for the following three years. Furthermore, initial operating losses can be carried forward for a maximum of five years. For foreign companies with advanced production technology or export orientation (i.e., more than 70% of sales exported), a further 50% tax reduction is granted after the five-year tax holiday. Royalty income is generally subject to double taxation under Chinese rules.

A 100% tax refund is allowed if the profits are reinvested by establishing or expanding the operation of an export-oriented or high-technologically advanced company (PricewaterhouseCoopers, 2002a). Preferential policies are granted to foreign companies that use materials for manufacturing export products; these are exempted from import and export tariffs. Moreover, the Chinese government reduced its import tariff on 5,300 items from 15.3% to 12% on 1 January 2002 to fulfill its commitment to the WTO. As a result, there was a reduction of more than 25% in the average tariff rates on electronic products to 10.7% (*People's Daily,* March 26, 2002). Table 5.3 summarises and compares the tax planning of Hong Kong and China.

SUMMARY

The purpose of this chapter was to provide a summary of the transfer pricing issues faced by the MNE. Transfer pricing is a critical element in the management of the MNE because inter-company transfers make up a large portion of international trade and the pricing of such transfers are becoming subject to increasing scrutiny by tax authorities around the world. In the first part of this chapter, three broad types of transfer prices were described: 1) market price, 2) cost-based or cost-plus methods, and 3) negotiated price. This part also sets out the challenge for the MNE in setting transfer prices that promote organisational efficiency and competitiveness while at the same time staying within the regulatory guidelines set by both the country of the home office and the countries in which the MNE has subsidiary operations. Effective management of these trade-offs consists of having the right

Table 5.3 Comparison of Tax Planning between Hong Kong and China

Regulatory framework	Hong Kong	China
Tax planning		
1) Corporate income tax rate (effective rate)	17.5%	33%
2) Tax holiday for enterprise engaging in production	N/A	2-year exemption and 3-year 50% reduction
3) Tax reduction (for exports of more than 70% of the products)	N/A	Additional 50% reduction in income tax, effective rate cannot be less than 10%
4) Investment tax refund	N/A	40% to 100% income tax refund for reinvestment of profits
5) Value Added Tax (VAT)	No VAT	Refund available for export goods, 100% for electronic products
6) Customs duties	No custom duties except for minor items	Import and export tariffs are waived for export goods

combination of transfer pricing and other management controls (e.g., organisation structure) in place. The second part of this chapter provided a summary of empirical research on transfer pricing and the regulatory guidelines set out by the OECD. Specific transfer pricing guidelines were also spelled out for MNEs with subsidiary operations in China.

QUESTIONS

1) What are the basic transfer pricing alternatives available to MNEs? Discuss the advantages and disadvantages of each.
2) How does the role of transfer pricing in a multinational corporation differ from that of a domestic corporation?
3) Explain each of the trade-offs in the international transfer pricing typology?
4) Give an example of how the competitive environment or organisation efficiency may dominate in determining the appropriate transfer price?

5) Explain how organisation structure may influence transfer pricing policy with respect to each of the factors that influence international transfer pricing.
6) Now that many countries are toughening their regulations on transfer pricing to prevent tax minimising and profit-repatriating activities, there seems to be little scope for transfer pricing strategy other than to set transfer prices at the market (arm's-length) price. Discuss.
7) What are the latest trends in MNE transfer pricing behaviour? Refer to the brief literature review in this chapter.
8) What are the critical risks to be aware of when setting transfer pricing policy for MNEs operating in China?

EXERCISES

1) **Transfer pricing game**

   This exercise requires participants that have experienced a working transfer pricing policy in an organisation with one or more subsidiaries.

   Presenters

   - Choose a firm with a transfer pricing strategy.
   - Draw a map of the inter-organisational flows and identify the transfer pricing strategy.

   Class

   - Ask questions about what determinants exist in a particular MNE. Use Table 5.1 as a guide for understanding which factors are likely to influence the scope and direction of transfer pricing policy.
   - Guess the type of transfer pricing practice in terms of the type of transfer price and the reasoning (key factors) behind such practice.
   - Provide a one-page summary of an MNE practice, detailing the main transfer pricing practice and the practical determinants.

2) **Scope (HK) Ltd.** Examine the following transfer pricing strategy used by Scope (HK) Ltd. Scope Ltd has the following import-export arrangement with its factory in China.

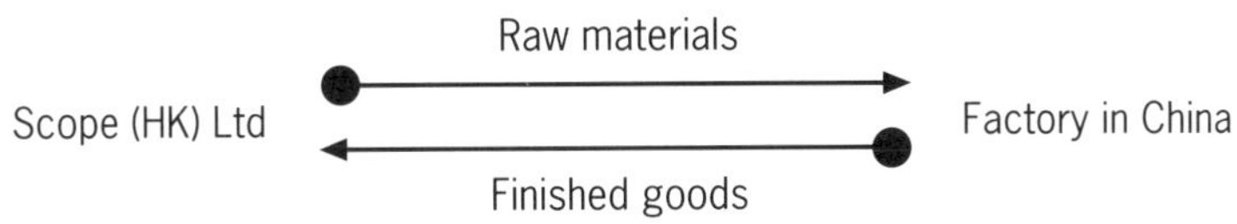

The following independent variables are ranked according to their importance in each transfer; 5 is the most important and 1 is the least important.

a) Sale of raw materials from the Scope (HK) Ltd to the factory in China

Independent variables	**Rank**
Accounting arrangement – ease of consolidation	5
Minimisation of taxation	1
Performance evaluation	1

b) Sale of finished goods from PRC factory to Scope (HK) Ltd

Independent variables	**Rank**
Minimisation of taxation	5
Avoidance of tax audits in both Hong Kong and China	5
Source of finance by the Hong Kong company	3
Profit repatriation from the factory in China	1
Performance evaluation	1
Market positioning towards domestic and non-domestic customers	1

i) What is the transfer pricing strategy that best fits this scenario? Specify the likely transfer price for:
   - raw materials
   - finished goods

ii) Indicate the reasons and factors that are most likely to explain the transfer pricing strategy shown.

3) **Engineering Co Ltd.** Review the following case for the fit between Engineering Co Ltd's transfer pricing strategy and the reasons for this strategy. Engineering Co Ltd is based in Japan (headquarters) and sells equipment and parts to Hong Kong. The Hong Kong subsidiary resells the equipment and parts to mainland China for the group's engineering service operations. The transfer pricing strategy is as follows.

Countries involved

	Japan	Hong Kong	Mainland China
Regulatory environment			
Corporate income/profit tax	Highest (47%)	Lowest (17.5%)	Middle (33%)
Tariff/import-export duty	N.A.	Nil	Yes
Other considerations (e.g., repatriation of profits, FX control and risks and political stability	Not important	Not important	Not important
Competitive environment			
Inflation	Not important	Not important	Not important
Differentiation strategy	Yes	Yes	Yes
Local financing	Yes	Yes	Yes
Organisation efficiency			
Existence of local partner	No	Yes	No
Pressure from workers/trade unions	Minimal	Insignificant	Insignificant
Performance evaluation	Not important	Not important	Not important

a) What is the transfer pricing strategy that best fits this scenario?
   i) Japan to Hong Kong
   ii) Hong Kong to mainland China

   Give reasons for your answers.

CASE STUDY 16

XYZ Group – Factors Influencing Its Transfer Pricing Strategy

CASE BACKGROUND

XYZ Group is a manufacturer of bedding products with head office in Hong Kong and a manufacturing operation in Shenzhen. The current transfer pricing policy for the Shenzhen subsidiary has been in force since incorporation. Due to good cost control, increasing amounts of profit are trapped in China. The implementation of the rules on transfer pricing in China has limited the scope of profit repatriation from the subsidiary. To avoid this constraint, the company has established a new subsidiary in Heshan for the production of the same products. Although the new subsidiary is located in the same province, it faces different local government policies, tax requirements and economic factors. This study examines whether the existing transfer pricing policy is applicable to the new subsidiary.

The company was established in Hong Kong in 1985, and has major customers in the US and Europe. In the early 1990s, the company successfully developed a strong customer base in the US, and it contributes about 80% of its total sales. As the turnover increased, the company decided to establish a new manufacturing operation in China to reduce its labour and operating costs. In 1992, XYZ (Shenzhen) Ltd, a wholly owned subsidiary in Shenzhen, was established. The production line in Hong Kong was maintained until the middle of 1996, when the entire manufacturing operation was moved to Shenzhen. XYZ (Shenzhen) Ltd contributes about 50% of the total production capacity of the group.

As the trading arm of the group, XYZ (Hong Kong) Ltd purchases products from XYZ (Shenzhen) Ltd and sells them to its customers. The current transfer pricing

I wish to acknowledge Ranco Chung Man Kit, for his assistance in preparing this case study. This case was developed as a basis for class discussion rather than to illustrate either effective or ineffective handling of an administrative situation.

rate is 75% of the sale price. In other words, if the Hong Kong company sells a product at US$100 to the customer, the Shenzhen subsidiary sells it to the Hong Kong company at US$75.

In view of the potential expansion of the market share in the US, the company further increased its production capacity in 2000. Heshan was selected to be the new location for the establishment of another manufacturing subsidiary. The major reasons for the choice were:

1) the average operating expenses were 20% to 25% lower than that in Shenzhen,
2) the land and building costs in Heshan were lower, and
3) although the income tax rate was 24%, which was higher than the 15% rate in Shenzhen, tax incentives were offered by the Heshan government, including a five-year tax holiday with full exemption from income tax for the first two profit-making years and a 50% tax reduction for the following three years.

Table 1 shows the factors that affect the transfer pricing decision.

Table 1 Factors that Affect Transfer Pricing Decisions

Factors	Regulatory environment	Competitive environment
1) Tax incentives	*****	
2) Transfer pricing rules	****	
3) Competition in a foreign country		*
4) Exchange controls	***	
5) High ad valorem tariffs[1]	*	

Key:

*: affects the least

*****: affects the most

[1] High ad valorem tariffs in China are only applied to imported goods. There is a refund of import duties when goods are exported up to a certain level. In the case study, the goods are for export.

TRANSFER PRICING ALTERNATIVES

The Selling Price Based on Transfer Pricing Policy

Since XYZ Group is small and the structure is simple, the major concern of the management was the regulatory environment. At the early stage of the establishment of the subsidiary, the turnover was small. The tax planning requirements were not so significant, but profit repatriation was a major concern due to the exchange controls and uncertain political situation in China.

The policy of transfer pricing between XYZ (Hong Kong) Ltd and XYZ (Shenzhen) Ltd was set at 75% of the usual sale price. The policy worked satisfactorily until recent years due to better cost control in the subsidiary, which resulted in a satisfactory profit. The manufacturing costs were reduced from about 65% of the selling price in 1993 to about 55% in 1998 with the increase in efficiency in XYZ (Shenzhen) Ltd. As the transfer price was based on the selling price, the extra profit earned remained in the Shenzhen subsidiary.

Considerations for the New Policy

With the establishment of XYZ (Heshan) Ltd, the senior management of the group wants to review the transfer pricing policy. They want to know whether the policy for XYZ (Shenzhen) Ltd can be used for XYZ (Heshan) Ltd. With the reformation of the legal system and the change of exchange control policy, profit repatriation is less of a concern, but with the growth of group profit, tax issues have become more significant. The CEO wants all group profit to be allocated to the new subsidiary to maximise the tax benefits that are offered by the Heshan tax authority. However, transfer pricing issues have been of great concern to both the Hong Kong and China tax authorities. A sudden change in the selling price to the Hong Kong head office could raise suspicions of transfer pricing irregularities. A balanced approach is required to satisfy the requirements of the tax authorities and enjoy the tax benefits at the same time.

New Policy – Cost Based

The major problem of the transfer pricing policy for XYZ (Shenzhen) Ltd is the uneven profit allocation by a discount on selling price as a result of improving cost efficiency. This method keeps profits inside China because cost reductions do not lead to selling price reductions. Consequently, a new transfer price based on manufacturing costs (the cost-plus method) is proposed, in which the transfer price to the Hong Kong head office is adjusted with costs and a constant level of profit in China is maintained. As a long-term policy, the method can offer a reasonable profit allocation for the Heshan subsidiary. Any extra profit as a result of increases in efficiency will go back to Hong Kong. This may happen with the Shenzhen subsidiary in the later stage of operation when the tax holiday is over. The profit will then be taxed at 17.5% in Hong Kong instead of the 24% full rate in Heshan. This is a trade-off for the transfer pricing mechanism (see Table 1). Among the various objectives of the policy, tax minimisation is the most important.

ANALYSIS

This case is analysed with hypothetical figures under the two transfer pricing policies. Because it is a long-term investment plan, a time frame of ten years is used. The major objective is to ascertain which method, selling-price-based or cost-based, is better for XYZ (Heshan) Ltd. Furthermore, an optimum transfer pricing rate can be fixed so that the company can balance the tax benefits and the requirements of the tax authorities.

The hypothetical figures are listed in Table 2. An annual turnover of HK$100 million is assumed. The variable manufacturing costs are 65% of the sales. The annual operation costs are fixed at HK$3 million for Heshan and HK$15 million Hong Kong. Zero inflation and zero growth are assumed, and hence a zero discount rate for the net present value of the tax liabilities. To simplify the analysis, the operation in Shenzhen is ignored. The hypothetical annual profit allocation is computed for Hong Kong and Heshan using the selling-price-based and cost-based transfer pricing policies. Based on the annual profit allocation that is computed in Table 3, the tax liabilities of the group over ten years are evaluated. In particular, the tax liabilities for Hong Kong and Heshan are evaluated. The results for the selling-price-based and cost-based transfer pricing policies are summarised in Tables 4 and 5, respectively.

The total tax liabilities of XYZ Group for the ten years are summarised in Table 6. To compare the sensitivity of the total tax payable to different transfer rates, the range and the variance of the total tax payable is computed under the two transfer pricing policies. Referring to Table 3, there are some extreme transfer rates that give a loss to one of the two locations. To eliminate the effect of the extreme figures, another set of ranges and variances is computed on the transfer price rate from 15% to 30%.

Table 2 Hypothetical Figures for XYZ Group

	HK$ million
Turnover	100
Manufacturing cost	65
Operating cost (for Hong Kong)	15
Operating cost (for Heshan)	3
Net profit before tax	17

Table 3 Annual Profit Allocation for the Different Transfer Pricing Policies[1]

		Selling price based		Cost based	
Net profit before tax (HK$ million)	*Transfer price rate*	*Hong Kong (HK$ million)*	*Heshan (HK$ million)*	*Hong Kong (HK$ million)*	*Heshan (HK$ million)*
17	10%	22.0	–5.0	3.5	13.5
17	15%	17.0	0.0	6.8	10.3
17	20%	12.0	5.0	10.0	7.0
17	25%	7.0	10.0	13.3	3.8
17	30%	2.0	15.0	16.5	0.5
17	35%	–3.0	20.0	19.8	–2.8

[1] The annual profit is computed based on the hypothetical figures in Table 2.

The range for the cost-based transfer pricing policy is HK$4.3 million, in comparison to HK$7.8 million for the selling-price-based policy. The variance also shows a greater difference, with HK$2.7 million for the cost-based policy and HK$11.3 million for the selling-price-based policy. If the two extreme rates are ignored, then the range for the cost-based policy decreases to 0.4 and that for selling-price-based policy decreases to 0.6. The variances are 0.03 and 0.07 respectively. The sensitivity of the total tax liabilities with respect to the transfer rate is very low for both methods. Hence, the transfer price rates have only a small effect on the total tax liabilities for the company's ten-year planning.

The cost-based method and the selling-price-based method are similar in terms of the long-term total tax liabilities. Under the analysis, manufacturing costs are kept at 65% throughout the ten years. Refer to Figure 1 for a comparison of the total tax liabilities against the transfer rate over ten years. Except for rates less than 10% and above 30%, the total tax liabilities are similar throughout the period.

The decrease in manufacturing costs as a result of the increase in efficiency in the later stage of XYZ (Shenzhen) Ltd has not been considered. To avoid the problem of the shifting of profit to the subsidiary, a cost-based policy is recommended. The extra profits will then be passed on to the Hong Kong company and be subject to the 17.5% profit tax instead of the 24% income tax in Heshan. The transfer price rate does not have much effect on the long-term total tax liabilities. However, a higher rate can be fixed so that the subsidiary will pay less tax in the early stage of the tax holiday. Refer to Figure 1 for the distribution of tax liabilities at different transfer rates under the cost-based policy over ten years. It is recommended that a

Table 4 Tax Liabilities under the Selling-price-based Transfer Pricing Policy[1,2]

Panel A: Tax liabilities (HK$ million) for XYZ (Hong Kong) Ltd under the selling-price-based transfer pricing policy

Transfer price rate	*Yr 1*	*Yr 2*	*Yr 3*	*Yr 4*	*Yr 5*	*Yr 6*	*Yr 7*	*Yr 8*	*Yr 9*	*Yr 10*	*Total*
10%	0.0	0.0	0.0	0.0	0.0	0.0	0.0	0.0	0.0	0.0	0.0
15%	0.0	0.0	0.0	0.0	0.0	0.0	0.0	0.0	0.0	0.0	0.0
20%	0.8	0.8	0.8	0.8	0.8	0.8	0.8	0.8	0.8	0.8	8.0
25%	1.6	1.6	1.6	1.6	1.6	1.6	1.6	1.6	1.6	1.6	16.0
30%	2.4	2.4	2.4	2.4	2.4	2.4	2.4	2.4	2.4	2.4	24.0
35%	3.2	3.2	3.2	3.2	3.2	3.2	3.2	3.2	3.2	3.2	32.0

Panel B: Tax liabilities (HK$ million) for XYZ (Heshan) Ltd under the selling-price-based transfer pricing policy

Transfer price rate	*Yr 1*	*Yr 2*	*Yr 3*	*Yr 4*	*Yr 5*	*Yr 6*	*Yr 7*	*Yr 8*	*Yr 9*	*Yr 10*	*Total*
10%	0.0	0.0	2.6	2.6	2.6	5.3	5.3	5.3	5.3	5.3	34.3
15%	0.0	0.0	2.0	2.0	2.0	4.1	4.1	4.1	4.1	4.1	26.5
20%	0.0	0.0	1.4	1.4	1.4	2.9	2.9	2.9	2.9	2.9	18.7
25%	0.0	0.0	0.8	0.8	0.8	1.7	1.7	1.7	1.7	1.7	10.9
30%	0.0	0.0	0.2	0.2	0.2	0.5	0.5	0.5	0.5	0.5	3.1
35%	0.0	0.0	0.0	0.0	0.0	0.0	0.0	0.0	0.0	0.0	0.0

Panel C: Tax liabilities (HK$ million) for XYZ Group under the selling-price-based transfer pricing policy

Transfer price rate	*Yr 1*	*Yr 2*	*Yr 3*	*Yr 4*	*Yr 5*	*Yr 6*	*Yr 7*	*Yr 8*	*Yr 9*	*Yr 10*	*Total*
10%	0.0	0.0	2.6	2.6	2.6	5.3	5.3	5.3	5.3	5.3	34.3
15%	0.0	0.0	2.0	2.0	2.0	4.1	4.1	4.1	4.1	4.1	26.5
20%	0.8	0.8	2.2	2.2	2.2	3.7	3.7	3.7	3.7	3.7	26.7
25%	1.6	1.6	2.4	2.4	2.4	3.3	3.3	3.3	3.3	3.3	26.9
30%	2.4	2.4	2.6	2.6	2.6	2.9	2.9	2.9	2.9	2.9	27.1
35%	3.2	3.2	3.2	3.2	3.2	3.2	3.2	3.2	3.2	3.2	32.0

[1] Zero inflation and zero growth are assumed.
[2] The tax liabilities are evaluated based on the annual profits computed in Table 3.

Table 5 Tax Liabilities under the Cost-based Transfer Pricing Policy[1,2]

Panel A: Tax liabilities (HK$ million) for XYZ (Hong Kong) Ltd under the cost-based transfer pricing policy

Transfer price rate	*Yr 1*	*Yr 2*	*Yr 3*	*Yr 4*	*Yr 5*	*Yr 6*	*Yr 7*	*Yr 8*	*Yr 9*	*Yr 10*	*Total*
10%	2.2	2.2	2.2	2.2	2.2	2.2	2.2	2.2	2.2	2.2	22.0
15%	1.6	1.6	1.6	1.6	1.6	1.6	1.6	1.6	1.6	1.6	16.0
20%	1.1	1.1	1.1	1.1	1.1	1.1	1.1	1.1	1.1	1.1	11.0
25%	0.6	0.6	0.6	0.6	0.6	0.6	0.6	0.6	0.6	0.6	6.0
30%	0.1	0.1	0.1	0.1	0.1	0.1	0.1	0.1	0.1	0.1	1.0
35%	0.0	0.0	0.0	0.0	0.0	0.0	0.0	0.0	0.0	0.0	0.0

Panel B: Tax liabilities (HK$ million) for XYZ (Heshan) Ltd under the cost-based transfer pricing policy

Transfer price rate	*Yr 1*	*Yr 2*	*Yr 3*	*Yr 4*	*Yr 5*	*Yr 6*	*Yr 7*	*Yr 8*	*Yr 9*	*Yr 10*	*Total*
10%	0.0	0.0	0.4	0.4	0.4	0.8	0.8	0.8	0.8	0.8	5.2
15%	0.0	0.0	0.8	0.8	0.8	1.6	1.6	1.6	1.6	1.6	10.4
20%	0.0	0.0	1.2	1.2	1.2	2.4	2.4	2.4	2.4	2.4	15.6
25%	0.0	0.0	1.6	1.6	1.6	3.2	3.2	3.2	3.2	3.2	20.8
30%	0.0	0.0	2.0	2.0	2.0	4.0	4.0	4.0	4.0	4.0	26.0
35%	0.0	0.0	2.4	2.4	2.4	4.7	4.7	4.7	4.7	4.7	30.7

Panel C: Tax liabilities (HK$ million) for XYZ Group under the cost-based transfer pricing policy

Transfer price rate	*Yr 1*	*Yr 2*	*Yr 3*	*Yr 4*	*Yr 5*	*Yr 6*	*Yr 7*	*Yr 8*	*Yr 9*	*Yr 10*	*Total*
10%	2.2	2.2	2.6	2.6	2.6	3.0	3.0	3.0	3.0	3.0	27.2
15%	1.6	1.6	2.5	2.5	2.5	3.3	3.3	3.3	3.3	3.3	27.2
20%	1.1	1.1	2.3	2.3	2.3	3.5	3.5	3.5	3.5	3.5	26.6
25%	0.6	0.6	2.2	2.2	2.2	3.8	3.8	3.8	3.8	3.8	26.8
30%	0.1	0.1	2.1	2.1	2.1	4.0	4.0	4.0	4.0	4.0	26.5
35%	0.0	0.0	2.4	2.4	2.4	4.7	4.7	4.7	4.7	4.7	30.7

[1] Zero inflation and zero growth are assumed.
[2] The tax liabilities are evaluated based on the annual profits computed in Table 3.

Table 6 Total Tax Liabilities of XYZ Group for Ten Years under the Different Transfer Pricing Policies

	Total tax liabilities[1]	
Transfer price rate	*Cost-based policy*	*Selling-price based policy*
10%	27.1	34.3
15%	26.9	26.5
20%	26.8	26.7
25%	26.7	26.9
30%	26.5	27.1
35%	30.8	32.0
Range	4.3	7.8
Variance	2.7	11.3
Range (15–30%)	0.4	0.6
Variance (15–30%)	0.03	0.07

[1] The total tax liabilities are summarised from Tables 4 and 5.

rate of 25% be adopted. Under this transfer rate, a large portion of the profit is allocated to Heshan. The tax paid in the early stage of the tax holiday will then be lowered. The cash flow will be increased and the financial burden may be smaller. However, as the tax will be increased after the tax holiday, this is only a deferral of the financial burden.

Although there are no great differences in the total liability over the ten years in using different transfer pricing percentages, the tax liabilities are spread differently. If the cost-plus percentage is high, then more profit will be allocated to Heshan and the company will pay less tax in the early stage of the tax holiday. However, if the percentage is low, then less profit will be allocated to Heshan and tax will be distributed more evenly over the period.

Figure 1 Tax Liabilities under the Cost-based Transfer Pricing Policy

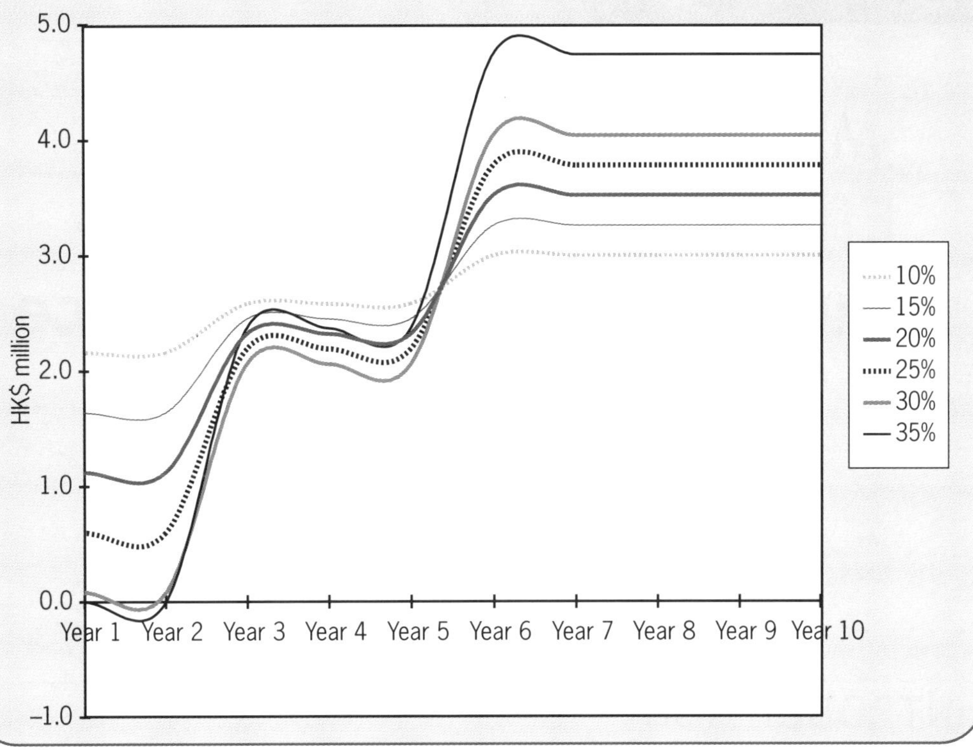

CASE STUDY QUESTIONS

1) What is the optimum transfer pricing strategy for the new Heshan subsidiary of XYZ Group?
2) How might the ending of the tax holiday change your analysis of the optimum transfer price?
3) What are the limitations of this analysis?
4) Would XYZ Group's transfer price strategy be the same if its proposed Heshan subsidiary was its first venture in China? Which factor (if any) would have a different influence on transfer pricing strategy?

CASE STUDY 17

MS Group – Organisation Efficiency and Regulatory Requirements: The Influence on Transfer Pricing Determination in a Competitive Environment

INTRODUCTION

MS Group is one of the largest processors and exporters of Chinese pearls in Hong Kong. It was also the first listed organisation to engage in the pearl business in Hong Kong. In recent years the demand for Chinese pearls has slowed. As a result, many Hong Kong suppliers adjusted their prices downwards to stimulate sales in early 2002. Many Chinese pearl suppliers in Hong Kong and China expect modest declines in sales in the near future. In view of this competitive environment, management is considering whether a change in transfer pricing policy between Hong Kong and China could help it maintain its market leadership. The current transfer pricing policy of the company is market based. To compete successfully and effectively, the management has considered moving to a cost-based or negotiation-based policy. However, the management is worried that such a switch could lead to

I wish to acknowledge the assistance of William Yau in the preparation of this case study. This case was developed as a basis for class discussion rather than to illustrate either effective or ineffective handling of an administrative situation.

increased performance rewards for the Chinese manager, an increment in the effort behind enforcing tax compliance in China and a distortion of management's perception of the profit margin.

CASE BACKGROUND

MS Group was founded in the early 1980s, and in the early 1990s, to take advantage of the proximity to the source of Chinese pearl supply and the abundant low-cost labour, it decided to establish its own pearl production facilities in China. MS (China) was established in Bao An, Shenzhen, in 1993 and commenced the business of pearl processing. The raw materials are purchased from pearl farms in Zhejiang and Jiangsu, and upon the refinement and bleaching processes, the finished pearls are sold to Hong Kong. MS (China) has enjoyed a tax holiday since 1998, the first profitable year, and to minimise the overall taxation expense within the group, a certain amount of profit has been shifted from MS (Hong Kong) to MS (China) by market-based transfer pricing. However, the tax holiday will expire in 2005.

Raw materials are procured in lots from farmers in Zhejiang and Jiangsu. The volume of procurement is usually in tonnes at a time. Due to such large volumes, the processing period usually lasts for three to six months. MS (China) then ships the finished pearls to Hong Kong in numerous lots. The finished pearls with the best quality are sent to Hong Kong, and then the next best and so on. The finished pearls are sent without billing, and when MS (Hong Kong) receives the goods, they are graded at the latest market price and the information is sent back to China. When MS (China) receives this information, it bills MS (Hong Kong) at a 70% discount. The transfer price formula is:

$$\textit{Transfer price} = \textit{Market price} \times \textit{Discount rate}$$

The ultimate selling price to the customer is billed according to the company pricing policy. The sales force is usually authorised to give a discount rate of up to 50% to 60% of the market price of the finished pearls to its customers. The selling price formula is:

$$\textit{Selling price} = \textit{Transfer price} \times \textit{Discount rate}$$

Table 1 illustrates the various transfer pricing scenarios.

Table 1 Alternative Scenarios for Proposed Transfer Pricing Systems

Assume the production of finished pearls of Grade A to C with the following details

Product	*Market Value per kg (a)*	*Weighted average Actual cost (b)*	*Proposed Standard cost (c)*
Grade A product	100,000	20,000	25,000
Grade B product	80,000	20,000	20,000
Grade C product	60,000	20,000	15,000

Original transfer pricing system – market-based method

Product	*Market value per kg*	*Discount rate (d)*	*Market-based transfer price (f)=(a)×(d)*	*Ultimate selling price to customer (g)=(a)×(e)*	*Discount rate to customer (e)*
Grade A product	100,000	30%	30,000	40,000	40%
Grade B product	75,000	30%	22,500	30,000	40%
Grade C product	50,000	30%	15,000	20,000	40%

Thus, the profit of MS (Hong Kong) and MS Group will be as follows

Product	*MS (Hong Kong) profit (g)–(f)*	*Profit margin*	*MS Group profit (g)–(b)*	*Profit margin*
Grade A product	10,000	25%	20,000	50%
Grade B product	7,500	25%	10,000	33%
Grade C product	5,000	25%	–	0%

(I) Proposed transfer pricing system – Actual cost-plus-based method

Product	*Market value per kg*	*Mark-up rate (h)*	*Actual cost-plus transfer price (i)=(b)×[1+(h)]*	*Ultimate selling price to customer (g)=(a)×(e)*	*Discount rate to customer (e)*
Grade A product	100,000	10%	22,000	40,000	40%
Grade B product	75,000	10%	22,000	30,000	40%
Grade C product	50,000	10%	22,000	20,000	40%

Thus, the profit of MS (Hong Kong) and MS Group will be as follows

Product	*MS (Hong Kong) Profit (g)–(i)*	*Profit Margin*	*MS Group Profit (g)–(b)*	*Profit Margin*
Grade A product	18,000	45%	20,000	50%
Grade B product	8,000	27%	10,000	33%
Grade C product	2,000	–10%	–	0%

Table 1 Alternative Scenarios for Proposed Transfer Pricing Systems (Cont'd)

(II) Proposed transfer pricing system – Standard cost-plus method

Product	Market value per kg	Mark-up rate (h)	Cost-plus transfer price (j)=(c)×[1+(h)]	Ultimate selling price to customer (g)=(a)×(e)	Discount rate to customer (e)
Grade A product	100,000	10%	27,500	40,000	40%
Grade B product	75,000	10%	22,000	30,000	40%
Grade C product	50,000	10%	16,500	20,000	40%

Thus, the profit of MS (Hong Kong) and MS Group will be as follows

Product	MS (Hong Kong) profit (g)–(j)	Profit margin	MS Group profit (g)–(c)	Profit margin
Grade A product	12,500	31%	15,000	38%
Grade B product	8,000	27%	10,000	33%
Grade C product	3,500	18%	5,000	25%

CASE ANALYSIS AND KEY ELEMENTS

Competitive Environment – Industry and Market Analysis

Recent demand for Chinese pearls has slowed in Europe and the US, and most Chinese pearl suppliers in Hong Kong and China expect sales to decline. Many Hong Kong suppliers have already adjusted their prices downwards by 20% to 30% to stimulate sales. This price war will lead to a drop in the group's market share and keen competition is expected.

The group uses a market-based transfer pricing system because it wants to shift its profit to China in view of the tax holidays and low tax rate. To retain profit in China, the market price that is charged to Hong Kong is quite high as compared to the actual cost of the goods, and this has recently meant that MS (Hong Kong) salespeople have found it difficult to negotiate the selling price of the end products with their customers while maintaining the pre-determined profit margin. The main customers are usually other major global corporations with professional purchasing functions, which easily recognise price disparities. The management has recognised the changing competitive nature of the market and is committed to maintaining a strong leadership position.

From an international transfer pricing theoretical perspective, an international transfer pricing system can be used to help the management by charging a low transfer pricing for goods. An MNE can set a low transfer price for goods shipped to the buying company to strengthen its financial and competitive position. In view of the group's situation, a cost-based transfer pricing system that offers a lower price to MS (Hong Kong) would reduce the purchase cost in Hong Kong and strengthen its competitive position.

Organisational Efficiency – Asset Specificity

The overall group operations are quite vertically integrated. MS (China) is responsible for procurement of the raw material and providing the finished products to Hong Kong after processing. MS (Hong Kong) is responsible for the export sales function. The group has invested over HK$20 million in MS (China) to develop the plants and factory, and employs over 700 workers.

From a transaction cost theory perspective, when the level of asset-specific investments in internal transfer is high, the corporate managers are most likely to protect the firm's economic interests by asserting control over the transfer by constraining the selling decision. In addition, as the level of asset-specific investment in the transfer by the component division increases, intermediate components will become increasingly customised and specific to the end product division. Consequently, market prices will become increasingly less relevant in providing information on the transfer pricing process (Colbert and Spicer, 1995). Taking into consideration the significant level of asset specificity in MS (China), a greater weighting should be given to manufacturing costs in the setting of the transfer cost. Hence, a cost-based transfer pricing system is more preferable.

Organisational Efficiency – Management Perception of Profit Margin

The profit margin of pearl processing is about 50% on the sales value in China, and the profit margin of the export business in Hong Kong is around 20%. The management has already factored this into the profit margin ratio.

MS Group is proposing a cost-plus-based transfer pricing system to replace the existing system. The proposed cost-plus-based transfer pricing will use the actual costs and mark them up to allow MS (China) to realise limited profit (see Table 1, Scenario 1). The realised profit will allow MS (China) to recover its normal operating costs plus an appropriate mark-up to earn a limited profit to deal with the Chinese tax authorities. This proposed system will rely on the accuracy and appropriateness of the valuation of the actual cost of the goods. MS (China) uses a simple weighted average costing valuation method, and as the procurement of the raw material is in lots, the actual cost of the products is calculated in lots. Due to the disparity in the grading of the products, MS (China) simply averages the cost of the items in the relevant lots to simplify the accounting. However, the current practice in the calculation of the actual cost means that the proposed cost-plus-based transfer pricing system will make the profit margin fluctuate unintentionally and distort the management perception of the profit margin ratio.

Taking into account the shortcoming in the implementation of the cost-plus-based system with actual cost valuation, the adoption of cost-plus-based transfer pricing with standard costs would give a more appropriate profit margin and retain the perception of the management (see Table 1, Scenario 1). Moreover, transferring at standard costs has the advantage of preventing the selling division from passing on its inefficiencies in the transfer price.

Organisational Efficiency – Performance Evaluation and Compensation Structure

The MS (China) operations are supervised by a general manager who is the elder brother of the group CEO. Although the daily operation of the company is quite autonomous, the determination of the transfer pricing for goods sold to Hong Kong depends on the decision of the senior executive in Hong Kong.

In evaluating the performance of MS (China), it is appropriate to evaluate its contribution to the objectives and goals of the whole group. It is also important to evaluate the contribution of foreign subsidiary managers to the performance of the MNE. However, a conflict appears when headquarters enforces a specific transfer price to be used by its subsidiaries to achieve certain objectives such as domestic and foreign income tax minimisation and foreign exchange risk reduction.

The operations of a foreign subsidiary may be evaluated as if they were completely autonomous, and subsidiary managers often have a great deal of freedom in making short-term decisions. However, they have less freedom in making decisions that directly affect other foreign subsidiaries and the group as a whole. As interdependence increases task uncertainty, the information that is provided by the transfer pricing system is vital for risk sharing and motivation.

Being a highly centralised organisation, the senior management determines how many units of output will be produced and how many units that the distribution department should be able to sell at a range of prices. Thus, the responsibility for profit performance is quite centralised, which implies that the performance evaluation system of the managers in China would be more meaningful if it depended on non-financial figures, such as the quality and quantity of the products. This kind of evaluation system could provide a fairer reward system to the managers while not having a significant effect on the overall transfer pricing system.

Regulatory Environment – Contemporary Transfer Pricing Issues in Mainland China

Chinese authorities, including the tax and customs administrations, have begun collaborating to combat unreasonable transfer practices as part of their effort to tighten up law enforcement. One noticeable change is that companies are now obliged to submit details of related party transaction along with their annual returns. Failing to submit such information may render a return invalid. Targets for investigation and audit are then screened and selected based on information in the returns. If a company is found to have conducted transactions with a related party on an unreasonable basis without proper substantiation and thereby reduced taxable income, then the tax authorities have the right to make appropriate adjustments. Another change is that custom rules now require importers to use proper value for import declarations, as opposed to custom-assigned values, which were used under the old procedures. Importers should be able to reconcile the custom values of their imports with the fair market prices in their accounting books and records. Obviously, these procedural changes are designed to prepare officials for stricter law enforcement. In certain circumstances, law enforcement agents seem to be willing to provide transitional relief such as tax amnesties to encourage taxpayers to adopt stricter compliance management.

In fact, the effective rate of income tax of MS (China) after the expiry of its tax holiday will be 15%, whereas the effective income tax rate of MS (Hong Kong) is 17.5%. Thus, the marginal cost of the differential tax rate is quite low. This implies that the shifting of profit back to MS (Hong Kong) by lowering the transfer prices with the cost-plus system would not have significant effect on the group's overall tax exposure, and it would help the management improve its competitive advantage. However, a carefully planned, well-reasoned and documented transfer pricing policy should be used as a tool to minimise the risk of tax audits by the Chinese authorities.

CASE STUDY QUESTIONS

1) What was the main factor that affected the transfer pricing strategy of the MS Group?
2) Which of the three general factors that influence transfer pricing strategy were significant in determining the transfer price in this case?
3) How are the influencing factors related? Are they complements or substitutes?
4) What limitations are associated with the analysis undertaken in this study?

CASE STUDY 18

ABC Group – How can a More Efficient Combination of Pricing and Resource Strategies be Achieved to Minimise the Group's Tax Liability?

COMPANY BACKGROUND

Hong Kong is renowned as a tax haven in the Asia-Pacific region. Currently, companies in Hong Kong are taxed at 17.5% on profits sourced locally. Hence, MNEs usually maintain a Hong Kong vehicle to reduce their group tax burden. ABC (Hong Kong) Ltd was formed to play this role. ABC (Hong Kong), a subsidiary of ABC (US) Co, is an electronic components manufacturer. Its customers come mainly from Asia and Europe. To take advantage of the lower production costs in China, ABC (Hong Kong) moved its production facilities to Shenzhen in 1996 by setting up a wholly owned subsidiary, ABC (China) Ltd. ABC (Hong Kong) and ABC (China) are collectively called ABC Group in this case study.

ABC (China) principally engages in production and employs over 400 workers. Most of the finished goods are sold through ABC (Hong Kong). With a reputation for superior product quality, ABC (Hong Kong) assigns only around 15 staff members to perform its marketing, after-sales service, logistics and finance functions. As a foreign company in a Special Economic Zone, and with its products classified as

I wish to acknowledge the assistance of Heizo Choi in the preparation of this case study. This case was developed as a basis for class discussion rather than to illustrate either effective or ineffective handling of an administrative situation.

technologically advanced and export oriented, ABC (China) is entitled to many tax incentives under the preferential tax policies offered by the Chinese government. At present, import and export tariffs on the material and final products of ABC (China) are waived. The company started to earn a profit in the first year of operation.

With an increasing number of manufacturing MNEs moving their production sites to low-cost countries such as China, Thailand and Malaysia, the demand for ABC (Hong Kong) products has been pushed up because of the company's proximity to these customers. The average annual sales growth over the past five years is about 8%. Most of the profits have been captured in Hong Kong, resulting in substantial Hong Kong tax payments. The current transfer pricing policy may not effectively match one of the company's paramount objectives – tax minimisation. The effective tax rate now charged on ABC China is only around 10%, which is actually lower than that on ABC (Hong Kong). Based on the existing practice, the group is not optimising its taxation benefits. It may be worthwhile to conduct a review to ascertain whether the group's tax liabilities can be minimised within the regulatory constraints, keeping in mind that careful attention needs to be paid to the potential risk of triggering a costly tax audit. Another factor to consider is the uncertainty of tax reforms upon China's accession to the WTO.

For the ABC Group, the objective of the transfer price is tax minimisation. The group has used the cost-plus transfer price method for a long time. The factors that affect the transfer price decision can be classified under regulatory environment, organisational efficiency and competitive environment. In terms of organisational efficiency, the group's performance evaluation is based on business lines, rather than on subsidiaries as separate entities. Each business unit is accountable for the profitability of its product line. ABC (China) was incorporated not for resource coordination, but rather to use it as a resource seeker. Given that there is no local partner, organisation efficiency is not an important driver of transfer pricing strategy for the ABC Group. In terms of competitive environment, ABC's products compete by brand name in the market. Therefore a price strategy is rarely necessary. Moreover, the parent company is committed to support their financial needs. Therefore, the competitive environment is not an important factor for the ABC Group. Hence, the focus of this study will be on examining regulatory factors, which are more important in influencing the group's transfer price decision.

CURRENT PRACTICE

ABC (Hong Kong) and ABC (China) are treated as associated companies by the Hong Kong Internal Revenue Department (HKIRD) and China's State

Administration of Taxation. The two companies incur selling, general and administration expenses (SG&A) of about US$2 million and US$600,000 annually. Three kinds of materials are required for production, namely materials X, Y and Z. The production mix is 40%, 30% and 30% respectively. Currently, around 70% of total material is purchased through ABC HK, of which material X is transferred at cost and material Y is transferred at a 15% mark-up on cost. ABC (China) purchases material Z directly from third parties overseas. About 90% of the final products are sold back to ABC (Hong Kong) for resale to third parties, with the rest sold in domestic markets (see Figure 1). At present, all sales from ABC (China) to ABC (Hong Kong) are marked up at 25% on cost.

Figure 1 Current Transfer Pricing Arrangement

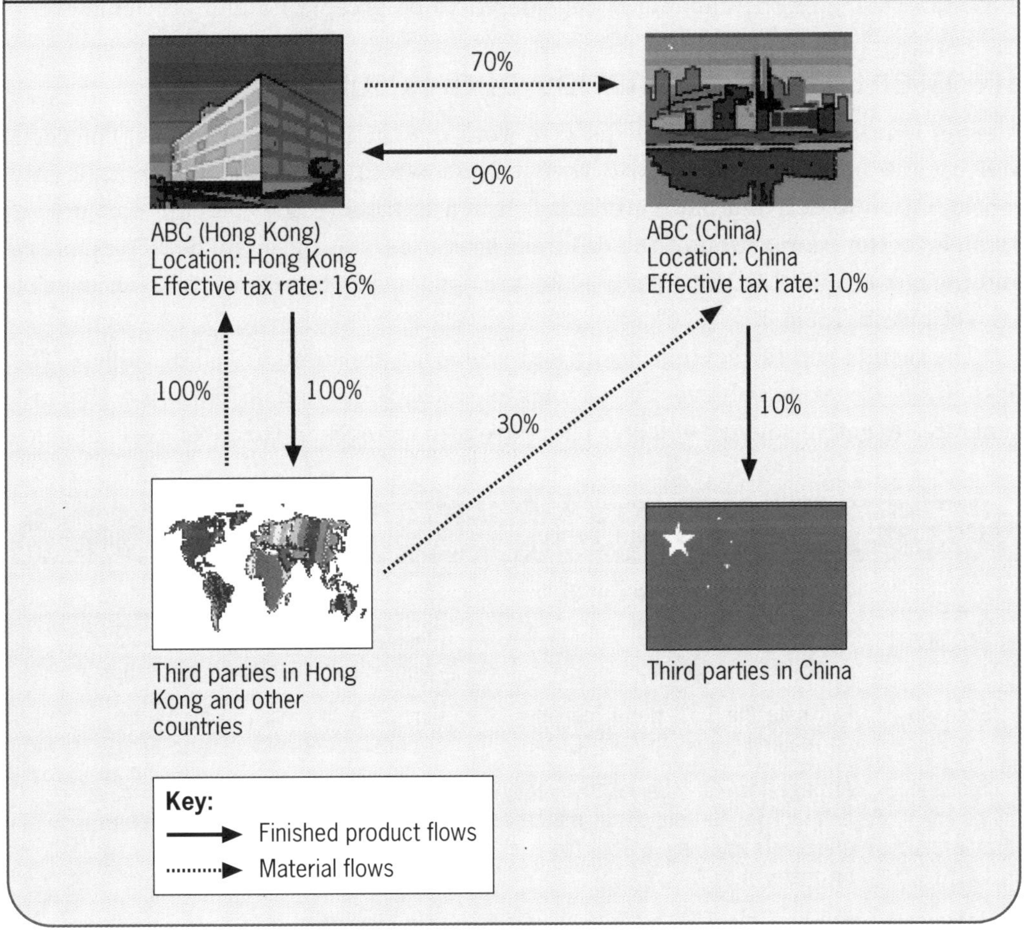

SCENARIO ANALYSIS

Setting Benchmarks

Transfer price violations are now being audited in many countries, including the US, Japan and European countries. China has become much more concerned about this issue in recent years. For Hong Kong, the transfer price issue is not so serious because the tax rate is comparatively low. Many MNEs consider retaining profits in Hong Kong rather than shifting them. Knowing that an aggressive change can trigger tax investigation, the management of ABC Group would prefer a mild shift of profits from Hong Kong to China to reduce the odds of being selected as an audit target by either jurisdiction before the certainty of tax reforms becomes clear. Hence, a 5% tax saving or thereabouts is considered to be acceptable and efficient.

Transfer Pricing Scenarios and Results

A set of hypothetical data will be used to work out the possible scenarios. The costs and benefits of each scenario will then be compared, taking the benchmark into consideration to derive a more efficient solution to achieve the company's objective. To allow better comparison of the different scenarios, sales growth, SG&A expenses and the current level of third party sales are assumed to be constant. The scenarios are set out in Table 1.

The results and tax savings of the four scenarios are summarised in Table 2. The first three scenarios achieve tax savings of 4.4%, 3.7% and 3.7%, while the last generates negative savings of 0.5%. There are also changes in turnover, costs of sales

Table 1 Different Transfer Pricing Scenarios

	ABC (Hong Kong)	ABC (China)
Scenario 1	No change	Increase the mark-up by 5% on goods sold to ABC (Hong Kong).
Scenario 2	Eliminate the 15% profit mark-up on materials sold to ABC (China).	Increase the mark-up by 5% on goods sold to ABC (Hong Kong).
Scenario 3	Arrange for ABC (China) to directly contract for the supply of material Y – effectively applying a 15% mark-up on material Y.	Increase the mark-up by 5% on goods sold to ABC (Hong Kong).
Scenario 4	Eliminate the 15% profit mark-up on materials sold to ABC (China).	No change

Table 2 Analysis of Different Scenarios

Scenario 1	Turnover	COS	GP	EBT	Taxation
ABC (Hong Kong)	US$'000	US$'000	US$'000	US$'000	US$'000
Current	75,473	56,691	18,782 (25%)	16,782 (22%)	2,685 (16%)
Proposed	75,473	59,405	16,067 (21%)	14,067 (19%)	2,251 (10%)
ABC (China)					
Current	42,200	31,800	10,400 (25%)	9,800 (23%)	980 (16%)
Proposed	44,914	31,800	13,114 (29%)	12,514 (28%)	1,251 (10%)
				Total tax liabilities in current practice	3,665
				Total tax liabilities in the proposed scenario	3,502
				Total tax saving (+)/increase (–)	163 (=+4.4%)

Scenario 2	Turnover	COS	GP	EBT	Taxation
ABC (Hong Kong)	US$'000	US$'000	US$'000	US$'000	US$'000
Current	75,473	56,691	18,782 (25%)	16,782 (22%)	2,685
Proposed	74,469	57,971	16,498 (22%)	14,498 (20%)	2,320
ABC (China)					
Current	42,200	31,800	10,400 (25%)	9,800 (23%)	980
Proposed	43,380	30,796	12,684 (29%)	12,084 (28%)	1,208
				Total tax liabilities in current practice	3,665
				Total tax liabilities in the proposed scenario	3,528
				Total tax saving (+)/increase (–)	137 (=+3.7%)

Scenario 3	Turnover	COS	GP	EBT	Taxation
ABC (Hong Kong)	US$'000	US$'000	US$'000	US$'000	US$'000
Current	75,473	56,691	18,782 (25%)	16,782 (22%)	2,685
Proposed	67,778	51,280	16,498 (24%)	14,498 (21%)	2,320
ABC (China)					
Current	42,200	31,800	10,400 (25%)	9,800 (23%)	980
Proposed	43,480	30,796	12,684 (29%)	12,084 (28%)	1,208
				Total tax liabilities in current practice	3,665
				Total tax liabilities in the proposed scenario	3,528
				Total tax saving (+)/increase (–)	137 (=+3.7%)

Scenario 4	Turnover	COS	GP	EBT	Taxation
ABC (Hong Kong)	US$'000	US$'000	US$'000	US$'000	US$'000
Current	75,473	56,691	18,782 (25%)	16,782 (22%)	2,685
Proposed	74,469	55,353	19,116 (26%)	17,116 (23%)	2,739
ABC (China)					
Current	42,200	31,800	10,400 (25%)	9,800 (23%)	980
Proposed	40,862	30,996	9,865 (24%)	9,265 (23%)	927
				Total tax liabilities in current practice	3,665
				Total tax liabilities in the proposed scenario	3,685
				Total tax saving (+)/increase (–)	(20) (=–0.5%)

(COS), gross profit (GP), earnings before tax (EBT) and tax savings. It may be advisable to consider the scenario that arouses the least attention from either tax bureau.

Scenario 1. For ABC (Hong Kong), turnover remains but COS increases due to the higher mark-up percentage for goods from China. Hence, GP decreases by 4%. For ABC (China), turnover increases but COS does not. Hence, GP increases by 4%. Under this arrangement, the tax savings is 4.4% or US$163,000. This scenario also generates the highest level of cash flow.

Scenario 2. For ABC (Hong Kong), turnover decreases due to the elimination of the mark-up on materials to China. COS increases due to the higher mark-up on finished goods from China. Consequently, GP decreases by 3%. For ABC (China), turnover increases but COS decreases. Hence, GP increases by 4%. Under this arrangement, the tax savings is 3.7% or US$137,000. Currently, the materials are directly transported from suppliers to ABC (China). The direct contracting of materials will not add further supply risks to ABC (China) because the change simply means the elimination of the Hong Kong intermediary in terms of paperwork.

Scenario 3. For ABC (Hong Kong), turnover decreases due to direct contracting for material Y by ABC (China), and COS decreases, due to the amount of material Y being taken out for ease of calculation, so GP decreases by 1%. For ABC (China), the situation is exactly the same as Scenario 2. Under this arrangement, the tax savings is also 3.7% or US$137,000.

Scenario 4. For ABC (Hong Kong), turnover decreases due to the elimination of the mark-up on materials to China. COS also decreases because the cost base of materials is lower. However, there is no change in the mark-up on finished goods from China, so GP increases by 1%. For ABC (China), turnover decreases and COS decreases correspondingly, so GP also decreases by 1%. Under this arrangement, the total tax liability increases by 0.5% or US$20,000 because the effective tax rate is higher in Hong Kong than in China.

In terms of the potential tax audit risks that are faced by ABC (Hong Kong), the drop of 4%, 3% and 1% in GP in the first three scenarios does not constitute a substantial change in the company's overall profit and tax payment, and hence should not arouse attention from the HKIRD. The potential tax audit risks that are faced by ABC (China) in the first three scenarios are not particularly high because most of the criteria for triggering tax audits do not exist. Moreover, ABC (China) makes more profits and thus pays more tax in all three scenarios. Furthermore, the GP ratio of ABC (China) does not vary to a great extent because third party sales in China are limited. After all, from the experience of ABC management, the variation of GP for such percentages is not so extraordinary as to cause any concern from either tax bureau.

CASE STUDY QUESTIONS

1) What is the optimum transfer pricing strategy for ABC Group? Explain.
2) Is the optimum transfer pricing strategy likely to trigger a tax audit? Explain.
3) To what extent did political risk factor into the final result? In what way can political risk influence the optimal scenario?
4) What limitations are associated with the analysis undertaken in this study?
5) What alternative mechanisms can be used to manage the organisational efficiency problems associated with the transfer pricing method chosen by ABC Group?

References

Abdallah, W.M. (1989). *International Transfer Pricing Policies: Decision-Making Guidelines for Multinational Companies*. New York: Quorum Books.

Agarwal, S., & Ramaswami, S.N. (1992). Choice of foreign market entry mode: Impact of ownership, location and internationalisation factors. *Journal of International Business Studies*, *23*(1), 1–27.

Al-Eryani, M.F., Alam, P., & Akhter, S. (1990). Transfer pricing determinants of U.S. multinational. *Journal of International Business Studies*, September, *21*(3), 409–425.

Anand, J., & Delios, A. (1997). Location specificity and the transferability of downstream assets to foreign subsidiaries. *Journal of International Business Studies*, *28*(3), 579–604.

Anderson, E. (1990). Two firms, one frontier: On assessing joint venture performance. *Sloan Management Review*, Winter, *32*, 19–30.

Anderson, E., & Gatignon, H. (1986). Modes of foreign entry: A transaction cost analysis and proposition. *Journal of International Business Studies*, *17*(3), 1–26.

Anthony, R.N., & Dearden, J. (1980). *Management control system*. Homewood, Illinois: Irwin.

Appleyard, A., Strong, N., & Walton, P. (1990). Management control of foreign subsidiaries. *European Management Journal*, September, 402–407.

Arpan, Jeffrey, S. (1972). *International intracorporate pricing*, New York: Praeger Publishers.

Aulakh, P.S., & Kotabe, M. (1997). Antecedents and performance implications of channel integration in foreign markets. *Journal of International Business Studies*, *28*(1), 145–175.

Austin, J.E. (1990). *Managing in developing countries: Strategic analysis and operating techniques*. New York: Free Press.

Bailes, J.C., & Assada, T. (1991). Empirical differences between Japanese and American budget and performance evaluation systems. *International Journal of Accounting*, *26*(2), 131–142.

Barth, S. (1997). Reengineering socialism. *World Trade Magazine*. Accessed at http://www.global-insight.com/wt9709a.htm on 1 April 2004.

Bauer, T.N., Morrison, E., & Callister, R. (1998). Organisational socialisation: A review and directions for future research. *Research in Personal and Human Resources Management*, *16*, 149–214.

BBC Monitoring Asia Pacific (2002, April). *Chinese premier tells Boao forum renminbi not to be devalued*. Accessed at http://proquest.umi.com/pqdweb on 8 November 2004.

Beamish, P.W. (1985). The characterisation of joint ventures in developed and developing countries. *Columbia Journal of World Business,* Fall, *20*(3), 13–19.

Beamish, P.W. (1993). The characteristics of joint ventures in the People's Republic of China. *Journal of International Marketing*, *1*(2), 29–48.

Beamish, P.W., & Banks, J.C. (1987). Equity joint ventures and the theory of the multinational enterprise. *Journal of International Business Studies*, Summer, 1–16.

Beiman, I., & Sun, Y. (2003). *Balanced scorecard and strategy execution.* Beijing, China: China Machine Press.

Bhattacharya, M. (1999). *How much do country, industry and firm matter? A meta-analysis of modes of foreign entry decisions*. Paper presented at the Academy of Management Conference Proceedings, Chicago, USA.

Biddle, G.C., Bowen, R.M., & Wallace, J.S. (1997). Does EVA beat earnings? Evidence on associations with stock returns and firm values. *Journal of Accounting and Economics*, *24*(3), 301–336.

Blodgett, L.L. (1991). Partner contributions as predictors of equity share in international joint ventures. *Journal of International Business Studies*, *22*(1), 63–78.

Borkowski, S.C. (1997). The transfer pricing concerns of developed and developing countries. *The International Journal of Accounting*, *32*(3), 321–336.

Borkowski, S.C. (2000). Transfer pricing advance pricing agreements: Current status by country. *The International Tax Journal*, Spring, *26*(2), 1–16.

Brickley, J.A., Smith, C.W., & Zimmerman, J.L. (1997). *Managerial Economics and Organisational Architecture.* New York: Irwin.

Brouthers, K.D., & Bamossy, G.J. (1997). The role of key stakeholders in international joint venture negotiations: Case studies from Eastern Europe. *Journal of International Business Studies*, *2*, 285–308.

Bruton, G.D. (2000). Foreign firms in China: Facing human resources challenges in a transitional economy. *S.A.M. Advanced Management Journal*, Autumn, *65*(4), 4–12.

Buckley, P.J., & Casson, M. (1976). *The future of multinational enterprises*. London: Macmillan.

Buckley, P.J., & Casson, M. (1988, Special Issue). A theory of cooperation in international business. *Management International Review*, 19–37.

Bushman, R.M., Indjejikian, R.J., & Smith, A. (2000). CEO compensation: The role of individual performance evaluation. *Journal of Accounting and Economics*, *21*, 161–193.

Campbell, A.J., & Verbeke, A. (1994). The globalisation of service multinationals. *Long Range Planning*, *27*(2), 95–102.

Carman, J.M., & Langeard, E. (1980). Growth strategies of service firms. *Strategic Management Journal*, *1*, 7–22.

Casson, M.C. (1987). *The firm and the market.* Oxford, UK: Basil Blackwell.

Chalos, P., & O'Connor, N.G. (2004). Determinants of various controls in U.S.-Sino joint ventures. *Accounting, Organisations and Society*, *7*, 591–608.

Chan, K.H., & Chow, L. (1997a). An empirical study of tax audits in China on international transfer pricing. *Journal of Accounting and Economics*, *23*, 88–112.

Chan, K.H., & Chow, L. (1997b). International transfer pricing for business operations in China: Inducements, regulation and practice. *Journal of Business Finance and Accounting*, *24*(9–10), 1269–1289.

Chan, K.H., & Chow, L. (2001). Corporate environments and international transfer pricing: An empirical study of China in a developing economy framework. *Accounting and Business Research*, 103–118.

Chan, W.A. (1999). Managing human resources across the border: Two cases of Hong Kong-based joint ventures in China. *International Journal of Management*, *16*, 586–593.

Chen, C., & Godkin, L. (2001). *Mianzi*, *guanxi* and western prospects in China. *International Journal of Management*, *18*(2), 139.

Chen, C.C., (1995). New trends in allocation performance: A Sino-U.S. comparison. *Academy of Management Journal*, *38*, 408–428.

Chen, H.Y., & Hu, M.Y. (2002). An analysis of determinants of entry mode and its impact on performance. *International Business Review*, *11*, 193–210.

Chen, S., & Dodd, J.L. (1997). Economic value added (EVA): An empirical examination of a new corporate performance measure. *Journal of Managerial Issues*, *9*(3), 318–333.

Child, J. (1984). *Organisation: A guide to problems and practice*. London: Paul Chapman.

Child, J. (1994). *Management in China during the age of reform.* Cambridge, UK: Cambridge University Press.

Child, J., & Faulkner, D. (1998). *Strategies of cooperation: Managing alliances, networks and joint ventures*. London: Oxford University Press.

Child, J., & Yan, Y. (1999). Investment and control in international joint ventures: The case of China. *Journal of World Business*, *24*(1), 3–15.

Chinese Cultural Connection. (1987). Chinese values and the search for culture-free dimensions of culture. *Journal of Cross-Cultural Psychology*, June, 143–164.

Chow, C.W., Deng, H.J., & Ho, J.L. (2000). The openness of knowledge sharing within organisations: A comparative study of United States and the People's Republic of China. *Journal of Management Accounting Research*, *12*, 65–95.

Chow, C.W., Shields, M.D., & Wu, A. (1999). The importance of national culture in the design of and preference for management controls for multi-national operations. *Accounting, Organisations and Society*, *24*, 441–461.

Christie, A.A., Joye, M.P., & Watts, R.L. (2003). Decentralisation of the firm: Theory and evidence. *Journal of Corporate Finance*, *9*, 3–26.

Chung, H.F.L., & Enderwick, P. (2001). An investigation of market entry strategy selection: Exporting vs foreign direct investment modes – A home-host country scenario. *Asia Pacific Journal of Management*, *18*, 443–460.

Colbert, G.J., & Spicer, B.H. (1995). A multi-case investigation of a theory of the transfer pricing process. *Accounting, Organisations and Society*, *20*(6), 423–456.

Cooper, H., & Johnson, I. (2000, May). Congress's vote primes forms in U.S. to boost China deals. *Asian Wall Street Journal*, *1*(7).

Cravens, K.S. (1996). Examining the role of transfer pricing as a strategy for multinational firms. *International Business Review*, *6*(7), 127–145.

Cyr, D.J. (1995). *The Human Resource Challenge of International Joint Ventures*. Westport, Connecticut: Quorum Books.

Cyr, D.J., & Schneider, S.C. (1996). Implications for learning: Human resource management in East-West ventures. *Organisation Studies*, *17*(2), 207–226.

Czinkota, M., Ronkainen, I., & Moffett, M. (1996). *International Business* (4th Ed.). New York: Dryden Press.

Daley, L., Jiambalvo, J., Sundem, G., & Kondo, Y. (1985). Attitudes towards financial control systems in the United States and Japan. *Journal of International Business Studies*, Fall, 91–110.

Doz, Y.L., & Prahalad, C.K. (1986). How MNCs cope with host government intervention. *Harvard Business Review*, *58*(2), 149.

Dunning, J.H. (1988). The eclectic paradigm of international production: A restatement and some possible extensions. *Journal of International Business Studies*, *19*(1), 1–31.

Dunning, J.H. (1999). The location and the multinational enterprise: A neglected factor? *Journal of International Business Studies*, *29*(1), 45–67.

Ehrbar, A., & Stewart III, G.B. (1999). The EVA revolution. *Journal of Applied Corporate Finance*, Summer, *12*, 18–31.

Erramilli, K.M., & Rao, C.P. (1993). Service firms' international entry mode choice: A modified transaction-cost analysis approach. *Journal of Marketing*, *57*(3), 19–38.

Fang, Tony. (1999). *Chinese business negotiating style*. Thousand Oaks, California: Sage Publications.

Feils, D.J., & Sabac, F.M. (2000). The impact of political risk on the foreign direct investment decision: A capital budgeting analysis. *The Engineering Economist, 45*(2), 129–143.

Firth, M. (1996). The diffusion of managerial accounting procedures in the People's Republic of China and the influence of foreign partnered joint ventures. *Accounting, Organisations and Society*, *21*(7–8), 629–654.

Franko, L.G. (1971). *Joint venture survival in multinational corporations*. New York: Praeger Publisher.

Gastanaga, V., Nugent, J.B., & Pashamova, B. (1998). Host country reforms and FDI inflows: How much difference do they make. *World Development*, *26*(7), 1299–1314.

Gerhart, B., & Milkovich, G.T. (1990). Organisational differences in managerial compensation and financial performance. *Academy of Management Journal*, *33*(4), 663–691.

Geringer, M.J. (1986). Criteria for selecting partners for joint ventures in industrialised market economics. Unpublished doctoral dissertation, University of Washington.

Geringer, M.J., & Frayne, C.A. (1990, Special Issue). Human resource management and international joint venture control: A parent company perspective. *Management International Review*, *30*, 103–120.

Geringer, M.J., & Herbert, L. (1989). Control and performance of international joint ventures. *Journal of International Business Studies*, Summer, *20*(2), 235.

Geringer, M.J., & Herbert, L. (1991). Measuring performance of international joint ventures. *Journal of International Business Studies*, *22*(2), 249–63.

Gomes-Casseres, B. (1990, First Quarter). Firm ownership preferences and host government restrictions: An integrated approach. *Journal of International Business Studies*, *21*, 1–22.

Groot, T.L.C.M., & Merchant, K.A. (2000). Control of international joint ventures. *Accounting, Organisations and Society*, *25*, 579–607.

Hagerty, B. (1997, April 10). Multinternationals in China use pay packages to lure talent. *The Wall Street Journal*, Interactive Edition.

Harms, P. (2000). *International investment, political risk, and growth*. Boston, MA: Kluwer Academic Publishers.

Harrison, G.L. (1993). Reliance on accounting performance measures in superior evaluative style: The influence of national culture and personality. *Accounting Organisations and Society*, *25*(4–5), 319–339.

Harrison, G.L., McKinnon, J.L., Panchapakesan, S., & Leung, M. (1994, October). The influence of culture on organisational design and planning and control in Australia and the United States compared with Singapore and Hong Kong. *Journal of International Financial Management and Accounting*, 242–261.

Hofstede, G.H. (1968). *The game of budget control*. London: Tavistock.

Hofstede, G.H. (1980). *Culture's consequences: International differences in work-related values*. Beverley Hills, California: Sage Publications.

Hofstede, G.H. (1983a). The cultural relativity of organisational practices and theories. *Journal of International Business Studies*, Fall, *13*(2), 75–89.

Hofstede, G.H. (1983b). Dimensions of national cultures in fifty countries and three regions. *International Studies of Management & Organisation*, Spring/Summer, *13*(1), 46–75.

Hofstede, G.H., & Bond, M.H. (1988). The Confucius connection: From cultural roots to economic growth. *Organisational Dynamics*, *16*(4), 4–21.

Howell, L.D., & Chaddick, B. (1994). Models of political risk for foreign investment and trade: An assessment of three approaches. *The Columbia Journal of World Business*, *29*, 70–91.

Huang, M., & Yu, H. (2002). *Special report on transfer pricing*. Beijing, China: Coopers and Lybrand.

Inkpen, A.C., & Beamish, P.W. (1997). Knowledge, bargaining power, and the instability of international joint ventures. *Academy of Management Review*, *22*(1), 177–202.

Isobe, T., Makino, S., & Montgomery, D.B. (2000). Resource commitment, entry timing, and market performance of foreign direct investment in emerging economies: The case of Japanese international joint ventures in China. *Academy of Management Journal*, *43*(3), 468–484.

Jensen, M.C. (1998). *Foundations of organisational strategy*. Cambridge, Massachusetts: Harvard University Press.

Jensen, M.C., & Meckling, W.H. (1995). Specific and general knowledge, and organisational structure. *Journal of Applied Corporate Finance*, *8*(2), 4–18.

Johanson, J., & Vahlne, J.E. (1977). The internationalisation process of the firm: A model of knowledge development and increasing foreign commitments. *Journal of International Business Studies*, Spring/Summer, 23–32.

Killing, J.P. (1983). *Strategies for joint ventures success*. New York: Praeger.

Kim, C.W., & Hwang, P. (1992). Global strategy and multinationals' entry mode choice. *Journal of International Business Studies*, *23*(1), 29–53.

Kobrin, S.J. (1982). *Managing political risk assessment*. Berkeley, California: University of California Press.

Kogut, B., & Singh, H. (1988). The effects of national culture on the choice of entry mode. *Journal of International Business Studies*, Fall, 411–432.

Korea Herald. (2001, August 15). Prospects grim for foreign direct investment amidst global slump.

Kwon, Y.C., & Konopa, L.J. (1993). Impact of host country market characteristics on the choice of foreign market entry mode. *International Marketing Review*, *10*(2), 60–76.

Lane, P., & Lubatkin, M. (1998). Relative absorptive capacity and inter-organisational learning. *Strategic Management Journal, 19*(5), 461–478.

Lecraw, D.J. (1984). Bargaining power, ownership, and profitability of transnational corporations in developing countries. *Journal of International Business Studies, 15*, 27–43.

Lee, J., Wu, X., & Kuo, D. (2004, February). Overview of China's impending APA rules: Transfer pricing in China. *Deloitte Touche Tohmatsu.*

Leitch, R.A., & Barrett, K.S. (1992). Multinational transfer pricing: Objective and constraints. *Journal of Accounting Literature, 11*, 47–92.

Lessard, D. (2000). Country risk and the structure of international financial intermediation. *International Finance-Contemporary Issues*, 451–470.

Lessard, D., & Lorange, P. (1977, July). Currency changes and management control: Resolving the centralisation/decentralisation dilemma. *Accounting Review*, 628–637.

Li, J.Y. (2000, November). Transfer pricing in China. *International Bureau of Fiscal Documentation*, 565–576.

Luo, Y. (1997). Performance implications of international strategy: An empirical study of foreign-invested enterprises in China. *Group and Organisation Management, 22*(1), 87–116.

Luo, Y. (1998). Timing of investment and international expansion performance in China. *Journal of International Business Studies, 29*(2), 391–407.

Martinsons, M.G., & Tsang, C.S. (1995). Successful joint ventures in the heart of the dragon. *Long Range Planning, 28*(5), 45–58.

Merchant, K.A. (1989). *Rewarding results: Motivating profit center managers.* Boston, Massachusetts: Harvard Business School Press.

Meyer, K.E. (2000). *Institutions, transaction costs, and entry mode choice in Eastern Europe*. Center for East European Studies, Working Paper, *34*. Copenhagen Business School, Copenhagen.

Milgrom, P., & Roberts, J. (1995). Complementarities and fit: Strategy, structure, and organisational change in manufacturing. *Journal of Accounting and Economics, 19*(2–3), 179–209.

Ministry of Commerce, PRC, Catalogue for the Guidance of Foreign Investment Industries. Amended in 2004, accessed from http://www.fdi.gov.cn/itlaw/lawinfodisp.jsp?id=ABC00000000000010453&appld=1 on 3 February 2005.

Mjoen, H., & Tallman, S. (1997, May–June). Control and performance in international joint ventures. *Organisation Science, 8*(3), 257–274.

Nagar, V. (2002). Delegation and incentive compensation. *Accounting Review, 77*(2), 379–395.

Nair, A.S., & Stafford, E.R. (1998, February). Strategic alliances in China: Negotiating the barriers. *Long Range Planning, 31*(1), 139–146.

O'Connor, N.G., & Ekanayake, S. (1998). Culture's influence on budget emphasis: some method issues and further evidence. *Asia-Pacific Journal of Accounting*, 241–266.

O'Farrell, P.N., Wood, P.A., & Zheng, J. (1998). Internationalisation by business service SMEs: An inter-industry analysis. *International Small Business Journal*, *16*(2), 13–33.

Osland, G.E., & Cavusgil, S.T. (1996). Performance issues in U.S.–China joint ventures. *California Management Review*, Winter, *38*(2), 106–130.

Ostroff, C., & Kozlowski, S.W. (1993). The role of mentoring in the information gathering process of newcomers during early organisational socialisation. *Journal of Vocational Behaviours*, *42*, 170–183.

Ouchi, W.G. (1989). The new joint R7D. *Proceedings of the IEEE*, *77*, 1318–1326.

Palenzuela, V.A., & Bobillo, A.M. (1999). Transaction costs and bargaining power: Entry mode choice in foreign markets. *Multinational Business Review*, Spring, 62–75.

People's Daily (2002, March 26). China reduces tariff levels.

People's Daily (2003). Overseas investment to China reaches US$52.7 billion. Accessed at http://english.peopledaily.com.cn/home.shtml on 10 November 2004.

People's Daily (2004). ADB forecasts China's investment growth to decrease by half in 2004, 2005. Accessed at http://english.peopledaily.com.cn/home.shtml on 2 February 2005.

Pfeffer, J. (1981). *Power in organisations*. New York: Pitman.

Pfeffer, J., & Salancik, G.R. (1978). *The external control of organisations*. New York: Harper & Row.

Porter, M.E. (1985). *Competitive Advantage*. New York: Free Press.

Prendergast, C. (1999, March). The provision of incentives in firms. *Journal of Economic Literature*, 7–63.

PricewaterhouseCoopers (2002a). Tax facts and figures of the People's Republic of China.

Pun, P. (2004). Guangzhou wages shoot up as labour crisis worsens. *The Standard Greater China's Business Newspaper*. Accessed at http://www.thestandard.com.hk/news on 3 February 2005.

Radebaugh, L.H., & Gray, S.J. (2002). *International accounting and multinational enterprises* (5th Ed.). New York: John Wiley and Sons.

Ring, P., & Van de Ven, A. (1994). Development processes of cooperative interorganisational relationships. *Academy of Management Review*, *19*(1), 90–118.

Root, F.R. (1994). *Entry strategies for international markets*. New York: Lexington Books.

Sarathy, R. (1994). Global strategy in services industries. *Long Range Planning*, *27*(6), 115–125.

SAT. (2003). *Report on the application and administration of section 482. IRS Department of the Treasury, Internal Revenue Service*, Publication 3218(4-1999). Accessed at http://www.irs.ustreas,gov.

Schaan, J.L. (1988). How to control joint venture even as a minority partner. *Journal of General Management*, Autumn, *14*(1), 4–16.

Sharma, V.M. (2002). Entry into Latin American BEMs: High or low resource commitment modes? *International Journal of Commerce and Management*, *12*(1), 41–68.

Shenkar, O. (1990). International joint ventures' problems in China: Risks and remedies. *Long Range Planning*, June, *23*(3), 82–91.

Stern, J.M., & Shiely, J.S. (2001). *The EVA challenge: Implementing value-added change in an organisation*. New York: John Wiley & Sons.

Stopford, J.M., & Wells, L.T. (1972). *Managing the multinational enterprise: organisation of the firm and ownership of the subsidiaries*. New York: Basic Books.

Sun, H. (1999). Entry modes of multinational corporations into China's market: A socioeconomic analysis. *International Journal of Social Economics*, *26*(5), 642.

Tallman, S.B., & Shenkar, O. (1994). A managerial decision model of international cooperative venture formation. *Journal of International Business Studies*, *25*(1/2), 91–113.

Tang, R.Y.W. (1992, February). Transfer pricing in the 1990s: The emphasis is on multinational and tax issues. *Management Accounting*, 22–26.

Teagarden, M., & Von Glinow, M. (1990). Sino-Foreign strategic alliance type and related operating characteristics. *International Studies of Management and Organisation*, *20*(1–2), 99–108.

Terpstra, V., & Yu, C.M. (1988). Determinants of foreign investment of U.S. advertising agencies. *Journal of International Business Studies*, *19*(1), 33–46.

Tomlinson, James W.C. (1970). *The Joint Venture Process in International Business India and Pakistan*. Cambridge, Massachusetts: M.I.T. Press.

Tse, D.K., Pan, Y., & Au, K.Y. (1997). How MNCs choose entry modes and form alliances: The China experience. *Journal of International Business Studies*, *28*(4), 779–808.

Usunier, J. (1996). *Marketing across cultures*. London: Prentice Hall.

Van Maanen, J., & Schein, E.H. (1979). Toward a theory of organisational socialisation. In B.M. Staw (Ed.), *Research in Organisational behaviour* (p. 209). Greenwich, CT: JAI Press.

Vanhonacker, W.R. (1997). Entering China: An unconventional approach. *Harvard Business Review*, *75*(2), 130–140.

Wagner, W.H. (1990, November–December). The measurement and control of trading costs. *Financial Analyst Journal*, *46*(6), 73–81.

Wang, P., Wee, C.H., & Koh, P.H. (1999). Establishing a successful Sino-foreign equity joint venture. *Journal of World Business*, *34*(3), 287–305.

Watson Wyatt. (2004) *2002 Incentive compensation in Asia.* Accessed at http://www.watsonwyatt.com/research/resrender.asp?id=AP-001&page=1, on 12 December 2004.

Weldon, E., & Vanhonacker, W. (1999). Operating a foreign-invested enterprise in China: Challenges for managers and management researcher. *Journal of World Business*, Spring, *34*(1), 94.

Whitley, R. (1994). *Business Systems in East Asia*. UK: SAGE Publications.

World Investment Report. (2004). *The shift towards services*. United Nations Conference on Trade and Development, New York and Geneva.

Yan, A., & Gray, B. (1994). Bargaining power, management control, and performance in United States-China joint venture: A comparative case study. *Academy of Management Journal*, *37*(6), 1478–1517.

Yan, A., & Luo, Y. (2001). *International joint ventures: Theory and practice*. New York: M.E. Sharpe.

Zahra, S., & Elhagrasey, G. (1994). Strategic management of international joint ventures. *European Management Journal*, *12*, 83–93.

Zeithaml, V., Parasuraman, L., & Berry, L. (1985). Problems and strategies in services marketing. *Journal of Marketing*, *49*, 33–46.

Zhao, H.X., & Zhu, G.T. (1998). Determinants of ownership preference of international joint ventures: New evidence from Chinese manufacturing industries. *International Business Review*, *7*, 569–589.

Index

Note: The letters *f* and *t* followed by page numbers indicate figures and tables.